The Market Revolution in America

Liberty, Ambition, and the Eclipse of the Common Good

The mass industrial democracy that is the modern United States bears little resemblance to the simple agrarian republic that gave it birth. The market revolution is the reason for this dramatic – and ironic – metamorphosis. The resulting tangled frameworks of democracy and capitalism still dominate the world as it responds to the financial Panic of 2008.

Early Americans experienced what we now call "modernization." The exhilaration – and pain – they endured have been repeated in nearly every part of the globe. Born of freedom and ambition, the market revolution in America fed on democracy and individualism even while it generated inequality, dependency, and unimagined wealth and power.

John Lauritz Larson explores the lure of market capitalism and the beginnings of industrialization in the United States. His research combines an appreciation for enterprise and innovation with recognition of negative and unanticipated consequences of the transition to capitalism and relates economic change directly to American freedom and self-determination, links that remain entirely relevant today.

John Lauritz Larson is Professor of History at Purdue University. For ten years, he served as co-editor of the *Journal of the Early Republic*. He is the author of *Bonds of Enterprise: John Murray Forbes and Western Development in America's Railway Age* (1984) and *Internal Improvement: National Public Works and the Promise of Popular Government in the New United States* (2001), as well as numerous essays on early American economic development.

Cambridge Essential Histories

Series Editor
Donald Critchlow, *St. Louis University*

Cambridge Essential Histories is devoted to introducing critical events, periods, or individuals in history to students. Volumes in this series emphasize narrative as a means of familiarizing students with historical analysis. In this series, leading scholars focus on topics in European, American, Asian, Latin American, Middle Eastern, African, and World history through thesis-driven, concise volumes designed for survey and upper-division undergraduate history courses. The books contain an introduction that acquaints readers with the historical event and reveals the book's thesis; narrative chapters that cover the chronology of the event or problem; and a concluding summary that provides the historical interpretation and analysis.

Other Books in the Series

John Earl Haynes and Harvey Klehr, *Early Cold War Spies: The Espionage Trials That Shaped American Politics*

James H. Hutson, *Church and State in America: The First Two Centuries*

Maury Klein, *The Genesis of Industrial America, 1870–1920*

The Market Revolution in America

Liberty, Ambition, and the Eclipse of the Common Good

JOHN LAURITZ LARSON

Purdue University

CAMBRIDGE UNIVERSITY PRESS
Cambridge, New York, Melbourne, Madrid, Cape Town, Singapore,
São Paulo, Delhi, Dubai, Tokyo, Mexico City

Cambridge University Press
32 Avenue of the Americas, New York, NY 10013-2473, USA

www.cambridge.org
Information on this title: www.cambridge.org/9780521709897

First published 2010
Reprinted 2010

A catalog record for this publication is available from the British Library.

Library of Congress Cataloging in Publication Data

Larson, John Lauritz, 1950–
The market revolution in America : liberty, ambition, and the eclipse of
the common good / John Lauritz Larson.
    p. cm. – (Cambridge essential histories)
Includes bibliographical references and index.
ISBN 978-0-521-88365-8 (hardback) – ISBN 978-0-521-70989-7 (pbk.)
1. United States – Economic conditions. 2. Capitalism – Social
aspects – United States – History. I. Title. II. Series.
HC103.L327   2010
330.973–dc22   2009008472

ISBN 978-0-521-88365-8 Hardback
ISBN 978-0-521-70989-7 Paperback

For Sue

Contents

Acknowledgments

This book is the fruit of two ambitions. Specifically, I set out a few years ago to craft a short account of the economic transformation of early America that was quick and readable enough to assign to undergraduates but still faithful to the complexity of the early American experience. I had in view no historiographical quarrels with either friends or enemies of the term "market revolution"; rather, I wanted to convey to the unfamiliar reader all that I believe took place in that transformative period. More generally, I discovered as I wrote that this narrative capped a thirty-year effort to *understand* the phenomenon in question. The intersection of capitalism and democracy lay at the center of my interests when I headed off to graduate school in the 1970s; it bedevils me still. The present text is an offering to that muse. We shall see if the smoke rises.

Because this book is the culmination of thirty years' consideration, I first must acknowledge the impact of the thousands of students at Earlham College and Purdue University who constituted my audiences through all the iterations of lectures and discussions about these things. As the woodsman needs the stone on which to grind his ax, the scholar must have students to whet his or her insights and give them focus. Many (if not most) of these contributors doubtless went away bewildered, but their difficulty in grasping what I tried to tell them inevitably helped me learn to tell it better.

More immediately, I have been assisted by individuals and resources common to the scholarly community. A sabbatical leave from Purdue University contributed significantly to my ability to see the forest comprising these many trees. Although I did not work on this project at the time, a year at the McNeil Center for Early American Studies as a Barra Postdoctoral Fellow helped clear my head and stimulate my aging mind. (Nothing sharpens the wits like the close company of very bright young people – although the more "senior" body finds them hard to keep up with.) Thank you to Dan Richter, Roderick and Michelle McDonald, and the McNeil Center community in Philadelphia.

Several delightful days' work in the reading rooms of the Library Company of Philadelphia brought to light important bits from the documentary record, for which I thank Librarian James Green and his able staff. A Summer Seminar for Scholars, sponsored by the National Endowment for the Humanities, hosted by the Library Company, and co-directed by my friend and colleague Michael Morrison, gave me yet another useful forum. The Program in Early American Economy and Society (PEAES), also hosted by the Library Company and expertly directed by Cathy Matson, thankfully has fanned interest in economic history when almost nobody else would. For all these institutional contributions, I thank Library Company Director John Van Horne.

Professional colleagues polish whatever rough edges are left from grinding away on the students, and for this I am grateful to the growing family of historians who sustain the Society for Historians of the Early American Republic (SHEAR). For all of my career, SHEAR conferences have been the most reliable venue for critical discourse on matters pertaining to the market revolution (not least the bitter quarrels over whether or not it occurred). Of particular importance in my education in these matters have been friendships with Harry Watson, Paul Gilje, Drew Cayton, Cathy Kelly, Peter Onuf, Christopher Clark, Cathy Matson, Dan Feller, Richard John, and Daniel Walker Howe. Clearly we do not see all things alike, but I see nothing without imagining these friends gathering themselves for the pounce.

At Purdue, Frank Lambert, James R. Farr, and Michael Morrison read drafts of this material with grace and generosity. One chapter survived the scrutiny of colleagues and graduate students at one of our History Graduate Student Association's Works-in-Progress seminars. Laura Bergstrom, Ray Krohn, and Mark Johnson provided research assistance specifically for this book; countless other students brought me tips and made me rethink explanations. My canine editor-in-chief,

Juneau, did not survive to see this book completed, although not for want of trying. His assistant, Ellie, soldiers on, but the top position remains unfilled.

As the project neared completion, Drew Cayton and Harry Watson gave me constant support and advice. My old friend and mentor, Hunter Dupree, and his wife, Betty Dupree, read the finished manuscript, urging me to throw out Chapter 4 and try again. (I did.) Because I wanted this book to make sense to people who did *not* obsess about its thesis every summer at the SHEAR meetings, I asked Mark A. Hermodson, Leon Trachtman, Lynne Eckhart, and John Eckhart to read it and tell me what they saw. I have made significant adjustments as a result of their input, for which I am grateful.

At Cambridge University Press, Lewis Bateman (as always) proffers a firm hand of support. Series editor Donald Critchlow provided encouragement. Emily Spangler makes things happen as they should. Andy Saff patiently worked through the final manuscript, picking out infelicities. From here, the project goes into the hands of people around the world whose names I will not know but whose labors will bring the product into being. To all of them, in advance, thank you.

As always, the buck stops here. Few subjects exercise our passions like political economy, and I have no doubt there will be dissenters. Errors may persist ("mistakes," as they say, "were made"), and some readers will find fault in what I write here or what conclusions I draw. The offering is mine, warts and all. I only hope it will advance our conversation – and perhaps our understanding – just a little.

Lafayette, Indiana

Introduction

What Do We Mean by a Market Revolution in America?

At the end of its War for Independence, the United States comprised thirteen separate provinces on the coast of North America. Nearly all of 3.9 million people made their living through agriculture while a small merchant class traded tobacco, timber, and foodstuffs (flour, rice, livestock, salted meat, and fish) for tropical goods, useful manufactures, and luxuries in the Atlantic commercial community. By the time of the Civil War, eight decades later, the United States sprawled across the North American continent. Nearly 32 million people labored not just on farms, but in shops and factories making iron and steel products, boots and shoes, textiles, paper, packaged foodstuffs, firearms, farm machinery, furniture, tools, and all sorts of housewares. Civil War–era Americans borrowed money from banks; bought insurance against fire, theft, shipwreck, commercial losses, and even premature death; traveled on steamboats and in railway carriages; and produced $2 to 3 billion worth of goods and services, including exports of $400 million.[1] This dramatic transformation is what some historians of the United States call the "market revolution." For antebellum Americans, this revolution stood near the center of the experience of what happened to the United States during its grand experiment in republican government. For many modern historians, it does so still.

---

[1] *Statistical History of the United States from Colonial Times to the Present*, ed. Ben J. Wattenberg (New York: Basic Books, 1976), 239, 885.

ATLANTIC NETWORKS

The market revolution sprang from widely shared causes and conditions that surrounded American Independence and drew significant new energy from that revolutionary development. But to understand either the American independence movement or the market revolution that followed, we must first review certain features of the process of colonization. The rebellious British colonies – like other Atlantic provinces – owed their existence to commercial exploitation and exchange reaching back to the sixteenth century. Shortly after the famous voyage of Columbus in 1492, Spanish, Portuguese, French, Dutch, and finally British adventurers probed the "New World" (new to them, anyway) for riches and opportunities. Where they could, they stole gold and silver from indigenous people and enslaved the natives to mine more of the same. In most of the Caribbean and North America, however, colonization came to depend on coarser natural resources (fish and fur) and on slave-grown crops of tobacco and sugar. So it was profiteering through long-distance trade, by a relatively small class of merchants and adventurers, that drove colonial development from the earliest days.

The kind of merchant capitalism that flourished in this Atlantic economic community linked networks of African slave traders, island producers of sugar and wine, mainland planters, fur traders, fishermen, and farmers. Some still worked through state-sponsored firms such as the Royal Africa Company or the famous British tea monopoly, the East India Company; but by the eighteenth century, most were free agents seeking profit wherever they could. True commercial pioneers, these adventurous individuals rode transatlantic winds of supply and demand in a game of profit and loss that was altogether different from economic life inside their own countries. Over time, this new wealth pouring in from the colonies could not help but alter relations among the imperial powers and between the landowners of Europe (who once thought of themselves as the sole custodians of national wealth) and a rising class of entrepreneurs. In the English case, this resulted in a struggle between friends of the monarchy at "court" and "country" squires who pledged to defend ancient customs and traditions – including Parliament's right to control royal spending. But the money and power to be had in the Atlantic commercial economy proved irresistible to governing elites. As a result, the early modern system of merchant capitalism sank deep roots into the structures of British governance and set the stage for wrenching upheavals to come.

To shape and control these colonial networks, England and its rivals imposed systems of regulation based on mercantilist assumptions. Believing that real money (gold and silver) was a finite commodity, mercantilist policy makers tried to direct commerce in ways that brought control of the money into national hands (where kings and queens might deploy it – through armies and navies if necessary – in the interest of the nation-state). Competition pitted *countries* against one another (not individuals or firms), and the point of the game was to keep the flow of money away from one's enemies. England's many imperial wars with its Dutch, Spanish, and French rivals (1652, 1664, 1672, 1689, 1702, 1739, and 1754) all related to this goal and produced, by 1763, a state of effective British hegemony over the Atlantic commercial system.

What differentiates colonial merchant capitalism from its mature, modern successor is the extent of penetration of market forces and values into the daily lives of ordinary people. Capitalistic in many ways, New World commerce did not wholly transform the economies from which leading players ventured. Its impact on some Africans and indigenous Americans was dramatic and immediate, but colonial trade touched poor farmers in the provinces and most consumers back home infrequently until the middle decades of the eighteenth century. Cash prices, contracts, and speculation – all hallmarks of the capitalist system – could be found in the world of colonial merchants no matter how primitive the structures and instruments of their transactions. (Bills exchanged in a coffeehouse instead of a bank or bourse were no less binding or capitalistic.) But the vast majority of free provincials as well as Europeans played out their economic lives in local communities where markets and exchange continued to operate as they had for generations. "Just" prices, sometimes fixed by law, kept food and household necessities affordable; local producers and vendors dominated trade; and an individual's good name and character ensured the support of neighbors regardless of fluctuations in distant, speculative markets. Even staple-crop planters, whose fortunes depended on long-distance market forces, often lived and kept their household books just as if they were country squires in rural England. Ironically, it was the slaves more than anyone who felt the sting of these early capitalist networks that reduced them to pawns at the base of colonial plantation commerce.

Supply and demand always threatened to derange local community markets, leading men and women into temptation from the earliest days in Jamestown and Boston; but these were not yet accepted as "iron laws," nor did they always trump questions of justice, tradition, and brotherhood. In the seventeenth century, sumptuary laws had tried (in vain) to stop rude men with ready money from buying the costumes of gentility. Private contracts freely made were still found unenforceable if the outcome (perhaps unforeseen at the time of the agreement) struck authorities as patently unfair. Widows and orphans relied on entitlements as innocent victims of misfortune; men could be punished by law and custom for exhibitions of naked greed. There was an undeniable difference between the embedded commercial values of the early colonial markets and the anonymous cash transactions of nineteenth-century capitalism.

The eighteenth century appears to hold the fulcrum on which modern capitalism leveraged its way into Anglo-American culture. However humane and benevolent it seemed in retrospect, early provincial economic culture produced by the eighteenth century a certain restlessness in British North America. Colonists bought more imported manufactures to replace homemade articles and the products of local artisans. Gradually, sugar, tea, and tobacco found their way into larger and larger consumer markets. American trade grew enormously in volume and importance to the mother country. When it served their interests, Americans labored contentedly inside the framework of protection and promotion laid down by the Navigation Acts; the rest of the time, they bribed and cheated their way around the rules. Once their "starving times" were lost to memory, men and women now born in America (some not even of British parents) focused their energies on bringing the provinces up to speed with British fashions. Planters built country seats and landscape gardens in pale imitations of the English rural gentry. They sent their sons to study at the Inns of Court in London. Merchants in Baltimore, Philadelphia, and Boston furnished their urban palaces with fine furniture, carpets, and wall coverings, ate dinner off English china, and served their guests imported wines. Colonists devoured English books and periodicals. And during the imperial wars, they rose to defend as their own the glorious British Empire.

If Americans saw themselves as partners in the eighteenth-century British Empire, English governors and metropolitan commercial patrons continued to treat them like dependent servants. American planters – landed gentry in their own minds – fell into the clutches of English and Scottish creditors who did not extend the same considerations they might offer great landed families in Britain. Seaport merchants lived off credits offered by London correspondents who could just as easily, without cause, call in or cancel their loans. Colonists created real new wealth, but England's reluctance to allow local banking or expand local currencies left them struggling with so little ready money that Virginians set prices in pounds of tobacco. No matter how steeped they were in English country values, Britons in America had been forced from the start to accommodate long-distance market forces influencing the price of everything from cooking pots to servants and slaves. (It is hard to imagine that buying and selling Indians and Africans as workers – and sometimes sexual playthings – did not erode traditional values in the colonies.) Finally, entrepreneurial innovation, even in the smallest degree, rewarded American colonists with greater prosperity and happiness than careful attention to tradition or mercantilist regulations. Long before Adam Smith codified the principles of liberal political economy in *The Wealth of Nations* (1776), many Americans – not just merchants but also urban shopkeepers, market farmers, small backcountry planters, and certain skilled artisans – had begun to experience aspects of modern "liberalism."

By the middle decades of the eighteenth century, commercial men in London and Glasgow and political leaders at Whitehall recognized the rising importance of imperial trade as a vent for consumer goods and not just a source of New World staples. Accordingly, they moved to close off "leaks" in the system and maximize the flow of wealth in ways that mercantilist theory prescribed – unaware (by and large) that it was leaks and lapses that accounted for much of the wealth pouring in from the provinces. Further, in the wake of two long wars, officials sought to ease the burden on taxpayers at home by capturing greater revenues from the parties they thought most benefited from imperial protection – the colonists. In other words, the governors of empire moved to integrate provincials who had grown accustomed to suiting themselves unseen by any regulators' eyes. Precisely because mercantilist thinking placed the state in control of economic conditions, when economic conditions began to change in the mid-eighteenth century, colonists turned to *political* science to explain their discomforts.

ROOTS OF REBELLION

A quick series of events in the 1760s transformed these underlying features of colonial history into the crisis that resulted in the American independence movement. In 1760, George III succeeded to the British throne. Determined to rule effectively, the young monarch set out to drive from his court the corruption that had typified governance during his grandfather's reign. Alas, his "reforms" brought an end to the lax ways that American merchants understood as customary – and *right*. The quick passage of the Proclamation Act (1763, closing the mainland western frontier to trespassing settlers), the Sugar Act (1764, *lowering* duties but sharply increasing enforcement in the Caribbean sugar trade), and the Stamp Act (1765, imposing a small but novel direct tax on colonists at home) signaled new and forceful hands on the reins of power. Colonists perceived this new energy in government not as reforming but corrupt and tyrannical. Borrowing deeply from the "Old Whig" or "country" critics of influence peddling at court, Americans took offense at these policy initiatives. The new king and his ministers, they concluded, intended to sacrifice the colonists to gratify their own whim and fancy.

The case for revolution was hardly self-evident in 1765, and the leaders of the independence movement labored for a decade, interpreting events and orchestrating responses, to cultivate rebellion. For many colonial residents, changes in the markets resulted in lower prices and better selections on the shelves of country stores. Backcountry farmers and upland planters found Scottish tobacco factors ready to exchange their crops for cash and goods without the services of wealthy tidewater "grandees" who previously held them in chains of "friendship" (that is, dependency). Economic rationalization of the empire hurt provincial elites more than ordinary people, and the burden of new taxes – soon to be the pivot of rhetorical rebellion – was altogether trivial for most colonists. But American radicals spun out a different story in which the king and his lackeys, stuffed with colonial revenue and freed from Parliament's restraining hand, had embarked (like the tyrant Charles I) on a campaign of absolutism to subvert that glorious, balanced wonder of political equipoise, the British Constitution. Members of the House of Commons claimed to represent all the people of the empire, including colonial subjects; but any fool could see that the people *in England* would abridge the rights of provincials if it served their convenience at home.

Viewed from the western end of the scope, the progress of this evil was shocking, and its ultimate end could not be in doubt. American elites – commercial men in Boston and New York, radical artisans in Philadelphia, planters in Maryland and Virginia – began discussing among themselves these dire prospects. Only one form of government they knew could frustrate this evil and survive in an imperfect world: republicanism. To America's revolutionaries, this meant rule by the people's representatives, who could not tyrannize the people because they shared with them a basic common interest. No sane man would tyrannize himself, and as long as the governors were drawn from (and returned to) the ranks of the governed, no durable, external schemes could gain any traction against the interests of the people. Independence would remove the immediate threat of enslavement through corruption, but only *republican* government could guarantee liberty (and with it, prosperity) forever in the newly formed states.

As luck would have it, Americans thought they were ready-made for republican government. If you overlook the Indians and slaves (a huge condition, yet one nearly all white colonists accepted), virtually all British colonists were commoners. Having no separate, hereditary ranks to accommodate, Americans met the first republican criterion: one universal common interest. Equally important was an independent citizenry, sustained by widespread ownership of property. Here again Americans seemed uniquely positioned: The vast majority owned land or a shop and a trade. That proportion diminished as one moved southward, but even where the labor force consisted primarily of black slaves (not included in such calculations), abject dependency among *white* households was nowhere near as common as in Europe. The final criterion, according to classical theory, was sufficient virtue that the people could set aside self-interest in favor of the common good. The heroic exploits of colonial founders – risking all to succeed while the rulers back home paid so little regard – indicated matchless virtue, at least in the first generation. And by the early 1770s, in the popular mind, the willingness of colonists to rebel against the greatest power of the age suggested an abundance of virtue still. In short, by 1775, when the shooting war began, America's leaders had translated economic grievances into a utopian quest on behalf of human liberty. Whatever material ambitions underlay anyone's decision to join the patriot cause (and these were numerous and usually ambivalent), an ideological hymn to liberty and equality bound them together. The promise of republican government conjured up a vision of a future more "free" than anyone had known, even in the extraordinarily free societies of British North America.

Dissonance probably best characterized Americans' economic values as they entered the imperial crisis and the Revolution. They thought they were restoring traditional rights and customs even while they lived on the ragged edge of a competitive commercial empire. They had not yet read Adam Smith (when they did, many were appalled by his startling view of economic life), and they had not yet fully rejected the mercantilist principles by which their world had been governed for a century. Still, their experience *as lived* had taught them something about freer markets, innovation, and economic liberty. Their obsessive reading in the tracts of Whig country critics of the Georgian court convinced them that royal favorites, not deserving entrepreneurs, gained the most from government policy. When they cried out for liberty and equality, they instinctively imagined a greater degree of economic freedom as one of the objectives of regime change. Thus a revolution *intentionally* political fostered an economic revolution in its turbulent wake. At the same time, the conflict between virtue and self-interest – an ethical conundrum at the core of republicanism – marked many arguments in the generation after independence and lay at the heart of people's experience of the market revolution.

SEARCH FOR THE CAPITALIST SYSTEM

Finally, what of capitalism and the capitalist system? Historians and economists argue bitterly over the meaning of these terms and when they apply to early American society. Much of the quarrel can be attributed to precise (but different) definitions that make it possible to date the "rise of capitalism" to the 1620s, the 1740s, the 1790s, or the 1830s. A second line of controversy swirls around slavery and the nature of slave-based enterprise within a free-market system. Generations of historians, building on theoretical distinctions rooted in the writings of Karl Marx, portrayed the plantation economies of the southern colonies and states as fundamentally different from the mixed commercial-agricultural systems found in middle and northern states. More recent students have called attention to hard-driving, man-on-the-make planters, especially in the new slave states of the antebellum West, and question just how "backward" slaveholders really were.

At the center of all these arguments lies the question: When did the cold calculus of the marketplace trump other considerations in the making of private decisions by ordinary individuals? Long ago, Marx predicted that market forces would displace sentimental, familial, religious, or humanitarian values in a mature capitalist system; but while the tendency has been in that direction, it remains unclear just when – if ever – such a total transition took place. Before the market revolution, there were markets, to be sure: Profits were taken, greed exhibited, goods produced and exchanged. But greed was not normative, and an individual's behavior might as often contradict as conform to the dictates of economic interest. After the market revolution, "hard-headed" economic logic sought to dominate the process of evaluating all things. Individual identity dissolved into anonymity, commitment into contract, vocation into work, a living into a wage. The transformation never was absolute or complete. Long after the market revolution, people continued (and continue still) to exhibit behaviors (labeled "irrational") that contravened the expectations of economists. But there must have been a tipping point in history before which people did not believe – or did not accept it as natural and inevitable – that the market should be the universal arbiter of interests. After that point, whether happily or not, people came to believe that social and material life likely would not (could not?) be otherwise. At that point, which may have lasted a generation, a year, or one "eureka" moment, people experienced the market revolution and entered an era of capitalist relations.

That market revolution is the subject of this book. It is this tipping point for which we search in the lives of antebellum Americans, when they came to believe (correctly or not) that impersonal market forces had disabled the fabric of personal, familial, and cultural connections by which people earlier had tried to mitigate the hard facts of material life. It probably does not explain every personal and political decision made during the antebellum decades, but this market revolution was on the minds of nearly everyone in the United States between the Revolution and the Civil War, and it colored (if it did not dictate) their reaction to a host of public issues ranging from banking and money to bankruptcy, land policy, tariffs, manufacturing, democracy, and the expansion of slavery.

What follows are chapters that recount both the unexpected, overwhelming force of economic changes *and* the positive aspects that made it difficult for people who experienced the market revolution to know whether they were rising in a privileged class or falling victim to an economic juggernaut. Chapter 1 explores the impact of political liberation on a people already "free" by the standards of the day. The "first fruits of independence" included basic policy foundations regarding private property, law, contracts, money, corporations, and the limits of entrepreneurial freedom to act. Chapter 2 then re-creates the whirlwind of innovation and "progress" that left an entire generation, by 1860, literally gasping with exhilaration. Chapter 3 revisits the same antebellum decades to examine the consequences of all this accumulating "progress" as it restructured "life as lived" for individual farmers and their children, artisans and factory workers, clerks and entrepreneurs, women, immigrants, free blacks, Indians, and slaves. Much about these changes appeared as loss to persons experiencing them, yet not everyone recognized "progress" as the cause or connected the dots between innovations that brought them improvement and those that cost them independence or security.

Between Chapters 1, 2, and 3 fall brief interludes dedicated to the phenomenon known as the "panic." Panic was the name for sudden economic downturns that later would be seen as recurrent features of the capitalist "business cycle." In the early nineteenth century, they could be interpreted either as wicked and purposeful attacks on virtuous innocents by greedy evil-doers or as accidental shocks in a dynamic new system nobody quite yet understood. Severe panics returned periodically (very nearly every twenty years after 1819) until the onset of the Great Depression in 1929, since which time modern governments around the world have exercised policy leverage over natural business fluctuations. Because they created "hard times" – high unemployment, plummeting prices, credit contraction, bankruptcies, and other painful forms of failure – these episodes became flash points in the contemporary struggle to adjust to and understand the emerging capitalist system. If people could recall a single moment when the market revolution engulfed them, odds are that moment belonged to a panic event.

Finally, Chapter 4 examines efforts to explain how all the contradictory experiences of the market revolution could exist as true stories told by a single people. Not surprisingly, antebellum analysts, caught in the heat of immediate and painful changes, often chose sides and roundly condemned either the capitalist innovators or their critics among the farmers, workers, and other dependent classes. Later on, economists and social reformers probed for the roots of industrial America in order to craft (or deflect) policies intended to ameliorate social disruptions. Eventually historians weighed in with their own formulations, some tending to look with favor on the positive aspects of modernization, others lamenting the supposed virtues of a world that was being lost. By now, the literature is rich and feisty, constantly reenergized by present-day actors who champion the "forward" march of global capitalism, and by new generations of critics who wonder why, as the rich get richer, the poor, while a little better off, become so powerless over their own economic destinies.

It is my contention that, for Americans between 1800 and 1860, the benefits and costs of the market revolution presented a complex picture indeed. For most people, their allegiances – whether for or against "progress" – remained shallow, fraught with confusion, and often vacillated back and forth in the real-time experience. The result was a kind of vertigo that afflicted antebellum Americans and made the "tipping point" of the market revolution practically invisible to most individuals until, in hindsight, they recognized the difference between their future and a cherished past. Historians prefer to impose coherent narratives on the past because this makes their stories useful, meaningful, and satisfying. Unfortunately, the stories (inevitably multiple and contradictory) that accompany the rise of modern industrial capitalism resist such coherent telling. Intertwined as they are with political democracy and bourgeois material prosperity, they instead tempt us, like the serpent in the garden, with promises of freedom and knowledge beyond what we really can master.

I

First Fruits of Independence

With political independence secured under the Treaty of Paris (1783), the American founders in the states and in the Union sought to restart a war-torn economy and find their way back into the Atlantic commercial networks. At first they sought prosperity, but not everyone agreed how best to achieve that end. Prior to the independence movement, the individual colonies had shared very little in each other's progress or prosperity. Their interests were hardly as uniform as republican rhetoric was wont to imply, and visions of the ideal future diverged significantly from place to place and from person to person in the immediate postwar period. Everyone hoped to be better off, of course, in the hands of their own governments, being taxed and regulated for their own interests and not those of a distant power. But individual incomes had fallen steadily since 1774, and nobody felt much in the mood to shoulder *higher* taxes and *more* burdensome government than had prevailed before the Revolution – even if such things might be good for the fledgling nation. America's radical leaders had led their neighbors in a separatist movement; now the time had come for them to deliver the promised benefits of liberation.

Three barriers immediately frustrated these objectives. First, the Americans were deeply in debt – to the Dutch, to the French, and to themselves. In addition to £10 million in specie loans, the Continental Congress and the various states had issued roughly £45 million in stocks and bonds plus £110 million in fiat currency, all backed by nothing but the promises of untested new civil governments.[1] Second, significant capital had been degraded or destroyed during the bleak years of the war. Crops had been burned or seized by passing armies, livestock consumed, woodlots pillaged. Thousands of farms were neglected by men dragged far from home to serve in the Continental Army. At least one hundred thousand slaves (worth perhaps $250 each) ran away from their masters in response to British promises of freedom.[2] Third, in a move that should have surprised nobody, Great Britain kicked the Americans out of the commercial empire. Bounties on rice and indigo vanished. Doors closed on West Indian markets for American grain, flour, wood products, butter, meat, and livestock. English creditors called in loans that American borrowers never had imagined having to pay in real money. These unfavorable conditions cast a pall over celebrations of the Treaty of Paris.

On the "plus" side, Americans enjoyed a number of advantages. Independence had gained them "good title" (in terms of European law) to a vast landed domain from Maine to Georgia and west to the Mississippi River. Richly endowed with fertile soil, dense forests, a temperate climate, and dependable rainfall, the land was laced with navigable rivers, streams, and inland seas that seemed designed by Providence especially to invite commercial development by promising easy transportation. (Of all the sites of European colonization since the voyages of discovery – called "Neo-Europes" by one insightful student of global imperialism – none presented more promise or fewer barriers to exploitation on a vast scale than eastern North America.[3]) In 1783, over 3 million whites and another seven hundred thousand black slaves occupied the Atlantic coast, but most of the interior remained about the same as the colonists found it. Americans were youthful – over half the population was under age twenty – and correspondingly energetic.[4] Among the whites, even common people

[1] Edwin J. Perkins, *American Public Finance and Financial Services 1700–1815* (Columbus: Ohio State University Press, 1994), 103.

[2] Peter C. Mancall, Joshua L. Rosenbloom, and Thomas Weiss, "Slave Prices and the South Carolina Economy, 1722–1809," *Journal of Economic History* 61 (2001): Table 1, 620–1, Table 3, 635.

[3] See Alfred W. Crosby, *Ecological Imperialism: The Biological Expansion of Europe, 900–1900*, 2nd ed. (New York: Cambridge University Pres, 2004), 9.

[4] *Statistical History of the United States from Colonial Times to the Present*, ed. Ben J. Wattenberg (New York: Basic Books, 1976), 14, 16.

enjoyed a comfortable living by European standards, and reproductive rates were so high that they approached the biological maximum. (African Americans held in slavery lived far less comfortably, of course; but with a better balance of women to men and less hazardous conditions overall, slaves in the United States still lived longer and reproduced more successfully than did their counterparts in the Caribbean or South America.) Finally, the Revolution, with its promises of liberty and equality, had planted in free people's souls a restless sense of entitlement that tended to accelerate habits of mobility and innovation, habits that, in colonial days, often seemed to contradict good order and tradition.

In the long run, the abundance of resources, conditions of personal freedom, and the youthful energy of the population guaranteed the return of prosperity and the extension of American agriculture across the mountains to the Mississippi. Young Americans could expect to continue their habits of breeding, moving west, and snatching an easy subsistence from undeveloped land. Almost everyone saw the new United States as a treasure house of opportunity, a great poor man's country. As George Washington put it: "I wish to see the sons and daughters of the world in Peace and busily employed in the more agreeable amusement of fulfilling the first and great commandment, *Increase and Multiply.*"[5] But the market revolution would not transform the economic system until engines of intensification began to reorder this agrarian paradise. Transportation improvements were needed to "vent" the surplus product of interior settlements. Home manufactures were wanted to reduce the country's appetite for European imports before the new nation sank into neocolonial dependency. Somebody – governments or private businesspeople – would have to mobilize capital, generate a currency, reactivate trading connections, and stimulate markets, especially for the staple crops grown by African American slaves throughout the southern states. After 1783, conditions were right for the market revolution to begin, but policy decisions and positive actions were required to set the process in motion.

---

[5] Quoted in John Lauritz Larson, *Internal Improvement* (Chapel Hill: University of North Carolina Press, 2001), 14.

ESTABLISHING VIABLE GOVERNMENT

Private solutions to economic problems could not be imagined until the state and federal governments set down a framework for civil society, law, property rights, and commercial transactions. There had to be deeds to turn land into property, money with which to pay debts, and courts in which to sue for failure to pay. Whether they still thought in mercantilist terms or had begun to embrace economic liberalism, early American politicians had little choice but to shape the institutions of law and commerce in their new self-governing republics. Consequently, institutional structures, land, debt, commerce, and money dominated politics throughout the new states and in the Congress of the Confederation.

For example, the Treaty of Paris recognized American claims to the back lands west of the Proclamation Line of 1763 – but which claims? Those of Virginia? New York? Massachusetts? Connecticut? North Carolina? At stake was control of the single most important capital asset in American hands. In Virginia and North Carolina, western lands were eyed lasciviously by legislators eager to pay off soldiers, retire war debts, and back up paper money with land warrants drawn against wilderness acres. In 1784, guided by Thomas Jefferson's far-sighted image of a truly national public domain, Virginia offered to cede its western claims to Congress provided other states agreed to do the same. The next year (1785), Congress passed a Land Ordinance creating the most rational, simple, accessible, democratic, and commercial land system the world had ever seen. Surveyors were ordered out into the wilderness to run lines and carve up the country into numbered squares with fee-simple deeds and unique legal descriptions that could be bought and sold at a distance by anyone with money (not just wealthy gentlemen with political connections and expert legal advice). It was the first triumph of national policy for the Confederation Congress.

Congress fared less well with other issues that generated conflicts among the states. While some states raised taxes to pay down their debts and support their currency, others issued fiat money (paper without sound backing), tossing into circulation a bewildering variety of notes without known value, many of them worthless outside the state of issue. Rhode Island flooded southern New England with fiat paper proclaimed to be "legal tender" for any transactions taking place on Rhode Island soil. New York, Connecticut, Pennsylvania, and New Jersey raised protective tariffs to prevent foreign goods slipping in through their neighbors. Several states sent agents to England to negotiate individual access to lost British markets. Nobody honored their "voluntary" obligations to the treasury of the Confederation, so Continental stocks, bonds, and currency fell into complete disgrace and soldiers mustered out with little more than fistfuls of worthless Continental dollars. Western lands had been ceded to Congress, but private parties and agents of states continued to purchase deeds from resident Indian nations, stirring up conflicts for which no countervailing peace-keeping force existed. The habit of the day, to refer to the United States as a plural entity – *these* United States – seemed all too apt by 1785 and 1786, as states bickered and balked at solutions to interstate problems. Virginia and Maryland could not even come to agreement over plans to improve navigation in the Potomac River, which formed their common border; and at a conference called at Mount Vernon by Potomac Canal booster George Washington, talk quickly turned to the need for a stronger national union.

The campaign to secure a "more perfect union" was neither spontaneous nor especially popular in 1786. Only broad-minded nationalistic leaders felt an urgent need for reform of the Articles of Confederation; only some of these thought a wholly new frame of government was necessary, and nobody thought it was authorized. Still the nationalists pressed on, and when the all-state Annapolis Convention of 1786 failed, they got permission from Congress to call another reform convention. Once gathered in Philadelphia in May 1787, presided over by George Washington and deftly steered by James Madison, that convention chose to lock the doors, ignore the delegates' instructions, tear up the Articles of Confederation, and draft a new constitution. Under the resulting new charter, built largely on a framework designed by Madison earlier that spring, a national government acquired most of what was missing in the old Confederation Congress: taxing authority over the people; sole control of federal land, money, and Indian policy; and legal supremacy in matters of contract and interstate commerce. States lost the veto implied by the Confederation's amendment procedure (it required unanimous approval), and sovereignty was lodged in a novel two-tiered structure that laid over the independent states a super republic for national purposes.

In September 1787, George Washington unveiled the Constitution of the United States with a solemn plea to embrace it as the last best hope for preserving the Union. The pamphlet war over ratification began almost immediately, and the collected numbers of "Publius" (known later as the *Federalist Papers*), refuting as they did all manner of objections, bear ample witness to the range, severity, and strength of opposition. Without the new Constitution, the institutional integration that followed in the next three decades might have been postponed or prevented altogether. Without such integration, the stage might not have been set for a market revolution in America before the Civil War, and so the triumph of the nationalists in this founding era plays a critical part in the story before us. That said, it need not have been the design or intention of Washington, Hamilton, Madison, or any others among the founding elites to set the stage for a capitalist revolution. "Progressive" historians since Charles Beard have tried to "blame" these ardent nationalists for the rise of an integrated modern economy, while friends of industrial capitalism often try to celebrate these men as having shared in superhuman wisdom – perhaps divine guidance. The record will sustain neither credit nor blame, but the consequences of the new regime and the policies laid down by Federalist leaders in the 1790s nevertheless shaped the coming decades profoundly.

NEO-MERCANTILIST POLICY BEGINNINGS

In 1789, the First Federal Congress met to begin making policies for the whole nation. Among its earliest acts were reaffirmations of the 1785 Land Ordinance and also the 1787 Northwest Ordinance, which outlined how to govern frontier settlements and admit new states to the Union. These two signal achievements of the old Confederation Congress institutionalized and helped accelerate the most widely shared ambition of the postwar American people: to go pioneering in the West without losing the rights, privileges, and protections of republican civil government. The easy commerce in land and guaranteed right to reenter the Union on equal terms with original states profoundly democratized the process of colonization itself, reducing the cost and the risk to ordinary men and women who sought new fortunes on Indian lands – or, as they preferred to see it, in the interior's "howling wilderness." The second most popular task before the national government derived immediately from this first: the pacification of Indians who owned and occupied western lands, title to which had now been promised to future pioneers. Indian pacification quickly became one of the most important tasks of the new federal government, but nothing much could be done for the West until the new government addressed the critical economic problems left over from the Confederation era.

Accordingly, the first Congress asked Alexander Hamilton, secretary of the treasury in Washington's administration and a leading architect of the new federal system, to propose legislation for breathing life into the postwar economy. Hamilton responded with an interlocking program of public finance. By design, his policies favored commercial interests, creditors, and contracts: Such were the engines of economic development. Most urgently required was the funding of the national debt. Since the beginning of the Revolution, the stocks, bonds, and currency issued by Congress and the several states had passed from hand to hand, depreciating drastically. In the postwar malaise, foreign loans went unpaid, while domestic creditors despaired of ever recovering advances made to provisional governments. To restore the public credit, Hamilton proposed to redeem at par all those outstanding securities (both state and Continental), even though their most recent sellers might have gotten only 10 or 20 cents on the dollar. That the debt must be paid few would question – but at par? James Madison pleaded for a system of discrimination that would differentiate original holders from speculative sharpsters; unfortunately, no practical method could be devised, while good business principles required that obligations be paid in full. For wealthy individuals who had mothballed their "worthless" paper – or speculators who quickly bought it up as rumors flew – the windfall was tremendous. For ordinary soldiers whose pay in Continental dollars had bought but a dime's worth of food and drink, the insult was insufferable.

In addition to funding the debt at par, Hamilton also proposed absorbing the unpaid obligations of the states into one huge pool of national debt. On its face, this appeared to relieve the pressure on many state governments still struggling to balance their accounts. Some critics objected that assumption profited states that had hitherto ignored their indebtedness, while diligent taxpayers in other states had shouldered their burdens and taxed themselves to begin restoring their credit. Others, more suspicious, noticed that the assumption scheme would sharply curtail the role of separate state treasuries in the arena of public finance. The cynics largely were correct, for Hamilton clearly wished to consolidate fiscal policy in the hands of the federal government. Furthermore, he had plans for the national debt that rendered its expanded size more of a blessing than a curse.

The third prop in Hamilton's program proved no less controversial: the Bank of the United States (BUS). Conceived for the purpose of turning debt into money, this nationally chartered corporation seemed like a brilliant – or was it malevolent? – solution to an age-old American problem. Chronically short of specie, the colonies-turned-states desperately needed a flexible currency that would hold its value across state lines, leaving gold and silver coins free to service the overseas trade. Thanks to funding and assumption, a large supply of new United States bonds stood out as premier investments for persons of means – especially if their owners actually *received* the promised semi-annual interest in gold. Once the value of this paper rose to par in the market (once they were "good as gold"), such bonds could take the place of specie in the vaults of the national bank while BUS banknotes greased the wheels of commerce and stimulated economic growth. Government payments backed up by taxation guaranteed retirement of the paper, so that in twenty years the United States could enjoy a money supply many times larger than its stock of gold and silver, having benefited all the while from the circulation of an expanded common currency. It was a confidence game (banking *is* in a way), and so it required management by scrupulous executives. Accordingly, Hamilton placed control of his bank in the hands of private directors, beyond the reach of elected politicians who might feel pressured to encourage inflation. Such a brazen repudiation of popular governance sparked howls of protest, as did the technical fact that the Constitution authorized neither banks nor corporations. Still, the treasury czar rammed it through Congress, then got George Washington to sign it by promising to locate the federal capital across from his farm at Mount Vernon.

Hamilton's reach exceeded his grasp in 1793 when he pushed for bounties to manufacturers. All but a tiny fraction of Americans earned a living directly from agriculture, and few saw much need to change that situation. At best, urban artisans hoped for import tariffs that would shield them from British competition while they grew into their role as suppliers to an independent people. But Hamilton wanted something different. Rejecting tariff protection because it endangered the revenue stream that paid for his bonds (and also because it favored the independent artisans who tended to oppose Federalist policies), Hamilton asked for a system of bounties for large manufactories that quickly could establish competitive output – and would be headed by wealthy gentlemen whose politics he trusted. His model for such development was the Society for the Encouragement of Useful Manufactures (SEUM) of Paterson, New Jersey. Launched in 1791, SEUM's cotton manufacturing enterprise was designed first and foremost to absorb $500,000 worth of new federal government stock (the only form of payment accepted for its shares). Foreign bank loans were intended to generate working capital, and the whole scheme may have served as much as a prop for government securities as a stimulus to cotton manufacturing. Stabilizing a securities market proved to be the central objective of Hamilton's entire fiscal program, including his support for manufacturing.

This Federalist strategy of balancing agriculture, commerce, and manufacturing might have garnered considerable support both inside and outside of Congress, but Hamilton's way of gathering that support affirmed the suspicions of urban artisans, country farmers, and southern planters that the Federalists favored the urban merchant class. Rumors flew that his funding scheme intentionally transferred wealth to the "paper jobbers" in order to strangle "country" interests (farmers, planters, artisans) before they gained control of their own governments. The design of the national bank, governed by a board stacked in favor of private investors, seemed proof of elitist intentions. Factor in Hamilton's fondness for a standing army and a navy fit for the high seas, and the image of a dangerous Anglophile usurper was complete. His undisguised distrust of popular democracy made him an easy mark for opponents of this Federalist agenda, but in truth most of the so-called Founding Fathers shared his desire to see property rights protected, credit restored, and governing institutions safely controlled by well-qualified gentlemen (George Washington called them the "Monied Gentry"). Hamilton's designs fostered relatively modern financial institutions and a capitalistic market, but they owed much as well to old mercantilist habits of trying to control economic outcomes with public policy. His personal zeal in promoting a nationalistic program triggered opposition from *within* the ranks of pro-Constitution nationalists.

What united Hamilton's political positions – and focused the hostility of his enemies – was the theory of "broad" or "loose" construction with which he approached the Constitution. In his mind, the dangers of disintegration facing the infant republic were so great that every fragment of power implicit in the new charter should be exercised and built upon immediately, before the inevitable jealousies of local interests and popular demagogues shook the Union to pieces. Other framers of the Constitution – led conspicuously by James Madison – took alarm at Hamilton's aggressive pursuit of power. First in Congress and then gradually outdoors among the voters, opposition to the Federalist program took shape. Funding and assumption drew the initial attack, but the Bank of the United States became the true bête noir of the opposition, requiring as it did an elastic reading of the Constitution to copy that centerpiece of English corruption, the Bank of England. Obsessed with Hamilton's latitudinarian justifications for his bank, Secretary of State Thomas Jefferson conjured up visions of a phalanx of "monarchists" conspiring to re-enslave the nation. When President Washington scolded his fellow Virginian for such hysterical accusations, Jefferson concluded that heroic efforts were required to stop this Federalist campaign before liberty itself was lost.

The opposition movement led by Madison and Jefferson soon claimed the moniker "Republican" and brought together into something like a political party several groups outside the core of Federalist support. Many came from the southern planter class, men who distrusted urban merchants, lawyers, and creditors, and jealously guarded the political autonomy that made them virtual kings on their own plantations. Common farmers, whose poverty prevented them from holding Continental paper long enough to profit from redemption, lashed back at the "unfairness" of the Federalists' funding program. Small artisans opposed to monopolistic structures such as SEUM gravitated toward the opposition, as did unvanquished Antifederalists, men who had opposed the Constitution all along and now hoped to block all consolidation of power in the national government. What the Republicans lacked in coherent objectives they made up for in rhetoric and zeal. "Usurpation" had been one of Britain's crimes in 1776, and usurpation by Federalist elites rekindled the same emotional response. It did not help that Washington condemned the popular Democratic-Republican Societies – grass-roots political clubs that seemed like the soul of popular self-government – and delivered a Farewell Address in 1796 filled with grave warnings against partisan activity. Go home and let us govern for you is what these people heard in Washington's screed against "party spirit" and "self-created societies." Wasn't self-creation, they responded, what America was all about?

Historians often marvel at what seems, on the part of Madison, to be an astonishing reversal of positions, from author of the *Federalist Papers* to leader of the opposition against the Federalist machinery. In reality, Madison moved very little while those around him tugged and pulled at the Constitution, trying to make it vastly more (or less) nationalistic than he personally had intended. In the face of disintegration during the 1780s, Madison wanted significant energy at the center; but Hamilton's ambitions for the national state quickly outran Madison's sense of proportion and he turned back into an enemy of institutionalized power. His friend and mentor in revolution-making, Thomas Jefferson, always had been philosophically more radical (Jefferson had missed the Philadelphia Convention and spent the ratification months in Paris enjoying the opening scenes of the French Revolution). A far better political scientist, the younger Madison nevertheless deferred to the charismatic Jefferson, and together they staged an electoral coup at the turn of the nineteenth century. Rallying under frankly democratic principles laid down in the Virginia and Kentucky Resolutions of 1798 – little government close to home, states' rights, frequent elections, and maximum personal liberty – they won the bitterly contested election of 1800 and immediately proclaimed a new "Revolution" restoring power to the people.

The political struggles of the 1790s matter so much to the story of the market revolution that followed because they unleashed forces of individualism, localism, and libertarianism that had not been central – or essential – to the original idea of republican government. Truly radical democratic sentiments had existed all along, to be sure, but revolutionary leaders from John Adams to Hamilton, Madison, and Jefferson all had envisioned a leading role for gentlemen of vision and experience. In a proper republic, representatives would *govern* for the masses, not as simple spokesmen for the common man but as wise and virtuous statesmen. The delicate balancing of power within the Constitution sought to institutionalize deliberative processes and block the emergence of naked class or interest group factions, but Hamilton's agenda seemed to threaten that ideal from day one. As a result, men such as Madison leaned back to the left, depriving the government of durable power rather than see it fall into the hands of ideologues. In doing so, they placed great confidence in popular elections, a kind of political market mechanism, as the one safe way to keep decisions from acquiring force over time and subverting the people's liberty. The exact same confidence gradually would sanction the economic market mechanisms described by Adam Smith in *The Wealth of Nations*. It was, after all, against mercantilism that Smith railed, against its corrupting effect on both government and the economy. As early Americans shied away from centralized power and neo-mercantilist systems of economic policy, they found themselves embracing, almost by default, the assumption that markets were somehow less corruptible – and therefore more desirable – than the policies of governments, no matter how carefully designed.

Thus began, under the leadership of Jeffersonian Republicans, the steady privatization of economic life in the new United States. Too much is often made of the "modern" economic thinking of the Federalists in contrast to the antique "agrarianism" of Jefferson's followers, giving rise to the logical assumption that his election somehow deterred or postponed the market revolution. In fact, Hamilton's program of top-down, government-driven economic promotion was old-fashioned and mercantilist compared to the more liberal views of many Virginians. If they praised free markets and private capitalists mostly to prevent the state from raising taxes (and they often did just that), Virginia planters nonetheless stood among the earliest Americans to sing such hymns to government nonintervention and widespread freedom of enterprise (for white men). In their minds, republicanism lost the elements of communalism that always had tempered its libertarian energies, and the American tendency to conflate political liberty with economic freedom or autonomous individualism began in earnest.

LIBERALISM EMERGES

One of the first places we see evidence of the liberalization of political and economic culture is in the American courts. Legal practices at all levels understandably reflected English customs regarding private property and contracts, since local jurisprudence in the colonies grew out of English common law. At the same time, colonial conditions never had matched English traditions exactly, and over time American judges had grown more flexible and tolerant of innovation as they struggled to solve New World problems in unprecedented ways. Once released from direct English oversight, American jurists and legislators blended what they read in Coke and Blackstone – the leading sources on English law – with elements from Locke, classical republican writers, natural law scholars such as Emmerich de Vattel, and their own seat-of-the-pants sense of what was fair and equitable. The emerging legal culture was eclectic, instrumentalist, and contentious, in part because so many forces moved in to help define "the law," and there was no priestly caste of legal scholars to prevent it.

Consider, for example, the evolution of the corporation in American law. England long had used corporations to carry on charitable work such as hospitals and schools. More durable than partnerships, and legally sanctioned by sovereign authorities, corporations survived the deaths of individual officers and made it possible to husband resources for public purposes over long periods of time. Just after the Revolution, some American states adapted the corporations to provide other services – bridges and turnpikes, for example. Public thoroughfares traditionally were charged among the duties of the sovereign, but the early American states were short of money and loath to raise taxes on their newly enfranchised citizens. Accordingly, in 1785, Massachusetts chartered a corporation to build and maintain a bridge across the Charles River at Boston. An extraordinary blessing to the city and its hinterland, the Charles River Bridge mobilized the wealth of private investors to provide an improvement the sovereign could not afford. In exchange, the incorporators collected tolls and enjoyed monopoly protection for several decades into the future. With the confidence of men who were sure they had found a mutual solution to a vexing problem, the authors of the charter listed in great detail the privileges and obligations of the parties – even to setting tolls for coaches, wagons, pedestrians, cattle, and sheep. Such confidence marked similar charters all over the new United States between 1783 and the early 1800s, documenting in the process the last moments at which people thought they could imagine the details of their future sixty, eighty, or a hundred years out.

What the parties could not know in cases such as the Charles River Bridge was how explosive growth and unimaginable change would blast the assumptions on which these corporate contracts had been made. Bridge tolls poured in, rewarding the incorporators handsomely and driving the market price for Charles River Bridge stock to five or six times its original value. At the same time, the fantastic development of Boston and Cambridge transformed this once-benevolent gateway into a punitive bottleneck. Forty-three years after the first charter – but still before the end of the term for which the owners had a right to the revenue – the state authorized a new *free* bridge to relieve congestion on the toll bridge. The owners – for whom Charles River Bridge was a business investment, not a public service – sued for damages, only to find the courts now favoring the pressing needs of the community over the technical rights of the original charter. Finally ruling in 1837 against the exclusive rights of the original corporation, the U.S. Supreme Court overturned the law's traditional embrace of prior rights in favor of "creative destruction," a novel doctrine that encouraged innovation as a public good and limited the capacity of any legislature to bind its successors to terms that would prove, in the end, unfavorable to the community.

A drift in this direction had been seen as early as 1803 in a New York case that overturned the rights of a miller to the flow of his river in favor of a new dam upstream that promised public convenience and economic growth. English common law still protected prior rights and discouraged changes that infringed upon traditional arrangements. But Americans were more innovative by necessity and never had accorded vested interests quite the sanctity they enjoyed back in England. In the early 1800s, with or without legislative reform, American law started to favor enterprise and innovation at the expense of vested rights or ancient customs, just as more people were enjoying personal agency in a democratic regime.

Nowhere was the use of legal or political power for business purposes more visible, controversial, and potentially mischievous than in the regulation of money. For centuries, Europeans had employed gold and silver coins minted by sovereign governments as a medium of exchange. Relatively scarce and durable, the worth of such coins – known as *specie* – could be verified by weight even if the issuing government tried to cheat a bit on face values. This made specie the preferred currency for international trade. But gold and silver coins were heavy, bulky, irreplaceable if lost (especially at sea), and easily stolen – all of which made them as inconvenient as they were reliable. Individual merchants long had done business by swapping promissory notes or bills of exchange, paper instruments backed by their own specie deposits, goods in transit, and the reputation of the man who issued the paper. But as trading networks grew larger, men were forced to do business with strangers and rely increasingly on third-party handlers of private securities (discounters), who evolved over time into bankers. Bankers substituted generic, institutional promises to pay for the private notes of merchants, severing the personal link between borrowers and lenders and erecting in its place an institution that guaranteed the value of its paper and charged a small commission for its services.

Some early banks were strictly private, issuing notes and discounting bills entirely on the authority of the owners. They enjoyed no government privileges, and nothing but their reputation for honesty and prudence guaranteed the value of their paper. (Stephen Girard opened such a bank in Philadelphia in 1812, after the demise of the first BUS. Primarily it served the local community of merchants engaged in trade.) Because banks affected the money supply, however, they challenged the traditional power of the sovereign to regulate the "coin of the realm." As a result, eighteenth-century governments typically restricted banking to a privileged few operators licensed by the state, and most of the new American states followed suit. State control enhanced and protected the profitability of monopolistic banking, which made it an attractive enterprise for the "friends" of government officials; it also gave banking the appearance (if not always the fact) of public oversight. But such licensing invariably made banking a hotly debated topic of politics, especially in a self-governing republic created in part to put down "corruption."

In addition to the controversial Bank of the United States chartered by Congress in 1791, most American states chartered a single state bank or very few private incorporated banks to meet the needs of their local economies. Such incorporated banks in theory put the tangible assets of investors (gold and silver used to purchase bank stock) in the vaults and issued paper notes that could be redeemed at the bank on demand. Because not all bearers of banknotes were likely to demand redemption at once, banks typically issued notes in excess of the actual value of their capital stock – often three, four, or five to one (a system called "fractional reserves"). Bank loans amounted to credits resting partly on existing wealth but also anticipating growth from real economic activity, allowing enterprise to grow more quickly than the supply of hard money might warrant. Just as important, bank credits placed into the hands of innovative borrowers the stored wealth of others who (for whatever reason) preferred *not* to engage in risky enterprises.

In the hands of cautious managers of high integrity, such banking practices were really quite safe, but there were also many ways to cheat the system and render the enterprise unstable. For instance, if stockholders purchased shares with anything other than gold and silver, the capital stock in the vaults accordingly was overstated. In notorious (and oft-used) schemes, directors granted themselves loans from the bank to buy their shares of stock – effectively backing paper notes with more paper IOUs and nothing else. In the absence of regulations to the contrary, bank directors made loans to friends or political allies without reference to their creditworthiness. In this way, lending practices profoundly affected access to credit for individuals, classes, or groups of people (political parties, for example). Unwilling to foreclose such loans because of the entanglements of "friendship," bankers might put their enterprise at risk. If banks collected savings deposits and then failed, depositors lost real money while defaulting borrowers might escape repaying their loans – an outcome that seemed especially unjust to ordinary people. Finally, unscrupulous banks could issue far more notes than they ever could redeem, risking a "run" on the bank if customers lost confidence for any reason.

All of these evils and more marred the early history of banking and explain why so many intelligent people (Thomas Jefferson, for instance) feared banks even when they desperately needed ready money. For the casual observer, banking looked like a shell game: The pea was *somewhere*, and the gamesman was probably a crook. Securing the formal blessing of government, in the form of a corporate charter, was one way that bankers tried to secure credibility and public confidence, even if they turned around and abused that trust immediately. For a hundred years – since the founding of the Bank of England (1694) and the

bursting of the South Sea Bubble (1720) that nearly destroyed it –
Americans had known that government-chartered banks could do great
good *and also* ruin unsuspecting innocents. What they did not yet know
in the early republic was how to secure the one without risking the
other. Consequently, the regulation of currency bothered early Americans in ways we find hard to fathom in the twenty-first century.

The problem was that only money – "good money" – could facilitate
transactions at a distance between parties who did not know each
other well. For generations, local transactions had been recorded as
debits and credits in the books of great planters or country storekeepers, but as people stirred after the Revolution, moving away from the
narrow circles of colonial life, they did business far more frequently
with total strangers. Possessing enormous tangible wealth (mostly
bound up in land or bulky agricultural produce) and eager to exchange
their surplus for goods and services, early Americans thus demanded
from their governments an adequate supply of money they could trust.
The trick was to authorize banking privileges without kindling that
speculative urge to cheat and swindle that seemed to accompany every
known scheme of paper exchange. Most states outlawed private banking and placed control of money in the hands of political or economic
leaders, who were sometimes corrupt and always targets of popular
hatred when currency restrictions were in order. Hearing a different
drummer, Pennsylvania turned out charters on an equal-opportunity
basis. Popular with voters, perhaps, such inflationary practices threatened to drive good money out of circulation altogether. Lacking clear
theoretical guidance, and deeply suspicious of lodging the power to set
values in *anybody's* hands, people toyed with all kinds of solutions. By
1815, over two hundred separate banks contributed to the American
money supply; in the next generation, the number tripled.[6]

Because it was huge ($10 million), conservatively managed, and
one-fifth owned by the federal government, the Bank of the United
States developed a regulatory power over this patchwork of smaller
banks. Through its branches, it could facilitate exchange of notes
between institutions across state lines; and although it did not exercise
direct restraint, its potential to do so may have discouraged expansive
practices by local bankers. Controlled by its directors (not by elected

---

[6] Perkins, *American Public Finance*, 272.

officials), the Bank of the United States remained politically unpopular – all the more so as foreign investors bought up its stock (although they could not serve as directors). In 1811, Republicans in Congress, prompted in part by their friends in rival institutions such as the State Bank of Virginia, allowed the charter of the national bank to expire. Then the return of war in 1812 and a run on commercial banks in 1814 produced a new financial crisis and justification for another national bank. In 1816, President Madison signed legislation chartering a Second Bank of the United States. Still a mixed, public-private corporation, this new bank might have restored order, but its managers lacked either the talent or inclination to use it in a disciplined way. (Ironically, when Nicholas Biddle tried to do precisely that, President Andrew Jackson declared the bank a "monster" and killed it dead!)

In the first two decades of the new century, land speculation soaked up much of this newly minted capital, and most of the time, real farm and plantation making quickly backed up the value of paper claims. Since the Revolution, tens of thousands of Americans had poured into the trans-Appalachian wilderness, bringing Kentucky (1793) and Tennessee (1796) into the Union and pushing many Indians north and west of the Ohio River. People clamored for land, still the universal standard of independence in this pre-industrial world, and a credit program offered by Congress gave purchasers four years to pay for frontier farms at $2 per acre. With extreme care, a farm family might harvest value quickly enough from frontier land to make the required payments (assuming they had access to markets for their surplus), but far more government land was sold to speculators hoping to profit from resale at rising prices before their loans came due. Everything depended, of course, on expanding markets for export staples that were grown ever farther from ready markets. Thus the flood of pioneers (and speculators) deep into the backcountry stimulated greater demands for transport services, money, and credit, in an early example of the spiral of connections that would drive the market revolution forward. As later generations eventually would learn, bull markets typically succumb to "irrational exuberance" (Alan Greenspan's term for the "dot-com" boom of the late 1990s). For early Americans, however, the land boom before 1819 – and a second in the 1830s – seemed positively irrepressible.

Cotton fueled the greatest excitement in this first American land boom, brought about by the perfection of a machine called the cotton gin. First designed in 1791 by Eli Whitney, this "engine" – universally called a "gin" – removed seeds from the lint of short-staple upland cotton, making it possible to prepare for market a crop easily grown with slave labor all over the lower South. Textile factories in England stood ready to buy cotton faster than planters could grow it, and by 1800 copy-cat factories in southern New England were bidding for a share of the crop as well. By the thousands, the children of tidewater planters marched their families and slaves into central Georgia, Alabama, Mississippi, and Louisiana, displacing Indians and hacking out plantations wherever rivers allowed the export of crops. Slave labor, widely thought to be a drag on the Chesapeake region at the end of the Revolution, found a new lease on life as westward-moving farmers bought up hands to make their fortunes on the cotton frontier. Swirling banknotes, steady demand, and rising prices for cotton, land, and slaves all contributed to the boom that peaked in the years just after the War of 1812.

Independent of the cotton-fueled land boom, population growth, frontier expansion, and rising productivity (from new land as well as improved production techniques) all stimulated rising expectations that quickly took the form of demands for improved transportation – "internal improvements." First, the post-revolutionary growth of the seaport cities – Boston, New York, Philadelphia, and Baltimore – brought investments in turnpikes, bridges, and river improvements designed to facilitate trade with each city's hinterland. Pennsylvania led the nation in turnpike charters in the 1790s; after 1800, producers of milk, butter, eggs, livestock, vegetables, and firewood found brisk markets in several cities they could reach (for a price) on brand-new turnpike roads. Baltimore labored to improve navigation in the dangerous lower Susquehanna River – an ambition that was fought every step of the way by Philadelphia interests who wished to see the produce of central Pennsylvania forced off the river and onto their new Lancaster Turnpike headed east. Boston merchants cast their eyes north toward the Merrimack River and central New Hampshire. Richmond mounted a project to bypass the falls of the James River and improve the downstream flow of goods to that Virginia city. New Yorkers dreamed of cutting canals through Lake Champlain to the St. Lawrence River and via the Mohawk River to Lake Ontario. Most spectacularly, friends of the new federal city, Washington, D.C., led by George Washington himself, pushed a Potomac Canal intended to bypass the Great Falls above Georgetown, cut through the mountains to Ohio, and pour the entire produce of the continental interior into a great national entrepôt.

Between 1789 and 1815, America's prospering Atlantic commercial centers turned their faces inward, greatly expanding their commercial reach into rural hinterlands and gathering strength for the next round of growth. But none of the large interregional projects imagined in this generation came to successful fruition. Neither local capital nor technical expertise proved equal to the tasks. What this first burst of excitement for internal improvement did, however, was to spread the assumption that distance from a port or other ready market was no excuse for leaving undeveloped rich interior lands. All along the rivers of Tennessee, Kentucky, Ohio, and upstate New York and the territories of Alabama, Mississippi, Indiana, and Illinois, farmers settled their families and cultivated corn or cotton, absolutely certain that sooner or later *something* would bring them access to markets for their surplus commodities. This rising confidence, of course, closed the circle for sellers of land on speculation: Who could resist getting in on the ground floor of an interior region that was *destined* to become the next big thing in American economic growth?

Robert Fulton gave this exuberance a mighty boost in 1807 when he launched a successful steamboat on New York's coastal waters. The immediate impact on commerce in the East was probably greater on the upstream side: The price of manufactured goods at interior landings fell dramatically as the cost of transporting things against the current dropped by an order of magnitude. But in the West the steamboat made an even more dramatic difference. Before the arrival of steamboats on interior rivers in the middle 1810s, once a year pioneer farmers and planters floated their surplus to market (often all the way to New Orleans) and then walked back home, carrying their profits (or drinking them up in taverns along the way). Steamboats perfectly suited the needs of western markets. Relatively cheap to build and operate, they did not require government funding or corporate sponsorship. Redesigned for western rivers, by the 1830s, shallow-draft, flat-bottomed (and later stern-wheeled) boats probed the channels and bayous of the Mississippi, Yazoo, Tombigbee, Alabama, Ohio,

Missouri, Illinois, Tennessee, and Wabash rivers. Interior ports such as St. Louis, Memphis, Louisville, and Cincinnati became urban centers in their own right, forwarding produce and importing merchandise for country retailers scattered across eight states. Bridging the gap between the walking world of the eighteenth century and the high-cost, high-tech networks later represented by canals and railroads, private independent steamboats kept the dream alive for several million frontier settlers whose demands for even better facilities would stimulate a second major wave of internal improvement in the wake of the Erie Canal.

Up in tiny Rhode Island, one more story began that looked at first like a sideshow but later restructured the fundamentals of American economic life. A Providence merchant named Moses Brown, a recent convert to the Quaker confession, went looking for a better way to invest the unholy fortune he had made from importing slaves. Geographically, southern New England was long on fast little rivers and short on agricultural potential, so Brown thought the future may lie in using water power to spin cotton yarn – the way they were doing it now in England. An advertisement placed in a New York paper brought an English mechanic, Samuel Slater, to Brown's door. In 1791 in Pawtucket, using money from Brown and his kin, Slater managed to reproduce working Arkwright machinery and spin yarn by water power. A quaint little operation employing a few women and children, Slater's Pawtucket mill seemed anything but revolutionary; yet a larger, purpose-built factory soon followed, and in the next decade copy-cat mills popped up elsewhere in Rhode Island and southeastern Massachusetts. The American textile revolution had begun.

Brown's and Slater's little mill introduced the fundamental aspects of industrialization that in 1791 had not been seen yet in any other context or system. First, the productivity gained as a result of applying power to new machinery proved simply astonishing. Complaining that he would ruin them with overproduction, Slater's mercantile partners – William Almy and Obadiah Brown – scrambled to distribute the yarn that poured from his little factory. To Slater's enormous frustration, they tried to curtail inventory by holding back supplies of raw cotton and cash for payroll. Patiently, Slater explained that you could not profit from water spinning if you laid off hands and closed the mill; you had to *expand* the system to realize its potential. Wholesale and

retail marketing, dying establishments, and finally large-scale consignment weaving operations – putting yarn out to country weavers who
turned it into cloth – quickly ensnarled whole communities in textile
production. As the problems of venting inventory were resolved, Slater
himself and other competitors copied the Pawtucket mill, reproducing
all over southern New England the same sequence of events. By 1809,
there were twenty-five cotton mills in Rhode Island alone turning
almost 15,000 spindles; by 1815, the number of mills reached one
hundred, boasting 76,792 spindles.[7] Several thousand individuals –
many of them children – worked in New England mills directly while
thousands more earned at least part of their living from making cotton
cloth. Economies of scale, system integration, forward and backward
linkages, labor discipline (Slater had to *teach* his Pawtucket work force
to come to work on time each day), and the perils of overproduction –
all hallmarks of industrialization – all could be seen within twenty
years of this relatively small experiment on the part of a Quaker with
a new-found conscience.

All these early pieces of innovation and change – the Hamiltonian
programs, the banks and early corporations, legal decisions, the system
of land sales and western development, the cotton revolution, turnpikes and canals, the invention of steamboats, the early mechanization
of textile manufacturing – all were begun to gratify a liberated people
or solve problems as old as the colonies themselves. During the first
generation after Independence, few of these things (except for banks)
seemed especially controversial, and none of them as yet could be
identified as elements of systems more powerful and self-defining than
the people and governments who brought them about. Yet these things
were critical components of a system of enterprise that, once
assembled, took on a logic and a life of its own and caused what we
now call the market revolution. The Jeffersonian creed of "little government close to home" had minimized the hand of consolidated
national authority, yet many of the pieces of a new order took root
with the help of popular state and local governments. Together, American governors managed to restore the public credit, finance revolutionary debts, establish an expansive currency, formulate a liberal

[7] Peter J. Coleman, *The Transformation of Rhode Island 1790–1860* (Providence:
Brown University Press, 1963), 86–7.

system of land distribution, creatively remodel useful legal instruments (especially corporations), encourage internal improvements (roads, bridges, and turnpikes), and protect innovations that simultaneously launched the cotton culture in the South (the gin) and factory system in the North (the spinning mill). None of this amounted to a market revolution – yet; but the stage was being set.

THE WIDER WORLD

Finally, persistent warfare between Britain and France contributed the historical conditions from which would spring the American antebellum market revolution. Beginning in 1793 and continuing with one brief interruption until Napoleon was vanquished in 1815, these two imperial powers struggled to control events in the Atlantic world and contain revolutionary upheavals at home. For the new United States, such a world war proved to be a godsend. Sheltered by the 1794 Jay Treaty, which guaranteed "neutral rights" and effectively reopened British ports to American merchants, the export trade of the United States almost tripled by the end of the decade. The French had thought, as a result of their assistance during our own Revolutionary War, that Americans were bound to favor them; but President Washington took advantage of the fact that the monarchy (with which we had signed treaties) had fallen to a new regime (republican, like ours) and disavowed all mutual commitments. As long as the Anglophile Federalists controlled the national government, Americans profiteered in the shadow of British power. The resulting "Quasi-War" with France from 1798 to 1801 may have complicated life for President John Adams, but it had little real impact on an export trade that by 1801 surpassed $90 million per year.[8] In other words, circumstances largely outside the control of the American people and their governments contributed greatly to renewed prosperity and economic growth in the critical first decade under the Constitution.

The advent of the Jefferson presidency in 1801 began a steady retreat from pro-British policies that eventually led the republic into another war with Great Britain. Ideologically hostile to the British, the Federalists, and the urban commercial elite, Jefferson came into office

---

[8] Wattenberg, ed., *Statistical History*, 886.

determined to roll back the edifice of national power built on Hamilton's platform. Thinking that the value of America's agricultural exports entitled him to dictate terms in the Atlantic trade, Jefferson walked away from the Jay Treaty, cut the army, and scuttled the navy. Unfortunately, Britain and France signed the Peace of Amiens late in 1801, and the neutral commerce on which Americans had fattened dropped by nearly half within the next year. When the belligerents resumed active warfare in 1803, commercial restrictions played a more important part in the struggle and caught the Americans in an increasingly complex web of hostile decrees, blockades, and entanglements. Americans might think of their riches as fruits of their own virtue and industry, but in truth they were riding waves of international opportunity in a world where they remained bit players. Still, the "neutral trade" flourished and federal revenue from taxes on trade poured into the treasury. A giddy President Jefferson (to whom the national debt seemed exactly as evil and burdensome as his own chronic personal insolvency) paid off Hamilton's bonds as quickly as possible and looked eagerly (in his second inaugural address) to a day when the debt would be gone, taxes reduced, and federal revenues diverted to internal improvement projects in the states.

By 1806, both Britain and France had moved to limit America's freedom to trade with their enemies, and while exports peaked in 1807, the risks and complications peaked along with them. Some fifteen hundred American ships were seized by one party or the other, and some members of their crews were pressed into service in the British navy. To avoid war and punish these insults by European powers, Jefferson finally demanded in December 1807 a complete embargo of American commerce – a non-exportation order he believed would "prove" that the world could not survive without American goods and services. Within the year, it had proved instead that America could not prosper without a suitable vent for its produce. The embargo was repealed (although not before New England Federalists talked of disunion), and the second Republican president, James Madison, found himself presiding over a slow descent into war. Against the advice of Treasury Secretary Albert Gallatin (a Republican but a realist), Congress let the national bank charter lapse just months before hostilities required Gallatin to raise millions for defense. Caught between the legitimate needs of the state in a mercantilist world and the ideological preferences of Republican partisans for private, liberal, economic arrangements that maximized personal freedom, the Jeffersonians steered the country into a cul de sac of war without many of the tools (army, navy, taxes, or central bank) they needed to fight it.

Trade fell to almost nothing between 1812 and 1814. Except for some privateers – private ships engaged in "legal" piracy under license from belligerent governments – the American merchant fleet sat idle, and people turned once more to local exchanges and semi-subsistence economic strategies to survive. The loss of exports hit agriculture hard, but the corresponding shortage of imported goods yielded a small bump in demand for home manufactures. While statistically not all that important, this wartime experience helped turn the attention of Republican politicians away from a purely export-driven economic vision toward a more balanced approach that included home market development and manufacturing alongside agriculture and the carrying trade. At the end of the war in 1815, commercial activity recovered dramatically; but all Americans faced new tax burdens for wartime debts, and those whose fortunes depended on manufacturing felt the bite of sudden competition from a pent-up wave of imports that hit the wharves of New York.

At the level of public policy, Congress soon was debating an interlocking set of proposals for renewing the national bank, raising protective tariffs to ease the pain for infant industries, and investing in internal improvements (roads and canals) to help bring distant agricultural lands into the market economy. Eventually dubbed by House Speaker Henry Clay an "American System" of policy, these steps toward a framework of economic nationalism suggested a more active role for government than true Jeffersonians supported, and a serious rift developed within the Republican party between the old agrarian, liberal wing and these new advocates of intentional growth and development. The national bank and protective tariffs made it through Congress in 1816, the latter even blessed by Jefferson in retirement at Monticello. But Virginia Republicans balked at federal aid for internal improvements (they feared empowering the national government by spending money in the states), which began a struggle with the economic nationalists that dogged politics for the next generation.

The postwar recovery brought surprising changes to the port of New York that helped bring that city to a central place in the American economic landscape. With an excellent natural harbor and access via the Hudson to an extensive hinterland, New York nevertheless had lagged behind Boston and Philadelphia in the late colonial period. The British blockade during the War of 1812 sealed off most of the city's seaborne trade until the spring of 1815, when news of the peace brought a parade of British ships loaded with imported goods. It was the British who selected New York for this postwar "dumping," but new state legislation quickly eased the terms on which such goods were auctioned off at the city's docks. Resident New Yorkers purchased whole cargoes, took title, and provided all the secondary services required to warehouse the inventory, break down bulk shipments, and distribute the merchandise to local and country merchants. This freed up the British vendors to load and sail almost immediately. Having attracted this incoming traffic, New York merchants took additional steps to accumulate export produce with which to fill those ships – especially cotton from the South and flour from upstate. Steamboats on the Hudson improved this traffic and set New Yorkers to thinking once more about opening the water-level route to Lake Erie. In 1817, the nation's first full-time indoor stock exchange opened in New York, creating a formal capital market for the ready exchange of paper assets. In January 1818, a handful of venturous traders took the simple but revolutionary step of adopting a regular schedule for sailing to and from England. Previously, men and merchandise waited impatiently (often for weeks) while masters found cargoes worthy of setting sail. The new Black Ball Line promised to sail on a specified day each month, rain or shine, fully laden or half empty. What with the auctions, warehouse services, insurance underwriters, banks, stockbrokers, and other innovative services, dozens of ambitious entrepreneurs were transforming New York port into the best place to do business on the American Atlantic coast.

By 1818, the postwar economic boom had restored the confidence of Americans that their fortunes were secure, their future bright, and their rich endowment of natural resources virtually "inexhaustible." New banks of issue opened throughout the country, pouring a flood of paper currency into the hands of eager investors. Shopkeepers loaded up on merchandise and tradesmen expanded their workshops. Speculators in urban real estate bid the price of town lots upward exponentially. Farmers took out loans to enlarge their holdings, buy slaves, build buildings and fences, spread manure, or clear more land. Turnpike and navigation companies sprang up to augment the transportation infrastructure – and to issue more paper securities. Land in the West sold briskly, fueled by the federal government's generous four-year credit program that required only one-quarter down (a great deal in a rising market). Cotton exports climbed while cotton prices shot up even faster; foodstuffs coursed down the natural waterways to feed both a hungry world and the burgeoning population of mobile Americans pouring into frontier regions. True, in 1817 President Madison vetoed the Bonus Bill, intended to jump-start a system of national internal improvements that would speed up this internal flow of goods and people. But New York State, in an act of extraordinary courage (some said folly), borrowed $7 million to start digging the Erie Canal at its own expense. Peace was at hand, freedom was widely enjoyed (by adult white males), and ambition found rewards – sometimes extravagant rewards – in rapidly developing markets. It must have seemed to Americans in 1818 that all the barriers to enterprise and personal advancement that had burdened old European cultures had been lifted here in the United States. All a man had to do was find a little piece of land, put his shoulder to the wheel, mind his personal habits, tend to his own business, and reap his just reward. Such was the promise, many believed, of liberty and independence in the new American republic.

Interlude: Panic! 1819

"Let every Shylock leave his hole, and in the open day boldly sharpen his knife, to take 'the pound of flesh' nearest the heart of his honest neighbor!" So wrote Baltimore journalist Hezekiah Niles about news from the Bank of the United States, in August 1818, that free exchange of notes among various regional branches would be suspended. Ranting wildly in graphic prose, Niles condemned the "Rag Barons" and their "paper system" for the "criminal" abuse of honest persons and taxpayers. Whatever suspicions he had harbored since 1816 about the wisdom of chartering a new national bank stood vindicated now that the crooks and swindlers in charge of this engine of currency manipulation had turned their "knives" upon the people, not just "skinning as heretofore" but cutting deep at the "arteries of the public body" to get "blood enough at once to swim in."[1] So began the national nightmare known to history as the Panic of 1819.

Part and parcel of the postwar economic boom had been a dramatic expansion of the American money supply. As exports recovered from the wartime disruption, productivity expanded, and the promise of rapid growth returned, state and local banks, especially in the West and South, multiplied their loans and note issues with little regard for specie reserves or underlying values. All banks had stopped converting paper money into coin during the late war, so there was no effective check on this proliferation of banknotes. The newly chartered Second

---

[1] *Niles' Weekly Register*, 5 Sept. 1818, 25. Emphasis in the original.

Bank of the United States was expected to bring about specie resumption in early 1817, but nobody had the legal authority to compel it. As a result, the new central bank joined the expansionists' parade, showering loans and notes on eager customers until its total liabilities outran the specie in its vaults by a factor of ten to one! By early 1818, confidence in American banknotes began to slide. Spanish silver dollars commanded a 4 percent premium in Boston, creating the absurd possibility of drawing specie from the banks at par and selling it back for a profit – over and over again. "Good money" drained away to speculators and reckless western banks while questionable paper piled up in the hands of more conservative banks and in accounts owed (but not paid) to the treasury or the Second Bank.

In the summer of 1818, as this unstable monetary whirlwind spun out of control, the Bank of the United States suddenly called for a drastic contraction of credit. In the circular of August 28 (to which Niles was responding in the previous quotation), the bank stopped the flow of coin from solid to shiftless branches. At the same time, the directors called in millions in loans and demanded payment of outstanding balances owed by the state and local banks. Debtors and debtor banks scrambled for cash, calling in their loans and liquidating everything they could, driving down prices for the cotton, foodstuffs, and western lands against which such loans had been taken. In just over one year, the total demand liabilities (funds on deposit plus banknotes in circulation) of the Second Bank shrank from $23 million to $10 million. As the credit crunch rippled throughout the immature American banking system, business crashed to a halt and tens of thousands of individuals watched in horror as the value drained from their assets like water through a sieve. Technically, the monetary correction may have been a good thing, considering the dangerous inflationary pressures of the day, but the Bank's draconian contraction set off a full-blown financial crisis the likes of which Americans had never seen before. As William Gouge put it in his sharply critical *Short History of Paper Money and Banking in the United States* (1833), "The bank was saved, but the people were ruined."[2]

---

[2] William Gouge, *A Short History of Paper Money and Banking in the United States* (Philadelphia: T. W. Ustick, 1833), 32.

There can be little doubt that the sharp contraction of the money supply is what triggered a downward spiral in American prices and employment. In 1816, there had been $68 million in banknotes in circulation; by January 1820, that number had dropped to about $45 million.[3] The sudden removal of so much currency at a time when everybody needed cash to repay their debts unavoidably drove down the price of everything. Town lots, in which speculation had been especially heated, fell quickly by 50, 60, even 80 percent. Missouri Senator Thomas Hart Benton complained that the cities of the West were mortgaged to the Bank of the United States: "They are in the jaws of the monster! A lump of butter in the mouth of a dog! One gulp, one swallow, and all is gone."[4] Export staples such as cotton, flour, and tobacco lost just over half their value between August 1818 and June 1819 – although the physical volume of exports did not decrease. Public land sales crashed from $13.6 million in 1818 to under $2 million two years later.[5] Thousands of individuals defaulted on their obligations to the federal land office. Falling agricultural prices made it impossible for farmers to repay their loans for capital improvements, exposing their means of a living to the danger of foreclosure. For want of cash, consumers stopped shopping and country merchants failed, awash in debt for expensive goods they could not sell except at a loss. Country people retreated into the semi-subsistence ways of their fathers, making do with homemade things and what they could gain from local barter and exchange.

Town people faced new forms of distress rendered disastrous by the sharp rise in the concentration of propertyless workers. Unemployment spiked in 1819 and remained high for at least two years after that. One 1820 report from Philadelphia estimated employment in major handicraft industries as down four-fifths from what had prevailed in 1815 – even before the big boom. Hezekiah Niles thought as many as fifty thousand people were out of work in Baltimore, Philadelphia, and New York. Textile manufacturers laid off thousands of

---

[3] Quoted in Murray N. Rothbard, *The Panic of 1819: Reactions and Policies* (New York: Columbia University Press, 1962), 7, 13.

[4] Quoted in Samuel Rezneck, *Business Depressions and Financial Panics: Essays in American Business and Economic History* (Westport, CT: Greenwood Press, 1968), 58.

[5] *American State Papers: Public Lands* (38 vols., Washington: Gales and Seaton, 1832–61), III: 371.

workers whose families had no other means nor even anywhere to go once evicted from company housing. It might be possible to blame real estate speculators or even overreaching farmers and planters for getting themselves into trouble, but what crime had these people committed? For the first time since Independence, on such a massive scale, Americans experienced widespread distress through *involuntary* unemployment – that is, those who *would* work could not find paying work to do. One young man in Poughkeepsie, New York, despairing of an honest living, stole a horse in order to spend eight years in the state prison. There, at least, he would have bed, board, and employment.[6]

What could explain this sudden disaster in a land of plenty? People blamed the banks, of course, but others saw the boom as a reckless spree by a youthful nation drunk on the promise of luxury. Mordecai Noah, editor of the Tammany newspaper, the New York *National Advocate*, likened the condition of the nation to an "overgrown and pampered youth, with a constitution unhurt and passions unrestrained, vaulting and bounding to ruin."[7] Writing even before the panic was upon them, Noah had warned that *"the want of industry is the foundation of the evil."* Easy money and high living tempted all, and Noah saw the hand of Providence looming over the country. Lazy wives and frivolous daughters came in for especially brutal criticism for seducing their husbands and fathers into the paths of ignoble extravagance. Fifty-dollar plumb cakes and thousand-dollar shawls, for Noah, summed up the complete loss of sensible values that obtained in the years before the panic. He further condemned urban life, especially the temptations offered to wage-earning urban clerks – unmarried youths, cash in hand, lured by all manner of vices, and bereft of the influence of home and elders to keep to the straight and narrow.[8]

At the core of Noah's critique were the old-fashioned values of the rural economy: frugality, economy, and self-reliance. He acknowledged that there had been shocks before in the local systems of credit and barter, but an honorable merchant always was left with the

---

[6] Rezneck, *Business Depressions*, 55–7.

[7] [Mordecai Noah,] *Address of the Society of Tammany, or Columbian Order, to Its Absent Members and the Members of Its Several Branches* (Cincinnati: Morgan, Lodge, 1819), 8.

[8] New York *National Advocate*, 2 Oct. 1818, 7 Nov. 1818. Emphasis in the original.

freedom to "prop up his tottering affairs to the best advantage of honest creditors." Modern banking and "currency brokers" (his term for the heartless enforcers of contracts who cared not *who* you were nor *to whom* you owed money) had loosed upon the people a species of predators without consciences. They turned the credit system into an evil snare. Go back to the ways of your fathers, Noah exhorted: "There are so many ways of earning a morsel of bread honestly, that want, arising from indolence should never be tolerated . . . it is by Providence ordained that man is to live by the 'sweat of his brow.'"[9]

For Noah and many others, the solution to "hard times" lay in retreating into the values of the moral economy that had obtained in the late eighteenth century: Eschew debt, avoid luxurious indulgence, suppress vicious habits, and tend to your own, autonomous living. Semi-subsistence agriculture perfectly matched this ethic, but semi-subsistence agriculture produced little surplus and did not grow the national economy. It contributed not a farthing to the engines of capitalist expansion on which national prosperity depended. Philadelphia booster and political economist Mathew Carey struggled to deflect the conversation in a more forward-looking direction. The present distress, Carey argued in 1819, offered no stimulus to industry: "There can be no industry without a motive: and it appears to me there is a great danger that our people will soon limit their exertions to the raising of food for their families."[10] Although Noah might applaud such retrenchment, Carey recognized that the system of economic growth would collapse without the further elaboration of the interdependencies, specializations, and divisions of labor that made the capitalist system effective. Do not retreat to the country, Carey cried: There were too many people on the land already. What the country needed was a program of home manufactures and a system of policy that protected home markets from exploitation by foreign capitalists. Banking reform was appropriate, but high protective tariffs would do more to engender a balanced economy and raise an "American system" of policy – the same thing Henry Clay was pushing in Congress – the point of which was to harness economic growth to American national interests.

---

[9] Noah, *Address of . . . Tammany,* 10; New York *National Advocate,* 3 Sept. 1819. Emphasis in the original.

[10] Quoted in Rezneck, *Business Depressions,* 55.

⸮risis of 1819, local institutions for poor relief found
. beneath the sheer volume of genuine distress. Some
.h stay laws, suspending foreclosures and debt repay-
ounds that prevailing low prices made forced liquida-
.nt to theft. Some people called for the destruction of all
for a return to easy paper money. A congressional inves-
the workings of the Second Bank of the United States found
the .   ,tuffed not with specie, but with IOUs signed by directors who
had loaned vast sums to themselves and their friends, ignoring what
safeguards had been written into their charter. But some forty members
of Congress held stock in the Second Bank, and none wished to see it
punished appropriately. Congress did reform the land system, restruc-
turing some landholders' debts, lowering the minimum price to $1.25
per acre, and eliminating altogether the four-year credit system. From
now on, buyers of public land would have to pay cash or find lenders in
the private sector. Throughout the country, debates raged over the sanctity of contract on one hand (without which the modern economy would
not flourish), and on the other the protection of innocent persons (a
traditional responsibility of the sovereign authorities) from predatory
swindlers and fast-talking cheats who seemed mysteriously immune
from the terrible sword of financial correction.

Clearly the Republic stood at the threshold of a new era. Prosperity
for all – the booming potential of a growth economy – lay down the
road toward the modern capitalist system; security for all – the enjoy-
ment of a modest "competence" without exposure to undue risks in
global financial markets – lay back the other way. State and local
governments fumbled the dilemma, while the federal government
blithely ignored "hard times" until they went away of their own
accord. Modern economists now have ways of explaining these cycli-
cal failures of confidence, but almost nobody in 1819 understood the
technical forces that had crushed the system of credit and so drastically
undermined prices. That cotton could be worth 24 cents one day and
11 cents the next made no sense: Cotton was a tangible product whose
properties and usefulness changed not a whit overnight.[11] One price
or the other must be dishonest – one puffed up by intoxicating

---

[11] *Statistical History of the United States from Colonial Times to the Present*, ed. Ben J.
Wattenberg (New York: Basic Books, 1976), 209.

speculation, or the other forcibly depressed by the actions of crooked dealers. Not a generation away from the mercantilism of old, most Americans either accepted the scoldings dished out by the likes of Mordecai Noah or angrily searched for the scoundrels who must have wrecked the markets and profited handsomely in doing so. The Panic of 1819 had been a "teachable moment" in the emergence of a market revolution in the United States, but few could decipher correctly the moral of the story.

Painful as it was, the Panic of 1819 did not quite dislodge the traditional frameworks of economic virtue and providential blessing with which early Americans interpreted their fluctuating fortunes. Careful students looking back catch glimpses of the modern phenomena that accompany the business cycle in mature financial systems, but no one on the ground in 1819 knew what to look for or how to understand these market forces that rose and fell of their own accord and seemed to obey the commands of no man. It still made more sense to view them (like the Biblical plagues of Egypt) as warnings from an angry God, or as proof of corrupt conspiracies, than to embrace them as natural and inevitable features of the new economic system. Therefore, by 1822, when prosperity returned on a more stable footing, a generation of American white men recovered their confidence that they could navigate new economic waters to their own eventual improvement.

2

Marvelous Improvements Everywhere

After two full years of hardship, the American economy began to emerge from the Panic of 1819, shaken by the experience but still possessed of the deep roots of optimism and promise that had been planted since the time of Independence. The foundations of American prosperity survived; fundamental resources, energy, and innovative habits persisted; and the shape of what might be was apparent to perceptive entrepreneurs. And even as the speculative boom of the late 'teens marched toward its disastrous resolution, crucial structural changes had begun that pointed the way toward an era of "marvelous improvements" that would capture the imagination of a generation and set the agenda for American economic growth through the rest of the antebellum period. Nothing better symbolized the pluck and drive, the audacious ambition, and the breathtaking confidence of men with little more than a layman's hunch about what they were doing than New York's magnificent Erie Canal.

THE RISE OF NEW YORK PORT

Since the late colonial era, New Yorkers had dreamed of improving the "water-level" route to the West that nature conveniently laid out within the confines of their state. From Maine to Georgia, elevations of two or three thousand feet separated the Atlantic from the interior waters – except in New York. In the Empire State, the east-west valley of the Mohawk River offered a link between the Great Lakes and the Hudson River – a route 360 miles long – with an elevation gain less than 600 feet. The easiest connections – to Lake Ontario and the St. Lawrence River – had been the object of two failed projects in the 1790s. (Had they succeeded, such canals only would have fed commerce into the hands of Canadian merchants.) Abandoning the wisdom of that earlier day, new visionaries boldly proposed a canal straight across the state to Lake Erie. Gentle grades and abundant supplies of water convinced surveyors in 1808 that an Erie route was practicable. Writing in 1811, New York Canal Commissioner Gouvernor Morris claimed that no greater object in the civilized world could be encompassed at so little expense.

Posting their first estimate at $5 million, New York's commissioners believed such a great undertaking must be a public work – indeed, a *national* public work worthy of the patronage of Congress. But sectional jealousies made federal assistance impossible, so New York decided to press on alone: If the nation would not avail itself of this rare advantage, the State of New York would – and reap the benefits. The War of 1812 intervened, killing all progress on the Erie project, but in the early days of the postwar boom, DeWitt Clinton breathed new life into the scheme, painting marvelous, even Biblical images of eastbound "boats loaded with flour, pork, beef, pot and pearl ashes, flaxseed, wheat, barley, corn, hemp, wool, flax, iron, lead, copper, salt, gypsum, coal, tar, fur, peltry, ginseng, bees-wax, cheese, butter, lard, staves, lumber," and returning with "merchandise from all parts of the world." Manufacturing establishments would spring up, agriculture and commerce flourish, villages, towns, and cities would "line the banks" of the canal and the Hudson River. "The wilderness and the solitary place will become glad, and the desert will rejoice and blossom as the rose."[1]

New Yorkers did not accept spontaneously their historic role as improvers for the nation. In fact, the project that would guarantee New York's commercial hegemony prevailed against the opposition of every single delegate from New York City. Nevertheless, in 1817 a state law authorized loans up to $7 million, pledging the salt tax, auction duties, and taxes on land along the canal to pay the interest until such time as tolls from the canal would render it self-supporting. Work began later that year. Lacking professional "engineers" (there

[1] Quoted in New York General Assembly, *Laws of the State of New York in Relation to the Erie and Champlain Canals* (2 vols., Albany: E. and E. Hosford, 1825), I: 129.

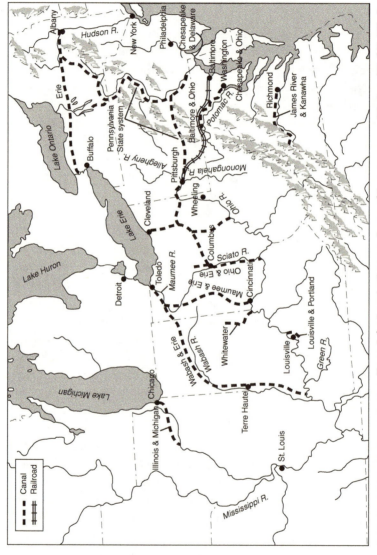

MAP OF CANALS AND RAILROADS. From John Lauritz Larson, *Internal Improvement: National Public Works and the Promise of Popular Government in the Early United States.* Copyright © 2001 by the University of North Carolina Press. Used by permission of the publisher, www.uncpress.unc.edu.

were almost none in the world worthy of the name), local men set about to make do with what they could learn on the fly. By trial and error, they discovered the inadequacies of wooden locks, the mysteries of hydraulic cement, and the relative merits of deep cuts and long embankments. They invented simple machines to pull stumps, cut roots, and handle soil. They learned how to "puddle" the ditch with clay slurries until it stopped "weeping."

Understandably, the Panic of 1819 raised a fright among friends of the Erie Canal, but New York had enough funds on hand to keep building as prices for labor and materials fell. By early 1820, 94 miles of the middle section had been completed, relatively close to budget, and eager users were contributing tolls to the fund intended for servicing debt. Over 200 miles were open by the end of 1822, and technical feats such as a long stone aqueduct over the Genesee River at Rochester bore witness to the talent of the men in charge. Ahead lay the most difficult parts: the narrow channel east of Little Falls where the Mohawk cut through rock to reach the Hudson, and a 70-foot escarpment at Lockport separating the broad interior from the Erie shore. But the cumulative impact of successful experimentation, steady financing, and a rising tide of traffic on the finished canal guaranteed victory over these final barriers.

By October 1825, the Erie Canal was finished. Swelling with pride, New Yorkers began a ten-day celebration. They had made the "longest Canal – in the least time – with the least experience – for the least money – and of the greatest public utility of any other in the world." As the ceremonial flotilla sailed slowly eastward from Buffalo toward New York City, bearing DeWitt Clinton together with a host of dignitaries and two kegs of Lake Erie water soon to be poured into New York Harbor, crowds thronged to share the excitement and ceremony of this wonderful achievement. Speakers everywhere praised the wisdom, public spirit, and energy of the people of New York. Congratulatory letters poured in. President John Quincy Adams declared the moment an "Event" in the "progress of human Affairs." Former president James Madison, whose Bonus Bill veto had forced New York to act alone, called it a "precious contribution" to the happiness of the country, "worthy of emulating" in other states. Thomas Jefferson thought the Erie Canal would bless New York's "descendants with wealth and prosperity" while proving to "mankind the superior wisdom of employing the resources of industry in works of improvement."[2]

Jefferson, of course, was correct. The Erie Canal diverted into New York City a river of gold far exceeding that which its early friends had predicted. Lured by the canal itself and the prospects of immediate access to markets, ambitious pioneers flocked into upstate New York. Lumber, grain, and flour flowed down into the city and out into the markets of the Atlantic world. Immigrants and trade goods found a better route to the Old Northwest, and farm exports from the Great Lakes basin added to New York's growing trade. In the city, merchants, bankers, warehousemen, shippers – entrepreneurs of all sorts – seized the opportunity to perfect and specialize their services, fostering round after round of business innovations that within a decade of the opening of the Erie Canal had made New York by far the best place in America to engage in commerce. So successful was the grand canal that everyone forgot it had ever been opposed. And so complete was the commercial transformation of New York that when the railroads of the next generation made it possible to divert trade virtually anywhere, New York captured the railroads instead. Nobody could know for sure in 1825, but with the opening of the Erie Canal, New York had redrawn the economic map of the United States forever in its favor.

The case of Rochester, New York, amply demonstrates the extraordinary local impact of the Erie Canal. A mere village of fifteen hundred in 1821, Rochester exploded into a city of ten thousand over the next decade. Once the canal reached Rochester, the town was awash in craftsmen, salesmen, laborers, speculators, lawyers, crooks, and clergymen, most of them strangers. According to one historian, in 1826 over one hundred new people arrived each day, and another hundred moved on – net gain: ten to fifteen.[3] In such a marketplace, supply never outstripped demand and economic rewards showered anyone with a "better idea" for meeting his neighbors' needs. Carpenters adopted new construction techniques; coopers and shoemakers routinized and subdivided traditional skilled crafts, inventing jigs, tools, and

[2] Quoted in John Lauritz Larson, *Internal Improvement* (Chapel Hill: University of North Carolina Press, 2001), 78–9.

[3] Paul Johnson, *A Shopkeeper's Millennium: Society and Revivals in Rochester, New York 1815–1837* (New York: Hill and Wang, 1978), 13, 17, 37.

frames that allowed less experienced (and less expensive) hands to do more work. (Shoemakers even put out pieces for needle assembly to low-paid women all over town.) Certain master craftsmen climbed *up* the ladder to become merchant-manufacturers, and once they had all the local people shod, these high-output shoemakers began exporting cheap brogans in barrels for sale to planters in the South, who eagerly snapped up the product to "give" to their slaves each Christmas.

In New York City, the rising volume of business since 1815 stimulated innovation even as the canal was being dug. The dumping of British goods at the end of the War of 1812 caused wholesalers to perfect New York's famous system of dockside auctions. Warehouses filled up everywhere as ships' cargoes were off-loaded, broken, sorted into lots, and resold for domestic distribution or directly to local retailers. The canal then closed a commercial loop by funneling agricultural commodities into the hands of these same merchants. Bankers and insurance underwriters further institutionalized their services; brokers cared less *who* their customers were than whether they paid with good money and fast. Robert Fulton's steamboats pushed upstream against the Hudson's currents to help make the Erie Canal not just a downstream "vent" but a two-way highway, ferrying imports back up the canal into the hinterland. After 1815, steam navigation quickly spread to interior rivers such as the Mississippi and Ohio, fed by New York expertise and investment capital.

On January 5, 1818, a sailing ship, the *James Madison*, operated by the Black Ball Line, weighed anchor for England into the teeth of a winter storm, inaugurating the world's first *scheduled* "packet" service across the Atlantic Ocean. Prior to this, ships had lain at anchor, sometimes for weeks, while captains rustled up cargo and passengers enough to pay for the trip across. Travelers caught in this uncertain system cooled their heels in the city and called impatiently day after day to see whether their voyage was about to begin. Information and correspondence idled in mailbags, losing pertinence (and value) with every passing hour. By the simple decision to sail on schedule, regardless, the Black Ball Line introduced a new standard of dependability that began transforming all sorts of business transactions. In the 1820s, buyers and sellers flocked to New York port because it was becoming *the* place to do business – and because they flocked there, it *was*. Coastal traders from New England, the South Atlantic, and

New Orleans congregated there to get the latest price information, the freshest European goods, the lowest prices on imports, and best contracts for outgoing produce. Twenty years after that first daring Black Ball departure, New York merchants had engrossed American domestic commerce, and even the cotton export trade that logically "belonged" to Savannah and Charleston passed through the hands of Manhattan brokers and speculators.

SCRAMBLING TO COMPETE

The staggering rise of New York port sparked an urgent competition in rival cities such as Boston, Philadelphia, Baltimore, and even fledgling Washington, D.C. (which harbored pretensions of becoming the emporium of the Republic). From the beginning a city of artisans, Philadelphia focused on expanding and retaining its hinterland commerce with state aid to numerous turnpikes, and on *preventing* improvements in the lower Susquehanna River that would siphon off Pennsylvania produce into Baltimore's lap. Baltimore and Boston each found niche markets in the China trade, developing fast "clipper ships" to trim down the length of the voyage, carrying California hides and Middle Eastern opium to Canton, and bringing to America supplies of tea, ceramics, and luxury textiles. The persistent demands of Caribbean sugar planters for food, lumber, and livestock fueled booms in mid-Atlantic flour, New York packed beef, Rhode Island horses and cattle, and (thanks to Frederic Tudor in Boston) New England ice.

None of this commercial excitement in the seaport cities kept pace with the growth of New York, and as the impact of the Erie Canal became apparent, frantic interests demanded interregional internal improvements as the only way to level this new playing field. Philadelphia pinned its hopes on canals winding along and between the Schuylkill, Susquehanna, and Allegheny rivers, trying to replicate, over a 2,000-foot mountain ridge, what New York had done across its "water-level route." Heading an internal improvement society, Mathew Carey launched a propaganda campaign on behalf of Philadelphia merchants to get state support for the "Main Line," a system that would rival New York's. Writing in 1825, he reminded Pennsylvania lawmakers that since 1817 Philadelphia's exports had dropped 40 percent! "Which of our legislatures," he goaded, "will have the honour" of doing for Pennsylvania what Clinton did for New York?[4] Urgency was everything. Virginia and Maryland already had chartered a new Chesapeake & Ohio Canal Company that someday would satisfy the commerce of southwestern Pennsylvania, thereby killing support in that region for state public works. New York's future branch canals promised to serve northern Pennsylvania counties with more "foreign" connections. Only quick action could prevent Pennsylvania being carved up into sections paying tribute to out-of-state capitals. Some critics wondered if the brand new system of railroad transport might not better suit their mountainous terrain, but Carey's group insisted there was no time to gamble on such untested pipe dreams.

In February 1826, Pennsylvania authorized its own interregional system of canals, but the story ended less happily than in New York. To gratify local interests, work was scattered in many directions. Engineers struggled to learn how best to conquer the towering Allegheny Ridge. By the time they adopted a portage railway as the only practical solution, hundreds of miles of canal were completed and the state was committed to an awkward, amphibious network. Through-service to the western waters – the grand objective of the Pennsylvania Main Line and its primary source of anticipated revenue – did not begin until 1834, long after interest on debt had overwhelmed revenues from unfinished branch operations. The system truly was an engineering marvel in its day, running 395 miles from Philadelphia to Pittsburgh (including 36 miles of Allegheny Portage Railway and 82 miles of railroad from Philadelphia to the Susquehanna), climbing 2,322 feet above sea level, with 174 locks, an 800-foot tunnel, and 10 inclined planes, 5 on each side of the primary ridge, equipped with stationary winding engines to haul up the barges. Unfortunately, the Main Line never serviced its own debt and never poured revenues into the coffers of the state the way the Erie did in New York. Perhaps most cruelly, the necessary substitution of railways for canals in parts of the Pennsylvania system helped demonstrate the merits of the railroads themselves; and once perfected by experience, railroads displaced the canals whose own perfection had been proclaimed so recently.

---

[4] "Fulton" [Mathew Carey], "Canal Policy – No. III," *United States Gazette,* 26 Jan. 1825.

At exactly the same time that New York was taking the plunge, Virginia also took up the question of state-sponsored roads and canals. Fiercely protective of their interests as taxpayers, Virginia's governing planter elites preferred to confine internal improvements to things chartered companies could hope to accomplish – usually local turnpikes. In 1817, the new round of debates produced an Internal Improvement Fund (filled with state-owned bank stock) and a Board of Public Works to assist private ventures by purchasing stock. Among the beneficiaries of these new state investments was the languishing James River Company, which promised somehow to link Richmond with the waters of the Ohio River. Meanwhile, in northern Virginia and southern Maryland, backers of the old Potomac Canal, leading from Washington, D.C., into the mountains toward Pittsburgh, turned again to Congress for patronage. This time, because of Erie, they prevailed, and the Chesapeake & Ohio Canal broke ground July 4, 1828.

Two final projects debuted in response to the challenge of Erie that proved to be prophetic: the Baltimore & Ohio Railroad and the Western Railroad of Massachusetts. In the case of the B & O, Baltimore merchants had felt threatened by Washington, D.C., and the city's powerful friends in Congress. Rather than let the Chesapeake & Ohio Canal divert Potomac Valley trade to the national capital, they struck back with a railroad project, funded largely by private investment, to run up the same narrow gorge and terminate somewhere near Pittsburgh. The result was a dramatic contest between two technological systems to seize the best ground and deliver superior service along this central route to the West. Breaking ground on the same day as the canal, the B & O became a laboratory for perfecting still-primitive components of a proper railroad. In a parallel story, Boston boosters launched a railroad project to cut through the rugged terrain of western Massachusetts and intersect the New York route where the Erie Canal met the Hudson River. Like the B & O, the Western Railroad turned into a proving ground for technical equipment and procedures, all of which would come into focus in their modern form during the railroad's first dozen years.

Even the infant states west of the mountains felt the seismic effects of the Erie Canal. Ohio launched an ambitious program to build two main canals across the state, linking Lake Erie with the Ohio River and opening an all-water circuit to New York City. Louisville, Kentucky, started work on a canal to bypass the mile-long falls in the Ohio itself. Indiana plunged into a huge internal improvement program centered on the Wabash & Erie Canal and a Central Canal tying the system into an Indianapolis hub. Illinois cut a major connection between the Illinois River and Lake Michigan at Chicago and added half a dozen railroad projects to facilitate commerce across the broad, level prairies of that state. Even boosters in Detroit's sparsely settled hinterland (Michigan would not become a state until 1837) laid grandiose plans to transect the lower peninsula and give steamers a "quick" portage between lakes Michigan and Erie. In other words, the 1820s and early 1830s saw an explosion of internal improvement projects wherever vacant land lured settlers who in turn demanded access to markets.

Throughout the South and in much of the Ohio and Mississippi valleys, steamboats on natural rivers promised similar results with far less risk or investment capital. With as little as $10,000, a steamboat operator could enter the game, cruising up and down the waterways, stopping at urban ports or private plantation landings, taking on cotton and other produce, disgorging imported goods, and ferrying news, prices, passengers, and slaves to and from interior points. Both planters and merchants lobbied for public investment aimed at clearing the shallow rivers of snags, brush, and mud banks; but much of the southern half of the country did not originally *need* expensive public or corporate systems of transportation in order to vent local produce. A mere seventeen boats plied the western rivers in 1817, but that number topped 100 by the time of Andrew Jackson's election in 1828 and hit 536 by 1840. Freight rates fluctuated wildly on the river, but overall riverboat transportation averaged roughly one-tenth the cost of overland transportation.[5] Maps of travel time and information flow prepared by geographer Alan Pred show dramatic improvements not just along big-ticket projects like the Erie Canal but all over the South and West, much of it due simply to steamboat penetration.

The excitement about antebellum internal improvements was driven as much from the middle ranks of society as from the top. Farmers and tradesmen at interior locations, especially in western

---

[5] Louis C. Hunter, *Steamboats on the Western Rivers: An Economic and Technological History* (orig. 1949; New York: Dover Publications, 1993), 33, 658.

New York, the Old Northwest, and the western counties of Virginia and North Carolina, begged their governments to help them gain access to lucrative markets. Time and again, frontiersmen complained about the "want of a market" as the "great evil" preventing local progress.[6] Of course, at the bottom of the economic ladder there were men who preferred a subsistence living. Plantations in the new cotton South often were surrounded by subsistence farmers clinging to the hills and marginal lands. Such farmers may have raised a small patch of cotton or tobacco to help pay taxes, but they *could* make do without commerce and they tended to fear expensive public works as well as banks and corporations. Some backcountry voters in North Carolina rejected better roads because they thought roads made it easier for merchants to reach out and cheat them. Nevertheless, much of the upper South saw backcountry farmers and merchants pushing together for roads and canals against the resistance of tidewater planters who paid more taxes and wielded disproportionate power in state legislatures. Despite the antibank, anticorporation rhetoric indulged by Jacksonian politicians during the 1830s, internal improvements, paper money, and other instruments of commercial modernization were broadly popular with more than just malevolent capitalist elites.

This is not to say there were no misgivings about the shape and institutions of the new market-oriented economy, but rather to suggest that the progress of the market revolution often was welcomed by individuals and classes of people who might – and did – at the same time recoil from some of its implications. On its positive face, the new economy wore the aspect of a rising domestic marketplace in which all were welcome to participate and fortunes could be had by any man (or even woman) with ambition, industry, and a little bit of capital. For many Americans by the 1820s and 1830s, this seemed to be the essence of the revolutionary promise made manifest in economic liberty and personal wealth. In the eighteenth century – and even in the first generation after the Revolution – men often had found it necessary to be sponsored and endorsed by established community leaders before they could launch new careers or embark on business ventures with any hope

---

[6] Quoted in Nathan Miller, *The Enterprise of a Free People: Aspects of Economic Development in New York State during the Canal Period, 1792–1838* (Ithaca: Cornell University Press, 1962), 7.

of success. But as networks of commerce expanded and institutions such as banks, wholesale firms, forwarding houses, and credit bureaus began to manage the flow of information among strangers, opportunities for entrepreneurs without patrons multiplied steadily.

LEARNING TO DEAL WITH STRANGERS

As much as it depended on improved transportation and communication, the rising American domestic market was not created or imposed by a single innovation or act of legislation. In a classic illustration of the principles explained by Adam Smith in *The Wealth of Nations*, thousand of buyers and sellers ventured out in search of each other and of personal gain in markets that presented an expanding universe. Competition and initiative characterized its dynamics, especially early on; efforts to control the flow of money, goods, or information – whether stemming from old-fashioned claims of local prerogative or new-fangled strategies to corner the market or distort its working – proved ineffective. In the China trade, where the information "float" ran forty to sixty days, American captains schemed to deliver instructions to resident agents before the ship had docked in hopes they could buy up tea before news of the latest "demand" hit the market. (By such shenanigans – plus occasional robbery and murder – Americans broke down the monopoly control of the British East India Company and brought reckless competition to the opium trade.) Closer to home, millers and butchers lost control of their "natural" local trade and accepted the price-setting leadership of larger urban dealers. Turnpikes invited private teamsters to use them, and when customers disliked the price or service, they turned to another hauler or did the work themselves. Taking umbrage at the sight of toll booths on what looked like public roads, many farmers and teamsters used illegal "turnouts" to bypass the gates, daring the "monopolistic" turnpike operator to take his customers to court.

Forwarding merchants in cities such as Pittsburgh traditionally had bound their country storekeepers, often through credit arrangements; but now, should a client grow restless, he could find another vendor in Philadelphia or Cincinnati, or a lender to supply him with cash so that he might shop with the "upper hand." Country customers found ready choices for disposing of their produce. They still ran up debts on the books of the nearest country storekeeper, but if they did not like the prices quoted when they offered up their butter and eggs, each retained the option of taking his surplus on to the next larger market and clearing his accounts with cash. Steamboats called for freight, knowing that another boat would land the next evening, making it easy for the shipper to wait if he did not like the captain's terms. The steady elaboration of complex markets tended to flatten the hierarchies of "friendship" and "connection" that had governed economic life in the eighteenth century. Smaller players gained equal access to news and transportation, leaving middlemen no choice but to compete with each other on price and quality of service. As a result, millers, hog buyers, and cotton factors all found themselves offering (albeit reluctantly) the same terms to the least of their customers that they once would have saved for their "best" friends.

By the early 1840s, these developments had produced an astonishing circulation of goods inside of the United States. Freight rates for commodities had fallen dramatically: on land, from $30 per ton-mile to something closer to $20; on steamboats, from $6 (upstream) to well under $2; and canal rates ranged between $2 and $3 per ton-mile.[7] Economic historians once suggested that interregional trade made possible by the transportation revolution allowed the antebellum sections to specialize – one in cotton, one in foodstuffs, and one in manufacturing. Subsequent research has shown this portrait to be exaggerated: Except for some of the densest cotton country in Alabama and Mississippi, most of the South remained self-sufficient in food until the late 1850s. Food exports from the Northwest did grow dramatically, but most of that produce shipped to New York and foreign markets.

With improved transportation, consumer goods (all sold on credit) flowed much more freely into agricultural communities. Frontier women retired their spinning wheels (or broke them up for kindling) and took to buying textiles from the store, bringing produce in exchange or paying cash saved from the annual sale of corn and hogs. Into the country came coffee, nails, window glass, mirrors, calico, lace trimmings, ready-made shoes, hats, blankets, kettles, books, and even musical instruments. Frontier planters in Mississippi and Alabama paid

---

[7] Jeremy Atack and Peter Passell, *A New Economic View of American History* (2nd ed., New York: W. W. Norton, 1994), 148; Hunter, *Steamboats*, 658.

their original capital debts for clearing the land and setting up production, then imported by steamship carved woodwork, Italian marble mantels, French wallpaper, huge mirrors, fine furniture, pianos, carpets, and damask draperies for the pillared mansions that by 1850 announced the "importance" of families who had staked their all on the cotton frontier. Self-sufficiency as a goal was replaced by interdependence: Indiana farmers sold corn and hogs and southwestern planters sent cotton into world markets while northeastern manufacturers shipped cotton and woolen cloth to the farmers and planters who no longer raised sheep or flax for themselves. The progress of market penetration can be traced in the price differentials between Cincinnati (deep in the interior) and New York: This "distance tax" (if you will) on a barrel of pork dropped from $9.50 in 1820 to just over $1.00 in 1860; for flour, from $2.48 to $0.28; and for corn, from 48 cents to 27 cents.[8]

All this dealing with distant strangers was made possible by the evolution of business institutions and facilitators that took advantage of the vast interstate free-trade zone that was the United States. Federal law required protection of contracts freely made between residents of different states, and by the 1820s both custom and jurisprudence had secured the assumption that citizens of all the states were playing by substantially the same rules. After 1822, in the hands of Nicholas Biddle, the Second Bank of the United States functioned de facto as a central bank, stabilizing the American financial markets. As a result, into the early 1830s the number of state banks in the system grew slowly, and the dozens of currencies they issued could be exchanged – or "cleared" – easily. After 1832, when Andrew Jackson's personal vendetta cost the national bank its charter, tens of millions of federal dollars were transferred to state-chartered "pet banks" scattered across the country. The number of banks grew sharply again, especially after 1849, when a dozen states followed the lead of "free-banking" states such as Michigan and New York in permitting anyone to open a bank without special legislative approval. Considered by many then (and most historians since) to be a reckless free-for-all of "wildcat" banking, the free-bank era actually generated a flexible and expansive money supply that served the economy remarkably well. The free entry and exit of banks into local markets depoliticized the "money question" (a little) and may have

---

[8] Atack and Passell, *New Economic View*, 168.

encouraged entrepreneurship independent of social or political connections. Force of habit and convenience continued to sustain the circulation of money except in moments of extraordinary crisis – such as the
Panic of 1837 and the lingering depression after 1839.[9]

In New York, the moralistic and evangelical Lewis Tappan had
developed a habit of keeping files on the personal character of his business connections. In 1841, he formalized this private gossip file into a
credit reporting bureau: Tappan's Mercantile Agency. By 1851, some
two thousand reporters gathered data on the debts, assets, character,
marriages, and drinking habits of borrowers all over the Union. The
service continued after 1858 as R.G. Dun & Company, and thanks to
its existence, retailers, wholesalers, factors, millers, meat-packers,
coastal importers, and large manufacturers wherever they lived could
study the same information about potential customers and form
responsible business judgments about persons they never had met. At
the same time, insurance underwriters increasingly guaranteed cargoes
in transit and inventories on hand from destruction, loss, or fire, allowing end users to assume somewhat greater transactional risks because
they were covered from behind. Such services, coupled with a steady
supply of dependable money, rendered anonymous dealings safer, more
efficient, and far more comfortable than had been the case in even
closely guarded colonial networks of friendship and connection.

Atop the whole emerging network sat New York City – a maze of
wharves and warehouses, banks, brokers, merchants, insurers, apprais-
ers, importers, manufacturers, and information peddlers, denser and
more reliable than their counterparts anywhere outside of London and
Glasgow. Having lured Liverpool's cotton buyers into their thriving
neighborhood, New York's cotton merchants started bringing only sam-
ples north to the city, selling bales that subsequently shipped directly
from Charleston or Savannah; only the money passed through New
York hands. Foodstuffs such as flour either shipped from New York
or referenced New York prices and quality controls. Imports headed for
interior points landed in New York to get the best price, quickest turn-
around, and best access to the web of domestic merchants who could
peddle the wares. Cotton factors in Mobile, Atlanta, or Memphis found
that they had little choice but to track prices in New York both for

[9] Ibid., 104–6.

outbound bales of cotton and for the incoming goods requested by their customers. By the last decade of the antebellum period – the era when railroads might have started to make a difference in commercial geography – New York had positioned itself so successfully that subsequent rivals never really stood a chance.

A THOUSAND CLEVER INNOVATIONS

While commercial interests assembled the framework for a burgeoning domestic marketplace, manufacturers steadily increased their own contributions to American economic growth. These were the first stirrings of the industrializing process; and even if they did not initially involve new machines or large-scale factories, they all shared common roots in technology and the processes of production. In the pre-industrial era, most things were made by skilled craftsmen – called artisans – working with their hands and hand tools. Master craftsmen typically owned their own shops and worked with the aid of a few journeymen (artisans in training) and apprentices (youngsters employed in odd jobs while they learned the "mysteries" of workshop production). The craft workshop was both a production center and a trade school: It made things, usually to custom order, and it produced the next generation of skilled craftsmen who carried on the industry. When local demand rose, it often was met not by the craftsman ramping up production, but by recently graduated "masters" opening new shops, effectively duplicating the means of production. Individual workmen knew every step in the production process and commonly worked on a piece from start to finish. No two products were exactly alike: Every piece was a "one-off" original.

Industrialization was a complicated process by which this regime of handicraft production gradually was altered to increase the productivity of capital and labor by *intensifying* output rather than simply multiplying the number of producers. One of the first techniques was division of labor, in which complex tasks were broken down into simple constituent parts and each part assigned to a worker who repeated it quickly and efficiently over and over again. Most of the gain came from routinizing movements, sometimes with the introduction of jigs or dies – templates that helped a worker repeat the same action to produce identical pieces. In some cases, routinization led to the development of new tools to perform the work; if appropriate, extra power from animals, water, or steam could be added to tools, turning them into machines and introducing the process of mechanization. Once machines became precise and accurate, they could produce interchangeable parts to be assembled by someone other than the parts maker without much customization. Sometimes inventors found ways to control the actions of complex machines so that they yielded identical products without operator intervention – a kind of automation first realized in France in 1801 by the punchcard-reading Jacquard loom. Finally, whole nests of machines and specialized, subdivided workers could be gathered in carefully laid-out, power-driven factories where, at some point in the industrializing process, economies of scale produced a significant drop in the unit cost of the goods compared to the same product made in an artisan's workshop. At this point, industrial production effectively replaced the handicraft system, the volume of output soared, prices typically fell, quality often improved, and control over the workplace passed from dozens or hundreds of independent masters into the hands of a few capitalists who owned the factories, the raw materials, and the finished merchandise, and who paid wages to workers for their labor.

In early America, manufacturing simultaneously followed both the traditional developmental path *and* the early road toward industrialization. All the major cities in the revolutionary era boasted traditional "man-u-factories" of every description: shoemakers, tanners, hatters, tailors, carpenters, joiners, cabinetmakers, coopers, wagonmakers, wheelwrights, blacksmiths, silversmiths, gunsmiths, watchmakers – the list goes on. Smaller country towns contained more limited arrays of specialists, but even in rural backwaters one could find a farmer-craftsman capable of making shoes for the children, beds for the loft, and stools for the weary pioneer's butt. Even in colonial times, the pressure of rising demand almost always had outstripped prevailing supply for manufactured articles. As a result, innovative craftsmen who were willing to try new techniques of production found few barriers (no product laws or restrictive guilds) and ready rewards (eager consumers) for their troubles. At the same time, high geographical mobility produced hundreds of new settlements on the frontier, to be supplied, at least before the antebellum transportation revolution, by the spread of *traditional* handicraft shops.

Deprived of foreign manufactures off and on by turmoil in Europe and then by the War of 1812, American producers in the early 1800s had stepped up their output, with positive results. With the return of peace in 1815, the British dumped huge stocks of goods on American markets, and the highly capitalized American industries – cottons and woolens, iron and steel – begged for protection by import tariffs from the "unfair" competition of European producers. The next year, Congress obliged, and the United States began to encourage (albeit feebly) domestic manufacturing. What really stimulated production in American workshops, however, was the relentless surge in demand produced by the growth and extension of the domestic marketplace itself.

Take boots and shoes, for example, one of the hand manufactures to undergo significant reorganization without big changes in tools or machinery. In Lynn, Massachusetts, cordwainers manufactured shoes with the help of apprentices working in "ten footers" – small workshops attached to the shoemaker's home. As market pressures rose, a new class of "shoe bosses" took to buying leather and putting it out among the artisans on contract. Masters and journeymen cut the leather into pieces, and the women inside the home sewed the uppers together and returned them to the shop for lasting. Division of labor was the novelty here: Bosses specialized in leather procurement and distributed the materials, the artisans and women divided the tasks of assembly according to levels of skill, then the bosses collected the finished shoes and sent them to mass markets in the cities or down South. To meet rising demand, bosses bought more hides and recruited more willing shoemakers in and around Lynn. Where transport was cheap, shoes from Lynn squeezed out local handicraft shoemakers. Away from the main arteries of commerce, local craftsmen continued to thrive in small shops – but theirs was a reprieve, not a pardon. In time, the bosses drew parts of the process into central shops under closer supervision. By the 1850s, when the sewing machine made it possible to mechanize production, these proto-shoe manufacturers simply moved their outdoor workers into one common factory building. By then, the railroad also made it possible to distribute shoes pretty much all over the nation, closing off the older, traditional avenue of craft expansion.

"Putting out" systems similar to that of the shoe bosses drew other rural people into the cash nexus during the early nineteenth century. Palm-leaf hats, for example, brought semi-subsistence rural people into the market economy. Weaved by hand, usually by women, palm-leaf hats were made of imported fronds "put out" by storekeepers, who then took finished hats in trade to balance people's accounts at the country store. At first, this was simply a variation on the traditional barter of butter, eggs, flax, firewood, and other local produce, but by the 1830s and 1840s, palm hats became a significant means by which rural New England families – especially poorer families with many hands and few capital resources – generated incomes over and above what they could squeeze from their marginal farms. In the early 1830s, one storekeeper in southwestern New Hampshire was marketing 23,000 hats per year made by some 250 country laborers. Output more than tripled in the next twenty years as upward of 800 area farm families entered the palm hat trade.[10] What had began as supplemental work for the quiet times at home had grown into regular enterprise without which these families would fail.

Similarly, early New England spinning mills generated yarn enough to keep every farmer with a loom for miles around busy weaving cloth. Either men or women could make cloth at home whenever time permitted without sacrificing other household routines. Because they earned more for weaving than for many other tasks they might do, rural people took to using cash to satisfy consumer needs. Many took the ultimate risk of abandoning marginal farms and moving into textile villages where father, mother, and children all worked for wages paid by the factory owners. Over time, most weaving moved into mechanized factories where power looms magnified the output and supervisors exercised control over when and how fast operatives worked. What seemed at first to augment the rural New England economy eventually took it over.

Time itself became an issue of greater precision around the turn of the eighteenth century; early factories rang bells to announce the beginning and end of a shift, but an appointment to close a deal (at noon sharp!) was best kept with the aid of a timepiece. Most people could not afford fine brass clocks, imported from England or France, at a cost of $50. In the late eighteenth century, some Connecticut craftsmen began making wooden movements for clocks, which opened a larger

---

[10] Thomas Dublin, *Transforming Women's Work: New England Lives in the Industrial Revolution* (Ithaca: Cornell University Press, 1994), 54.

market and set the stage for a true revolution in production. In the decade after 1793, in Plymouth, Connecticut, Eli Terry perfected a "hand engine" for cutting the teeth of the wooden gears and pinions that made it possible to build twenty-five clocks at one time. In 1806, he set up a "factory" with water power to turn the machinery and contracted with his retail peddlers to turn out four thousand clocks in three years. The price of a movement plummeted from near $25 to $4: Itinerants sold Terry's full-size clocks, case and all, for $25. The demand for handmade artisan clocks collapsed, and copycat factories popped up in half a dozen Connecticut towns. Terry then turned his attention to miniaturizing the clockwork, perfecting by 1816 the first "Pillar and Scroll" shelf clock, twenty inches high, which (at $16) became the standard timepiece for the next generation. In less than twenty years, Terry had revolutionized his industry. In 1837, one of Terry's former employees, Chauncey Jerome, developed a new clockwork made of stamped brass pieces that in turn put wooden clocks out of business. By the end of the antebellum era, Americans could buy a nice shelf clock for $4 and a bargain model for 75 cents.[11] Now people could actually expect each other to *know* the time of day.

Time was money in the market economy, and money usually was paper. The burgeoning demand for banknotes, as well as stationary, forms, account books, journals, newspapers, and the other paper products required by commercial societies, was met in the early Republic by another set of technological breakthroughs. For centuries, paper had been made in mills close to good sources of pure water for power and for pulp. The process involved several discrete steps reflecting significant division of labor and specialized expertise, but into the 1820s the only machines were found in the "beating room," where rags were shredded into fiber pulp. Subsequently, "vatmen" filled and drained the screens. Then "couchers" deftly flipped the soggy sheets onto drying felts, stacked one or two hundred such paper sandwiches, and squeezed them out with a screw press. The couchers then turned these sheets over to other hands, who separated the sheets from the felts; hung them up to dry; and then sized, smoothed,

---

[11] Chauncey Jerome, *History of the American Clock Business for the Past Sixty Years, and Life of Chauncey Jerome* (orig. 1860; e-book Project Gutenberg #12694, ed. Robert Shimmin, 2004); John Joseph Murphy, "Entrepreneurship in the Establishment of the American Clock Industry," *Journal of Economic History,* 26 (1966): 172–4.

trimmed, sorted, counted, stacked, and wrapped the sheets for delivery. Several towns in Berkshire County, Massachusetts, specialized in paper manufacturing, and around 1827, imported machines began appearing in these mills, eliminating more and more of the skilled handwork.

Mechanization proceeded gradually in the Berkshire paper industry in the context of extensive entrepreneurial reorganization of the business. If the fine source of clean water, well-developed networks of rag collectors, and existing communities of skilled workers first made these mills profitable, improved transportation (steamboats on the Hudson, the Erie Canal, then the arrival of the railroads) triggered market expansion, especially in New York City, that tempted Berkshire paper manufacturers to grow and improve. The steady adoption of "labor-saving" machinery at first improved the working lives of Berkshire papermakers and boosted both the quantity and quality of the paper produced. Local sources of rags became inadequate, and soon these country firms were importing bales of rag-stock from New York and even Europe, burrowing deeper into market economy all the while. In 1827, the Lafflins of Lee, Massachusetts, installed the first "cylinder" machine that actually formed a continuous roll of paper from the pulp. Market-savvy decisions by several independent manufacturers continued to feed the growth of the business until the 1840s and 1850s, by which time the widespread adoption of the superior (and more expensive) Fourdeinier machinery brought the rag paper industry to maturity.

Innovation in paper manufacturing primarily was driven by the explosion of paper use, especially for commercial purposes. Organized as it was in multiple small firms, the Berkshire industry succeeded in filling demands for a wide variety of specialty papers – for banknotes, writing paper, legal documents, stock and bond certificates, and bookkeeping supplies. The fragmentary nature of demand for many kinds of finished product kept antebellum mills from enjoying the huge economies of scale that later rewarded giant chemical wood-pulp paper manufacturers. Instead, innovations and machines yielded modest gains one after another without displacing wholesale the need for skilled hands and clean water. As New York City became the commercial hub of the United States, its paper suppliers stepped up to meet demand; in response, New York simply grew bigger and more demanding. Because commerce involves transactions between two parties or more, New Yorkers' addiction to commercial paper infected their customers everywhere. Once the railroads locked in the primitive networks of antebellum commerce, paper products took their natural place alongside other manufactured goods in the flow of merchandise across the country.

Commerce also stimulated journalism, which in turn required abundant sources of cheap paper to churn out newssheets dedicated to prices, markets, advertising, technology, and business information. American printing and publishing already had gone through one revolution by the early nineteenth century: The creation of popular republican governments had caused an explosion in political printing beginning in the revolutionary era. In Philadelphia, the number of printers and their output nearly doubled between 1770 and 1790 and doubled again by 1805.[12] Printers scrambled to ramp up production, exploiting apprentices and unskilled labor in place of proper journeymen – which set off some of the earliest labor confrontations in the new United States. Newspapers sprang up all over the country, and thanks to the 1792 Post Office law, they were exchanged among editors free of charge. Eventually some journalists took aim at a regional or national audience. Joining Hezekiah Niles's *Weekly Register* (started in 1811), we find Arthur and Lewis Tappen's New York *Journal of Commerce* (1827), D. K. Minor's *Rail Road Journal* (1831), Freeman Hunt's *Merchant's Magazine* (1839), J. D. B. DeBow's *Agricultural Review and Industrial Monthly* (1846), not to mention consumer-oriented periodicals such as Louis A. Godey's *Ladies Book* (1830) and general news magazines such as *Harper's* (1850) and *Leslie's Weekly* (1855).

The supply of cheap and plentiful paper solved only half the problem for early American printers: The technology of printing itself remained a serious bottleneck. The standard hand presses from the revolutionary era produced no more than two hundred sheets per hour, severely limiting both the size and circulation of papers. By the late 1820s, new machine presses cranked out one thousand sheets per hour and soon steam presses multiplied *that* number by a factor of five or six! Historians credit the convergence in the 1830s of steam presses, new paper-making technology, chemical bleaching (to make paper from

[12] Rosalind Remer, *Printers and Men of Capital: Philadelphia Book Publishers in the New Republic* (Philadelphia: University of Pennsylvania Press, 1996), 153–7.

colored rags), improved transportation, and mass-market journalism with transforming the tiny local cells of radical Yankee abolitionists into a noisy sectional movement. The appearance in Charlestown, South Carolina, of copies of William Lloyd Garrison's fire-breathing abolitionist sheet, *The Liberator*, helped set the stage in the early 1830s for direct confrontations between southern states and the federal government.

One hallmark of the industrializing process in America was the widespread substitution of iron and steel for wood in the construction of tools and machines. Since the early colonial period, Americans had craved locally made iron products for the simple reason that they were heavy and expensive to import. Raw "pig iron" was made in a furnace located near ore deposits and hardwood forests for making charcoal (the fuel preferred for smelting iron). Some molten iron was cast at foundries into canon, anchors, blacksmith's anvils, hollowware (pots and kettles), and mill and ship's findings; the rest was hammered into wrought iron bar from which other iron products were made. In 1800, most iron consumer products still were made to order by thousands of local blacksmiths, who manufactured everything from kitchen tools to plow shares, axes, door hinges, wagon tires, and lantern hooks. The tools of the smithy were simple: a forge and bellows for heating the iron, a hammer and anvil for pounding, and a variety of chisels and dies for cutting and shaping hot pieces of iron bar.

Exploding demand for nails, hinges, iron straps, shovels, plows, and other metal wares encouraged innovative smiths to create dies and jigs for producing hundreds of nearly identical copies and to harness water power to drive their bellows and operate trip-hammers capable of pounding out far greater quantities of red-hot iron than even the burliest blacksmith could handle. One humble beneficiary of early American inventive energy was the ax, an indispensible tool for deforesting North America that acquired its modern shape and form by the 1830s. Another was the common nail – originally wrought one at a time by a blacksmith but after 1780 produced on various hand-powered machines for cutting nails from iron plates. Ezekiel Reed of Bridgeport, Connecticut, is credited with the original breakthrough, but as so often was the case, many hands – perhaps dozens – were employed trying to improve nail-making machines. Finally, in 1807, Reed's son, Jesse, fashioned a device that could cut and head nails in a single operation. Purchased and installed in two factories by Boston

merchant Thomas Odiorne, Reed's machine quickly set the standard for mechanized nail manufacturing in the antebellum decades, and mass-produced nails hit the market just in time for the housing booms that occurred after the Panic of 1819 and the opening of new transportation routes.

Another site of significant creativity and innovation was the manufacture of small firearms. Either imported from abroad or custom-made by skilled gunsmiths, firearms before the Revolution were comparatively expensive, sometimes finely worked, and never exactly alike. As with so many things in the early United States, post-revolutionary demand sent buyers – especially the federal government and underfunded new state militias – searching for cheap, reliable guns. In 1794, at the site of a revolutionary-era weapons depot in Springfield, Massachusetts, Congress established the first federal armory, where forty-odd craftsmen turned out about 250 muskets per month. Demand pressure fueled by appropriations of ready money from governments to purchase thousands of arms stimulated managers at Springfield and another federal armory at Harper's Ferry, Virginia, to adopt or invent elaborate divisions of labor, water-powered machines, and ever-more standardized components. Independent producer Eli Whitney contributed further to the mechanization of gun manufacturing. By the early 1820s, the armory at Harper's Ferry made ten thousand muskets per year, and Springfield even more.[13] In the 1840s, Samuel Colt perfected the mass-produced revolver that would "win the West" in the hands of Texas Rangers. (It won him a prize at the international exhibition in 1851 at the Crystal Palace in London.) Although dozens of craftsmen and inventors contributed to these innovations, Whitney, Colt, and the American arms industry famously took the credit for "inventing" the modern "American System" of manufacturing using power, machines, and interchangeable parts.

Precision machinery made it possible to make small arms and other mechanisms out of interchangeable parts, but where did precision machinery come from? The answer could be found in the textile industry, where the earliest machine builders in America found themselves quickly required to repair and perfect the complicated implements that

---

[13] Merritt Roe Smith, *Harpers Ferry Armory and the New Technology: The Challenge of Change* (Ithaca: Cornell University Press, 1977), Table I, 342.

filled the earliest cotton factories. David Wilkinson set up a machine shop near Samuel Slater's first mill in Pawtucket, where he constantly improved both the textile machinery and the devices with which he made such machines. (In 1798, for example, he invented a slide-rest lathe for cutting screw threads.) The rapid deterioration of wooden machinery created powerful incentives to fashion equipment out of brass, iron, and steel, which required more precise fabrication of hard metal parts. Improved grinding and milling machines, drills, metal planes, and machine tools of all types poured forth from workshops in France, Great Britain, and America. These innovations allowed tool-makers to perfect rough castings and fit components to the narrow tolerances required for durable complex mechanisms running at ever-faster speeds. Everything from clocks and watches to farm machinery and railway locomotives benefited over and over again from the constant improvement of the tools for making machines.

Innovations such as these resulted from the efforts of dozens, maybe hundreds, of clever individuals striving to solve irritating day-to-day problems within the systems of prevailing technology. But innovations did not take root and transform whole industries or interlocking systems until calculating individuals (maybe the inventor, maybe not) found ways to make inventions commercially successful. Problem solving plus profit seeking: That seemed to be the winning combination. The presence in the early United States of such a multitude of free agents both in the technical trades and in the entrepreneurial community helps explain the timing of this explosion of creative development. Neither the inventors nor the entrepreneurs necessarily saw themselves engaged in the construction of complex new systems; indeed, their blindness to the big picture doubtless made it easier to celebrate each little triumph without taking stock in the cumulative impact. What legal historian J. Willard Hurst famously called the "release of energy" that followed American independence helped make possible this flourishing of tinkerers, while the paucity of organized, traditional, legally protected "vested interests" made it difficult to stand in the way once an upstart brought forth another tidbit of "progress."[14]

---

[14] James Willard Hurst, *Law and the Conditions of Freedom in the Nineteenth-Century United States* (Madison: University of Wisconsin Press, 1956), 3.

LINKAGES AND SYSTEMS

Textiles led the way to large-scale mechanization and mass production in manufacturing as cotton and wool mills spread throughout New England. At first these were typically small firms – partnerships of merchant capitalists who placed between $10,000 and $30,000 into the hands of skilled craftsmen (also partners at first, but over time increasingly hired managers) who built, installed, and oversaw the use of the machinery. Bound to locate near convenient water-power seats, many of these small Slater-style mills were built at rural sites that required the owners to install not just a factory but a town as well. To recruit a workforce of women and children, Slater found that he had to lure whole families with convenient rental housing, farm work for the husbands, company stores, churches, and Sunday schools. Marginal farmers traded agrarian poverty for real cash wages and the promise of a rising standard of living. The mills grew slowly before 1808, but the disappearance from American stores of British-made textiles between 1808 (the Embargo) and 1815 (end of the War of 1812) created boom conditions during which cotton manufacturing more than tripled in New England. Even before the rise of power weaving and integrated factory production, cotton textiles employed between ten thousand and twelve thousand wage workers.[15]

Technological evolution, market pressure from price competition, and the possibility of harvesting economies of scale created incentives for further innovation in the textile industry. Francis Cabot Lowell of Boston visited integrated factories in Lancashire and Scotland and returned in 1813 to introduce their model of industrial organization at Waltham, Massachusetts. Since the perfection of mule-spinning machinery in the 1790s, weaving had been the big bottleneck in textile production. Lowell dreamed of a large-scale firm that brought the whole process, from "breaking" the baled cotton to finishing the cloth, into one commercial operation. He secured a corporate charter from the state of Massachusetts, partly to facilitate capital formation, partly to gain the endorsement of the commonwealth for his potentially revolutionary enterprise. In 1814, the resulting Boston Manufacturing

---

[15] *Statistical History of the United States from Colonial Times to the Present*, ed. Ben J. Wattenberg (New York: Basic Books, 1976), 139.

Company began turning out coarse, cheap, uniform cotton cloth ("slave cloth," it would be called). The return of peace in 1815 and the subsequent flood of cheap British textiles into American markets made the timing of Lowell's experiment especially fortunate. Mill owners great and small petitioned Congress for tariff protection, which they received in 1816, but Lowell's integrated enterprise proved better situated to weather the storm than did the myriad Slater-style firms. The dramatic success of the Waltham plant led its investors to venture a much larger establishment on the Merrimack River at a new town they named Lowell. Here they erected an enormous water-power facility and arranged huge factories around it to create the first American industrial city. The factories at Lowell turned out not only great quantities of cotton cloth but also whole sets of new textile machinery with which competitors opened additional factories all over New England. As mechanization and integration progressed, total factory employment in cotton soared to 122,000 by the time of the Civil War.[16]

Not wanting to stir up negative visions of English working-class degradation, the entrepreneurs at Lowell quite intentionally recruited young, unmarried women to work in the mills and live in carefully chaperoned boarding houses supervised by their employers. To these "mill girls," the arrangement offered cash wages, leisure-time activities, excitement, independence, the company of peers, and a temporary escape from life in a rural farmhouse crowded with overweening parents and younger children. To the parents of the girls, the company offered assurances that the environment would be wholesome and chaste, while their daughters' wages allowed a little cash to flow back to hard-pressed Yankee farms. The arrangement was presumed to be temporary: Cash saved would enhance the marriage prospects of girls who in a few years hoped to return to the country and marry the sons of farmers when their patrimonies matured. In this way, the large-scale industrial city took root in an American social landscape that did not freely welcome it. Once installed, the logic of integrated production, economies of scale, and the pressure of price competition tempered the fabric of this new industrial system, and it began to exercise a powerful influence not just on Lowell but on all the other textile factories – including the quaint rural village operations designed on the Slater model.

[16] Ibid.

Too much can be made (and *has* been made) of this quasi-utopian story of manufacturing at Lowell. Manufacturing, including textiles, grew apace in many American cities while evincing neither the charm of the picturesque "mill village" or the benevolence of Lowell "girls' clubs." In the three decades after 1815, New York City became the most productive manufacturing center in the United States thanks to the dramatic expansion of "manufactories" and urban putting-out networks employing tens of thousands of working people. Straddling the polar examples of Lowell and the Slater-style village mills, Philadelphia's textile industry comprised small family firms or partnerships, lining the banks of the Schuylkill River northwest of the city center and the Delaware River north into Kensington, but also scattered about the metropolitan area. By 1820, some thirty-nine firms, each employing anywhere from six to two hundred workers, produced checks, ginghams, plaids, drillings, bagging, hosiery, duck, twine, trim, and fringes. Thousands of skilled handloom weavers worked in backyard shops, making cloth from yarn they purchased outright from the spinning mills. As was the case with boots and shoes, hats, nails, clocks, and firearms, textiles for mass consumption became steadily more standardized and cheaper, and returned a slimmer margin of profit as industrialization proceeded. But in Philadelphia, the decentralization of entrepreneurship, together with the broad range of specialized products produced, kept skilled artisans alive and small firms viable throughout the antebellum period, resulting in a middle path toward industrialization that one historian calls "proprietary capitalism."[17]

By the middle of the 1830s, the shine was fading visibly from the textile revolution. Total value and quantity of goods manufactured climbed steadily, but price competition and capital demands for expensive new technology produced razor-thin profit margins. The big cotton barons, more likely heads of corporations now than partners or sole proprietors, cut wages and lengthened hours, raised rents, eliminated "perks" that ran up overhead, and began to resemble the industrial "Gradgrinds" for which contemporary England was famous. A bitter strike at Lowell in 1836 (discussed in Chapter 3) punctuated the

---

[17] Philip Scranton, *Proprietary Capitalism; the Textile Manufacture at Philadelphia, 1800–1885* (Cambridge, UK: Cambridge University Press, 1983), 83, 97–9.

change of mood. In Slater-style villages, once-independent yeomen found their women and children working for lower rates while their own agricultural employment – a luxury peripheral to the mill owner's interests – disappeared. Indebted to their employers for store credit and past rent, such families could neither bargain nor protest, nor even escape their employers' grasp. At Lowell, long hours and declining living conditions left girls haggard and worn, while rising rents consumed what savings they had hoped to lay aside. The farm boys of their dreams found younger women still at home ready enough to be their brides, leaving some unmarried middle-aged women "spinsters," potentially for life. Desperate for cheap, tractable workers, mill owners gradually turned to immigrant workers, whose expectations some-times were lower, less rooted in artisanal traditions or in American revolutionary promises of liberty and social equality.

Cutthroat competition, not community standards, set the price of yarn or cloth. Factory masters could no more ignore the effect of market forces on their inputs than could the workers when they looked in their pay packets. Industrialization had transformed the textile industry, and there quite literally was no turning back. Tens of thou-sands of consumers had given up the tedious household production of cloth; other tens of thousands had traded farming or other pursuits for employment in textile factories. The final impact of industrial produc-tion was just as profound (and irreversible) as the introduction of guns, cloth, and steel edge tools to pre-contact Native Americans. And like the Indians, American consumers became dependent on goods and services they did not – and could not – provide for themselves.

By the 1830s, metal machines were replacing wood in nearly every application, and machine shops stood ready to tackle problems asso-ciated with making large-scale equipment. Harvesting small grains was one of the most important challenges, and in that decade a Virginia blacksmith, Robert Hall McCormick, and his sons began experiment-ing with a mechanical reaper. In 1837, Cyrus McCormick patented a workable horse-drawn reaper that could be operated by two men. McCormick and his brothers continued to perfect the ungainly con-traption into the 1840s, finally building a factory in Chicago in 1847 for the purpose of mass producing their machine. By this time, John Deere had perfected a steel plow (1837) that made it easier to break the tough sod of the tall grass prairies in Illinois and Iowa. Level ground and larger fields – plus the arrival of railroad transportation on the prairies – made this expensive equipment more feasible for farmers by the 1850s. Even so, it took the Civil War's spike in demand, coupled with the drain of manpower into the army and the development of companion machines (especially hay rakes and seed drills), to secure the development of horse-powered mechanized agriculture.

Steam engines – both locomotives and stationary power plants – also matured after 1830, reaching by the 1850s relatively modern, recognizable forms that allowed their widespread adoption by railroads and manufacturers. By 1845, steam locomotives had replaced horse power on all the nation's railroads, thanks to the efforts of determined inventors such as Laomi Baldwin of Philadelphia. A jeweler by trade, Baldwin had opened a machine shop in 1825 that made bookbinding tools and calico-printing cylinders. Steam power was something of a hobby at first, but in 1832 he demonstrated his first practical locomotive ("Old Ironsides") and within a decade he was known as the leading producer of railroad locomotives. Rival engine makers took heart, the pace of innovation quickened, and steam power – seen for a generation primarily on boats – took up residence in the urban industrial landscape. By the mid-1840s, locomotives chugged in and out the centers of most northern cities, while stationary engines liberated manufacturing from its dependence on rural water-power seats. The adoption of special grates made it possible to burn Pennsylvania's hard anthracite coal, which greatly multiplied the energy available for home heating, heat-using industries, and transportation as well. Within another decade, smoke and noise had altered the urban scene (not for the better), and these twin hallmarks of the modern capitalist transformation took root in the American experience.

Urbanization, itself a function of industrialization, likewise became a stimulus as ever-larger concentrations of workers required housing, furniture, carpets, light, heat, food, fuel, housewares, clothing, transportation, and entertainment. Overwhelmed with opportunity, house carpenters modified time-honored construction techniques (and the respectful divisions of labor that separated carpenters from joiners, cabinetmakers, and other ancient specialists) in order to throw up houses fast enough to answer burgeoning demand. Balloon frame construction (hollow walls constructed of light studdings instead of heavy framing timbers, on which were "hung" rafters and floor joists) made the biggest impact, allowing builders to close in a house in record time, making use of prefabricated windows and doors. (Alas, such houses burned down with astonishing speed as well.) Retail merchants of every description crowded the growing cities, testing the waters of demand (calculating) and forwarding orders to whichever innovative producers they thought could fill them on time. Butchers, bakers, and vendors of produce, dairy products, whisky, beer, and rum proliferated, boosting the demand signals reaching their suppliers: millers, milkmaids, fish mongers, brewers, distillers, and the growers of vegetables. Cartmen hauled firewood in and horse manure out day after day in thankless succession. Acceleration in each occupation fostered acceleration in others, forward and backward, until the rhythm of life itself seemed to increase with each passing hour. Towns filled with strangers; strangers grew rowdy in taverns and pubs; crime, disorder, and irreligion became epidemic. All of this brought out howls of despair from "respectable" middle-class merchants and manufacturers, who in turn moved to quieter neighborhoods, bought new houses and things like carpets and pianos that marked their escape from center-city squalor.

FACTORIES IN THE FIELDS

Economic growth in a market economy needs more than acceleration to become self-sustaining, and the prime mover behind American prosperity in the nineteenth century remained agricultural produce – especially slave-grown cotton. Between 1793 (when the cotton gin made it possible to process short staple cotton) and 1850 (when the census first recorded the data), some 30 million acres of land were brought into production in Georgia, Alabama, Mississippi, Louisiana, Arkansas, and Texas, mostly dedicated to cotton.[18] Roughly 1.3 million African American slaves powered these new "factories in the fields" (half the slave population of the United States), and while they gained a great deal of their own "fuel" from food grown on the plantation, southern staple-crop specialization also profited partly because

---

[18] Michael Williams, *Americans & Their Forests: A Historical Geography* (Cambridge, UK: Cambridge University Press, 1989), 119.

of meat and grain surpluses flowing out of the family farms of Pennsylvania, New Jersey, Virginia's central valley, and the Old Northwest. Ambitious planters hacked their way through the cotton belt in the space of a single generation. In the process, they displaced seventy-five thousand Indians – Cherokee, Choctaw, Chicasaw, Creek, and Seminole – and clear-cut miles of old-growth timber.[19] Most American cotton wound up in British industrial hands, but the demands of the burgeoning South for food, shoes, clothing, tools, transportation, commercial services, and investment capital yielded the same kind of growth pressures inside the United States that had swelled the fortunes of the British Empire in the last decades before the Revolution. At the same time, rising domestic markets steadily lowered the "cost" of pioneering on the cotton frontier by bringing convenient goods and services to new plantations within a few years – or even months – of their creation.

Cotton plantations themselves remained technologically simple throughout the antebellum period, with the single exception of the all-important cotton gin. Forests were cleared by slaves wielding axes, stumps were burned, and roots were grubbed out with shovels and hoes. New fields were plowed with single-bottom equipment drawn by one or more mules. Planting was done by hand, as was the periodic weeding ("chopping") with hoes that helped give the cotton plant its priority claim on water and soil nutrients. Harvest was the most labor-intensive part of the process: Phalanxes of slaves, dragging long bags, moved through the ripened fields, prying the valuable fluff from its boll, now split, dry, and razor sharp. How carefully this was done affected the value of the product, because cotton stained with blood from the fingers of the pickers or full of trash and hulls from careless handling commanded a lower price at the local exchange. Back in the plantation yard, the cotton gin removed seeds and debris before the lint was pressed into bales and wrapped with hemp bagging. Now the bales were ready to be stacked on a steamboat and started on a journey to Lowell or Liverpool. As the cotton culture moved westward, the size of cotton fields increased, but the process changed little between 1800 and the Civil War. Few economies of scale advantaged the larger planters over their

---

[19] Wattenberg, ed. *Statistical History*, 24–37, 460.

less wealthy neighbors, except at the end of the process, when crops were ginned and baled for market. As a result, white men made money growing cotton with just a few slaves – or with hundreds – and shared in that regard a common interest in perpetuating the slave labor system.

One technological innovation that kept slave-grown cotton profitable was the western shallow-draft steamboat. Steamers of different sizes, some drawing as little as 12 inches of water "light" (30 inches loaded), plied southern rivers and bayous, bringing foreign and domestic consumer goods right to the plantation docks, picking up their 500-pound bales of raw cotton, and relieving the planters from having to waste time shopping in town. The greater impact of the market revolution in the South, however, came through intangible changes in techniques of doing business, instruments of credit and commercial transaction, even ways of telling time. Specialized cotton factors orchestrated the planter's business: watching the cotton exchanges; tracking prices; combing markets for advantageous stocks of consumer goods; and trading (and speculating) in banknotes, promissory notes, bills of exchange, warehouse receipts, and other commercial paper, all greasing the wheels of cotton marketing. Planters seemed to focus their own attention on trading land and slaves – the two most essential components of their production system.

Historians of slavery once dismissed it as economically foolish, a backward agricultural system, but scholars in the recent generation have found more flexibility in planters' approach to slave labor and more evidence of smart attention to business on the part of the masters. Excellent studies now portray low-country rice plantations where bound men and women under the "task system" of management practically ran extremely complex enterprises for owners who often did not even live on the premises. Africans probably taught American planters everything they knew about rice cultivation, including how to construct elaborate waterworks for flooding and draining the fields. In Louisiana, some sugar planters employed labor management strategies (including careful attention to family connections) starkly different from the harsh systems seen in the West Indies. Throughout the South, slaves were leased and hired for all sorts of tasks, often working on their own recognizance and expected faithfully to carry back to their masters the cash wages of their labors.

In theory, no slaveholder could embrace the Smithian model of human economic motivation (the rational pursuit of self-interest) when trying to mobilize a chattel work force, but in a striking case in Virginia, we see skilled slaves at an iron forge earning bonus incentives and overtime pay, piling up money in savings accounts from which they withdrew small sums to give each other presents or cashed in the whole to buy their freedom. Southern railroads employed slaves, as did canals and manufacturing firms, mocking the conventional wisdom that slave labor was incompatible with enterprise and industry. Plantation masters adopted clocks and watches and "time discipline" just about as readily as northern factory bosses, even as they struggled to resist the democratic implications of the free-labor system of which it was a part. Finally, numerous studies on plantation management suggest that many planters paid close attention to the costs of production, the value of their capital assets (including "their people"), and the financial success of their enterprise over time. (Many others, of course, did not, which affirmed in a way that the master-slave relationship was more calculating than sentimental, even if short-sighted.) Rarely fitting the caricatures of the day – antique, backward-looking patriarch or brutal, slave-whipping sociopath – planters struggled like other Americans to square their social and racial assumptions with the challenges and opportunities thrown up by new market forces. At the same time, recent work on the slave trade has revealed a planter class intensely aware of the way that buying and selling black laborers made white men *white*, commodified human beings, and denied the humanity of slaves for the pleasure and profit of the master class.

THE FLOW OF INFORMATION

Beneath or behind all this profitable activity lay a dramatic revolution in communications that expanded the effective playing field for human interactions from a circle 5 or 6 miles across (a day's round trip on foot) to a continental scale. Admittedly, long-distance trade and transportation had been fostering social and economic intercourse for three hundred years when the nineteenth century began; but such linkages in the age of sail remained painfully slow and only occasionally impinged on the lives of most ordinary people. (It can be argued that the forced relocation of African laborers from their homes to New World plantations affected them daily ever after, but slaves were not free participants in the transactions that made early modern merchant capitalism possible.) After the formation of the American Republic, a series of interlocking improvements increased the circulation of information, in velocity and volume, in ways that encouraged and facilitated social mobility, economic ambition, and the willingness of persons to do business with strangers at a distance.

The first piece of this new communications network was the United States Post Office, which had been launched back in 1792 on an explicit mission to make the circulation of news and information as free and easy as possible all across the United States. Two early decisions helped make the postal system an extraordinary force for national integration: First, newspapers – *all* newspapers – were granted ready access to the post at trivial expense; and second, Congress adopted the habit of never turning down citizen petitions for new routes and post offices. Although it clearly benefited business, this early support for an expansive postal system did not spring from commercial considerations; in fact, private letters (mostly business communications) paid very high postage to subsidize the comparatively free flow of newspapers. It was the widespread "republican" suspicion of elected politicians, gathered in far-off Washington, that fostered the popular conviction that liberty itself depended on cheaply spreading the news. Political rivals on the national stage required information about their enemies and their enemies' constituents all over the Union; state and local officials demanded frequent communications from their representatives in Congress; and common voters, especially as the suffrage expanded to include all adult white males, had to be informed and inflamed about their favorite candidates and party tickets. As a result, by the early 1830s, the post office employed 8,700 individuals (three-fourths of all federal employees) and delivered 16 million newspapers a year – which number doubled by 1840. Current newspapers could be found in the farthest corners of the antebellum wilderness practically from the first days of settlement. The touring French aristocrat Alexis de Tocqueville found that the residents of frontier Michigan Territory were better informed than the common people of northern France, which had been settled since time immemorial.[20]

If the circulation of news was encouraged for political purposes, it nevertheless revolutionized business as well. Those newspapers were filled with prices and other market-related information, subjecting buyers and sellers everywhere to real market forces. Information worked like electric current in the capitalist free-market system, flipping switches and setting up situations. The arrival of a bushel of wheat in New York increased the supply – and theoretically depressed the price – of that commodity for New York buyers. Knowing what wheat sold for in New York helped farmers in Ohio or Illinois decide what to plant and what to expect in return for their produce at harvest time. Knowing what goods were for sale (the earliest mercantile "ads" typically printed detailed lists) piqued demand among country people and broke down consumer satisfaction with the limited choices available in local self-sufficient markets. Wherever information flowed freely, price competition began to exercise its influence on how people valued what they bought and sold: The value of a gallon of whiskey or a pair of shoes moved toward an equilibrium price, minus the cost of transportation.

Delivering the mail, of course, turned out to be a major impetus behind campaigns for improved transportation. Better postal service depended on the condition of local roads, which stimulated local officials and taxpayers (some more than others) to clear the roads, drain the mud holes, and build bridges and culverts where small, erratic streams threatened to cut off delivery for days or weeks at a time. Better roads, together with the availability of lucrative federal contracts for carrying the mail, encouraged private stagecoach lines to beef up capacity, speed up service, and move toward dependable schedules. Of course, once people became acquainted with better service, they demanded its continuation and further improvement. Competition thus repaid successful innovations that helped improve the circulation of people and information using whatever technology – primitive or experimental – was available. By the 1850s, letters and newspapers might travel by sailing ship, steamboat, canal boat,

[20] Richard R. John, *Spreading the News: The American Postal System from Franklin to Morse* (Cambridge, MA: Harvard University Press, 1995), 1.

railroad, and stagecoach before winding up in the locked "portman-
teau" of the lowly, mounted, rural post rider.

The postal service was not the only beneficiary of improved transportation, and when taken in combination with all sorts of private
conveyances and transportation services, the internal improvements
boom of the first four decades after 1800 yielded a truly remarkable
transformation of the network even before the steam railroad brought
industrial-strength speed and power to the system. Taking advantage
of Macadamized roads (well-drained roadways, free of stumps, and
paved with compacted broken stone), turnpikes with bridges and culverts, steamboats on natural waterways, and regular packet services on
brand-new man-made canals, purveyors of information – newspapers,
magazines, politicians, private businessmen, curious tourists, immigrants, and traveling family members – decreased the "information
float" (the time lapsed between sending and receiving messages). Scholars' calculations suggest that, in 1840, information and passengers
spread out from New York City between five and twenty times as fast
as they had fifty years before.[21] Distances seemed to be dissolving, and
for the first time, New Yorkers could reach their countrymen on the
Mississippi more quickly than they could reach Liverpool or La Havre.

Still profoundly fragmented, this relatively "low-tech" network
comprised hundreds of separate routes, conveyances, and facilities
and employed thousands of independent forwarding merchants, livery
agents, wagon masters, stage drivers, steamboat captains, canal boat-
ers, mule skinners, warehousemen, teamsters, dock workers, cartmen –
individual sellers of services knit together by market transactions the
complexity of which absolutely boggles the modern mind. Nevertheless, the volume and velocity of information in motion, as well as
passengers and freight, mushroomed and created a demand for the
faster, cheaper, and more dependable integrated services that would
be offered by the railroads within a decade. (In the absence of bureaucratic procedures or mathematical models derived from fluid mechanics, no one could imagine bringing all these transactions into a stable,
predictable order. Markets were the only way known to connect innumerable buyers with innumerable sellers efficiently.)

---

[21] Alan R. Pred, *Urban Growth and the Circulation of Information: The United States
System of Cities, 1790–1840* (Cambridge, MA: Harvard University Press, 1973), 64, 74.

Far from satisfactory by the standards of the next generation, this network by 1840 succeeded in teaching people to expect to know what went on half a continent away, order goods shipped a thousand miles, and consume things routinely that could not be grown or made at home. By the middle 1840s, at the same time that thousands of Americans were striking out on foot with ox-carts and wagons on the life-threatening six-month trek to Oregon and California – the last example of a style of emigration made famous by Daniel Boone six decades before – other Americans already were learning to board "the cars" for Boston or Philadelphia and return home the same day, shopping bags in hand. Some wags fretted that high-speed travel – "we flew in the wings of the wind at the varied speed of fifteen to twenty-five miles an hour, annihilating time and space" – might endanger human organ systems; but technological enthusiasts and commercial boosters deployed the most extravagant language to describe the world that lay just around the corner. Liberty, equality, world peace, and the diffusion of intelligence would all advance in the face of railroad transportation, while the "stock of human misery" must surely decline.[22] As if to prove prognosticators right, in 1844 Samuel F. B. Morse transmitted his famous first telegraphic message – "What hath God wrought" – across his wires stretched between the Capitol in Washington and the Baltimore railroad station. Space and time, it seemed, truly had been obliterated. By 1850, ten thousand miles of telegraph wires made it possible for merchants to forward information instantaneously while commodities themselves moved more slowly toward their destination (*one thousand bushels wheat shipped today*-stop-*due New York Thursday*-stop). Thereafter, market forces acquired an even greater influence on all kinds of economic transactions.[23]

Everybody knows that railroads accomplished this second revolution, this "annihilation of space and time," but few remember the long gestation of railroad technology nor the tremendous amount of experimentation (and failure) that finally produced the familiar "Iron Horse." Start with the roadway itself. The key to a railroad's energy advantage lay in the smooth, firm, parallel rails on which the cars and

[22] James A. Ward, *Railroads and the Character of America, 1820–1887* (Knoxville: University of Tennessee Press, 1986), 62, 110.
[23] Daniel Walker Howe, *What Hath God Wrought: The Transformation of America, 1815–1848* (New York: Oxford University Press, 2007), 696.

engines ran. Early English railroads were built on solid foundations, parallel stone walls set deep in the ground, like the footings of a building, onto which iron rails were pegged to carry the flanged wheels of the railway carriages. The first American experiments copied this design but found it inappropriate for the American setting. First, the extreme temperature variations in North America (north of the Chesapeake at least) produced frost heave that threw stone foundations out of alignment. Second, stone construction proved so expensive and slow that the vast expanses of the new United States never could have been crossed using English-style techniques. By the early 1830s, American railroad builders had settled on cheaper, more flexible roads, with wooden rails spiked together on wooden cross-ties or "sleepers" (to maintain their parallel orientation), set firmly on top of a Macadam-like bed of broken stone, and topped with straps of iron spiked onto the top edges of the wooden rails. The rapid deterioration of these "strap-iron" rails (not to mention the deadly "snake-heads" that resulted when iron straps broke, curled up, and penetrated the floor of a carriage, sometimes impaling passengers inside) stimulated further experimentation until the industry settled on the rolled-iron "T" rail seated in "chairs" that were spiked to the cross-ties.

Motive power likewise took almost two decades to evolve into its familiar form. In 1830, many railroad promoters still considered horse power to be more dependable and effective than the steam-powered locomotives being bragged about loosely by wild-eyed enthusiasts. The first American locomotives looked a little like four-wheeled gun carriages with water tanks mounted where the canon should be. Inventors had significant problems to solve. They needed a firebox on board and a boiler filled with water through which tubes could carry hot air to produce the steam. They needed precisely milled pistons and cylinders with which to convert the steam into reciprocal mechanical action, which was then transferred to the wheels by levers and cranks. Steamboat builders had pioneered solutions to many of these engine-building problems, but locomotives had to pack more power in a small package than did any steamboat engine. Of what could you make the fire tubes that would not burn out or corrode too quickly? How to build a frame that would not be wrenched apart by the alternating horizontal forces of the drive gear pushing back on the right, then left, then right again?

How to balance the driving wheels with counterweights so that the cranks will not have "dead spots" and at the same time turn smoothly enough to minimize any downward beating action that would hammer the rails to pieces? Finally, the locomotive had to develop enough power to carry itself and large quantities of wood and water and still pull a payload adequate to reimburse its cost of operation.

These technical elements, along with dozens of other details, all had to be resolved and then settled upon because an effective railroad system – unlike an individual steamboat – had to use identical rails, identical wheels, perfectly interchangeable cars and engines, a common mechanism for coupling cars together, and an operating system to coordinate the whole across time and space in a choreographed performance unlike anything tried by any enterprise before. For the first twenty years of railroad development, these difficulties were tackled on a very small scale. With the exception of the sprawling Baltimore & Ohio and the Western Railroad of Massachusetts, most early companies operated short lines between two terminal cities – and found coordinating such relatively closed systems trouble enough. Scheduling trains in both directions on a common single track required a level of attention to time and speed never before considered by teamsters or stagecoach drivers. Safety and convenience placed a monopoly of operations in the hands of the railroad company, which also owned the road, such that carrier and route – always two separate entities before – now were combined in a single business enterprise.

Early managers of railroads imagined their business as moving goods between terminal cities – for example, between Boston and Providence. But in practice, customers desired to ride or ship goods from all points along the line to one or the other terminal, and even from one intermediate place to another. Railroad managers quickly learned that they had to do business at dozens of different points on the map, handle all kind of goods as well as human passengers, and charge reasonable prices for their services as well as the use of the road for trips of a mile, ten miles, or a hundred. Employees worked not in a shop or factory, but on board the train itself, or out along the line doing maintenance of way, where supervision was difficult if not impossible. Gradually, it dawned on people that a railroad was something like a ship, something like a factory, something like a stagecoach line, something like a turnpike, and something like a municipal government charged with keeping the peace and collecting taxes over an expanse of geographical territory.

Even as railroaders met the challenges of managing a short-line company, one more step was required before the railroad as a *system* of transportation would come into its own: the integration of separate two-point links into a chain, and then a web or network, of common connections. In the early 1840s, the technical difficulties receded quickly, and by the late 1840s the business and management systems were coming into focus. It was in the 1850s that this last stage of integration kicked in to create the first long-distance interregional "trunk lines" connecting New York with interior markets – especially that breakneck upstart city on the lake, Chicago. In upstate New York, half a dozen short lines following the Erie Canal first made traffic interchange agreements, issued tickets to passengers for through passage from Albany to Buffalo, and pulled each other's freight cars rather than unload and reload goods at the points where two companies met. Bookkeeping nightmares resulted, forcing supposedly rival firms into closer and closer cooperation, until it made no sense at all for connecting lines to compete with each other. Mergers, leases, and capital investment by one firm in another pointed the way toward consolidation into long lines or systems that would challenge rivals *in parallel* between major distant markets while blunting market forces and eliminating market transactions between the points of the line *in series*. Before the outbreak of the Civil War, the New York Central, the Erie, and the Pennsylvania trunk lines established integrated service between the East Coast and Chicago and were rapidly filling out feeder links inside the regions they served as well as probing farther west into the prairies of Illinois and Iowa.

THE STEALTH ADVANCE OF PROGRESS

The cumulative effect of all these developments was the emergence and articulation of what we recognize as the modern capitalist economic system. All of it sprang from the extraordinary abundance of the natural American environment. Compared to Old Europe, North America had presented its European colonizers with a rich storehouse of resources that were being used only lightly by indigenous populations. Colonial Americans often remarked on their great fortune in "possessing" such a vast portion of the Creator's blessings, but in the nineteenth century, as the *rate* of wealth accumulation rocketed skyward due to technological innovations, people assigned more and more of the credit to human ingenuity and the enterprise of free Americans. The dramatic returns to industry that marked the experience of early Americans easily might have been curbed by scarcities of food, fuel, or rainfall at any time during the antebellum era. But significant limits never appeared, and the rapid development of frontier land and transportation silenced passing concerns about deforestation and soil exhaustion. Prosperity began to look boundless: A profligate "mother nature" seemed willing to gratify her children no matter how much they demanded.

Almost imperceptibly across several decades, structural changes in the means of production and patterns of exchange knit themselves in interlocking combinations. Face-to-face commercial transactions, so typical of rural village life in the late eighteenth century, evolved into institutional exchanges dependent more on cash and facilitating middlemen. Where villagers once exchanged eggs, butter, and firewood for yarn, shoes, or furniture directly from the person who made them, they soon passed all produce through the books of the country storekeeper and eventually bought their shoes, chairs, and dry goods from craftsmen they never met who worked in factories in unimaginable eastern or northern cities. Without delay, the overworked pioneer housewives hung up their spinning wheels and purchased ready-made woolens and cotton cloth as supplies became available. Not for a moment did they think that by dropping the extraordinary tedium of spinning, knitting, weaving, and sewing all of their family's textiles, they would usher in a new economic system that profoundly restricted their liberty or independence. Yet such was the effect of the encroaching web of market transactions that characterized their lives.

One of the earliest signs of market penetration was the rising export of surplus crops. Early subsistence farmers produced their immediate needs at home and only raised cash with exports to pay taxes or purchase coffee, powder, lead, and window glass. However, as their accounts at the store began to mount, farmers raised more chickens for sale in town, more wheat for sale at the local flour mill, and more hogs and cattle that could walk to distant markets, in order to balance their purchases. Farm women made butter and cheese for the nearest urban community where folks had no cows of their own. Some farmers brought the storekeeper firewood or forest products such as barrel staves. Others worked together to drive large herds of livestock to regional cities such as Cincinnati, where animals were slaughtered and processed for further export in national or international markets. Storekeepers, like it or not, found themselves wholesaling produce for export in order to stock their shelves with retail merchandise, and these primitive entrepreneurs often promoted industry and transportation improvements in desperate efforts to move out commodities brought to them by customers eager to purchase their wares. What stood out in the frontier progression from subsistence to export economy was the invisibility of the process and the relative innocence of each individual whose choices drove the transformation forward.

Farther up the chain of entrepreneurial innovation, "likely" young men (and this *was* mostly a man's business) took positions as clerks, where they learned elementary commercial skills. Some became managers of branch stores capitalized by their employers; some saved enough from their wages to buy a stock of goods and go out on their own. In larger towns and cities, the burgeoning volume of trade fostered specialization, and wherever transactions became numerous, the need for paperwork and records multiplied. Institutional procedures replaced family connections or personal acquaintance among buyers, sellers, employers, and employees. Banks replaced family, friends, and local notables as the primary sources of business capital, and by the 1850s, Lewis Tappan's credit reporters were making formal ratings of merchants in Chicago, Cincinnati, and French Lick, Indiana, for the benefit of lenders and vendors in Boston, New York, and Philadelphia. Partnerships remained the preferred instrument for larger businesses, but in most states, general incorporation laws made the once-scarce corporate charter readily available for groups interested in manufacturing, mining, turnpikes, insurance, sometimes banking, and experimental railroad development.

What made these commercial changes both permanent and irreversible was the contribution of industrialization, which fostered ever-more elaborate divisions of labor and corresponding interdependencies. In the same way that Indians who gave up their stone-age technology became utterly dependent on hatchets, knives, and firearms, antebellum Americans who traded cash wages for rural self-sufficiency enjoyed efficiencies at the expense of independence.

It took not a generation for the skills of self-sufficiency to begin to atrophy, and, frankly, few antebellum Americans indulged nostalgic dreams of a return to simpler times. Progress promised ease and prosperity, and most Americans were all too familiar with the "charms" of pre-industrial material life to see it as a virtue alongside modern ways.

Without anybody wishing it so, the increasing scope of commercial transactions, the specialized divisions of labor, the growing distance between buyers and sellers, the institutionalization of relations, and the proliferation of intermediaries disembedded individual transactions from contexts in which the common welfare or "commonwealth" of whole communities once had seemed self-evident. Not that folks were any more (or less) inclined to abuse their neighbors, but how was one to know who *was* his neighbor in a complicated nexus of actors and agents he never saw or knew by name, where prices, commissions, and the terms of trade seemed always to be set by somebody else? This was, of course, the genius of the free commercial marketplace: It depersonalized transactions, stripped them of all but economic information, and opened the game to anyone with something to sell or the wherewithal to buy. The result, overall, was a decline of what we might call "diseconomies" or wasteful transaction costs, but this rationalization came at a price in terms of community welfare and social relations. Individuals who bore their neighbors no ill will now found themselves required to raise prices, call in loans, lower wages, or fire employees because competitive forces left them no choice. Once the market revolution had produced a certain level of complexity and interdependence, the most moral or ethical of entrepreneurs found themselves powerless to stand against a panic or a boom.

In the countryside, the market revolution generated problems even for families engaged in the once-timeless and uncomplicated business of farming. Even before the Erie Canal was built, farmers along the Hudson River had worried that their "natural" advantage as suppliers to a fast-growing Manhattan population would be erased by cheap transportation reaching into the Genesee Valley. So it was, after 1830, that the breadbasket shifted westward, forcing farmers nearer the city into meat, dairy, and vegetable production – more valuable enterprises, perhaps, but far more dependent on immediate market forces, transportation costs, and innovative competition. Within a generation (by the 1850s), Genesee farmers felt the same displacement, as foodstuffs from Michigan, Ohio, and Indiana rode eastward on railroad trains that favored long hauls over short ones. Caught in the middle, upstate New York farmers found themselves too far from the city for butter and meat but not far enough to sell flour and corn in competition with new western sources. Butchering, traditionally a decentralized local enterprise (and an asset to the neighborhood), became "meat packing," as it grew in scale, transforming locales – sometimes whole towns – into nearly unlivable scenes of carnage and offal. Cincinnati became known as "Porkopolis," a city in which the odds stood "five hundred to one" (said English tourist Frances Trollope) that a woman could not cross the street without "brushing by a snout fresh dripping from the kennel."[24] Even rural marriages felt the strain of accommodating the capitalist system, as dairying, traditionally women's work and supplemental to household income, began to surpass grain farming as the primary source of support for many families in regions close to major cities.

Americans could hardly fail to notice the extraordinary flood of "improvements" that marked the four decades before 1860. Material conditions changed at an ever-increasing pace. More significantly, people who had once feared change began to embrace it, not as evidence of decay but as the natural condition of human beings in an age of "progress." No metaphor better captures the accumulated force of these "marvelous improvements" than that of a whirlwind. Coming ever faster and spiraling outward, discrete acts of innovation and entrepreneurship contributed to a rising sense of things spinning out of control. Foreign tourists repeatedly remarked about the frantic pace of change in the United States. Writing in 1835, Francis Lieber likened ten years in America to "a century in Spain." How could people endure feeling "all the time as if tied to the wing of a windmill?"[25] Outside observers even questioned whether this freedom, mobility, and chaos might not be harming Americans' health. But to domestic eyes, progress itself did not seem patently evil, even if one or two elements caused displeasure.

[24] Frances Trollope, *Domestic Manners of the Americans,* ed. John Lauritz Larson (orig. 1832; abridged ed., St. James, NY: Brandywine Press, 1993), 53.
[25] Quoted in Marvin Meyers, *The Jacksonian Persuasion; Politics and Belief* (Stanford: Stanford University Press, 1957), 122.

When the men and women who experienced this whirling phenomenon began to feel giddy, they had a good chance of seeing it as thrilling
rather than alarming or clearly dangerous.

Falling together in the 1850s with a suddenness that startled most
observers, all these disparate changes and adaptations seemed to assem-
ble themselves into a giant, interlocking network of institutions, expectations, and behaviors that all found their coordination in market forces.
With prices set by impersonal market mechanisms, vendors no longer
dickered with their customers. Market quotations from New York, New
Orleans, or even London seemed to establish the value of everything in
the most remote country villages. Banks, transportation companies,
insurers, and large mercantile houses held the better cards in whatever
bargaining went on in these complex commercial networks, leaving the
individual entrepreneur on the defensive, afraid of being bested, and
determined to recover his losses from the next most vulnerable "chump"
in the game. Whatever mutuality may have existed in the "moral economy" of traditional networks of community exchange (and there clearly
was some), it was disappearing from the commercial culture of the
antebellum United States (especially in the North) as the sectional conflict drew nearer.

The impact of this progress, of course, was never uniform: Real
people suffered absolute as well as relative distresses under this chaotic
economic regime. From time to time, when the business cycle triggered
a panic or a downturn in trade, a chorus of voices rose to protest the
destruction of traditions, the loss of brotherhood, the heartless triumph of naked greed. But the return of prosperity generally rekindled
people's optimism, boosted their expectations, and buoyed the hope of
so many (sometimes against available evidence) that every American
stood to gain from the market revolution. Many Americans believed,
at almost every step along the path through this wonderland of change,
that progress energized their birthright of liberty, and that the benefits
of freedom lay not in fighting what seemed inevitable, but in riding the
tiger into a future they hoped would reward their acquiescence.

Interlude: Panic! 1837

The years 1835 and 1836 showed a spike in American prosperity like nothing ever seen before. Cotton and foodstuffs poured forth into the markets of the world; investment capital flowed back in a virtual torrent as rich men in Europe and Britain scrambled to own a piece of the rising economic phenomenon that was the United States. Land sales boomed, cotton prices soared (driving up the price of land and slaves as well); the vast continental interior succumbed to parades of pioneers who stripped the land of timber, replacing it with cotton, hemp, wheat, corn, cattle, and hogs. Brilliantly, the tools of the market revolution – productive machinery, transportation improvements, easy credit, and marketing facilities – delivered fortunes to thousands of entrepreneurs and promised the same to tens of thousands more who lined up to emulate the successful. Then, between February and June 1837, it all fell to pieces again. Brokers failed in London, Paris, and all over the United States. Investment houses returned bills unpaid, leaving their correspondents holding worthless promissory paper. In May, banks in New York, Philadelphia, Providence, Baltimore, and New Orleans suspended specie payments and called in their loans. Suspension of payments interrupted credit, and the absence of credit brought to a halt the flow of goods and services throughout the system.

The Panic of 1837 cut a wide swath of injury largely because so many households now depended on the integrated market economy. There were, of course, high-stakes gamblers caught in the panic, but these were not a primary source of concern. Tens of thousands of city dwellers who worked for wages suffered most desperately with no means to pay rent or purchase food and fuel. Agricultural households could subsist on their own resources – unless they owed money, as thousands did, for the purchase of land, improvements, tools, livestock, or common necessities charged against the income from next year's crops. Shopkeepers and tradesmen usually owed others for stocks of goods or raw materials, while their inability to collect receivables forced businessmen with no other faults to fail. Men of property whose conduct had been impeccable nevertheless were ruined by the sudden demand that they pay off creditors with cash. Merchants and manufacturers who stood ready to supply what markets demanded found themselves paralyzed for want of financial means to carry on business.

Men and women who remembered the last such general catastrophe in 1819 quickly braced themselves for the worst. Many others, however, had risen to wealth since the early 1820s; these stood dumbfounded as the downward spiral flushed away half or two-thirds of their new fortunes. As they had for generations, moralists inveighed against "high living" and the "ravenous" desire "of acquiring wealth without labour." One likened the "commercial system" to the whore of Babylon: "All nations have been maddened, 'intoxicated with the wine of the wrath of her fornication.'"[1] Fearing violence among the disappointed, some clergymen urged the faithful to suffer in patience: "Lay up treasure in Heaven. . . . Godliness with contentment is a great gain."[2] "Speculation," of course, caught the brunt of the criticism, but the last twenty years had shown that the vice of speculation could scarcely be distinguished from innovation and risky investment. Horace Greeley saw speculation as a "natural phase" of economic growth; when successful, wrote Richard Hildreth, "however wild it may have appeared in the beginning," speculation was pronounced an "excellent thing" and commended as *enterprise*.[3]

---

[1] Orestes Brownson, *Babylon Is Falling: A Discourse Preached in the Masonic Temple to the Society for Christian Union and Progress on Sunday Morning, May 28, 1837* (2nd ed., Boston: I. R. Butts, 1837), 4.
[2] Quoted in Samuel Rezneck, *Business Depressions and Financial Panics: Essays in American Business and Economic History* (New York: Greenwood, 1968), 84.
[3] Horace Greeley, quoted in Rezneck, *Business Depressions*, 85; Richard Hildreth, *History of Banks: To Which Is Added a Demonstration of the Advantages and Necessity of Free Competition in the Business of Banking* (Boston: Hilliard, Gray, 1837), 160. Emphasis in the original.

Compared to 1819, analysis of failure in this new crisis displayed a profoundly ambivalent aspect. Nobody wanted to encourage reckless borrowing and personal default, yet there were, as one Cincinnati clergyman observed, "many honest failures in business, which ordinary prudence cannot prevent." Others disagreed and blamed most failures on "mistakes" originating in "personal character."[4] At stake, in part, was the matter of who should take care of needy dependents, but underneath it all lay a chilling question: In what kind of world could honest, frugal, hard-working, God-fearing people fail to support their families? As unemployment mounted in the winter of 1837–1838, especially in manufacturing centers such as Philadelphia and New York, howls of protest arose from the suffering poor. More comfortable persons worried that social unrest was imminent. Always drawn to hyperbole, Orestes Brownson feared the start of revolution: "What will be the issue of this fearful and protracted war of equality against privilege?"[5]

Like almost everybody troubled by this return of financial disaster, Brownson interpreted the crisis in terms of political power. Encouraged by Jacksonian rhetoric to see market forces as tools used by bankers and monied "aristocrats" to defraud hard-working people, Brownson quickly blamed the Second Bank of the United States. True, the bank had been sentenced to death, but it still clung to life as a Philadelphia corporation, obedient as ever to the will of its "evil" president, Nicholas Biddle. Brownson desired in its place an "independent treasury" – a source of money controlled by government and not beholden to private banks – which proposal found favor with Jackson's party and his presidential successor, Martin Van Buren. In this version of the story, the people's war against the "monster bank" had been won, but not before Biddle knocked down the pillars of his unholy temple in one final wicked act of vengeance.

Biddle, not surprisingly, saw things differently. In November 1836, he published an open letter to Congressman (and former president)

---

[4] Quoted in Edward J. Balleisen, *Navigating Failure: Bankruptcy and Commercial Society in Antebellum America* (Chapel Hill: University of North Carolina Press, 2001), 25–6,

[5] Brownson, "Prospects of the Democracy," *Boston Quarterly Review*, January 1839, in *The Works of Orestes A. Brownson*, ed. Henry F. Brownson (20 vols., rpt. New York: AMS Press, 1966), XV: 38; idem, *Babylon Is Falling*, 6.

John Quincy Adams, blaming Jackson for derangement in financial markets that barely had begun. When Congress had adjourned (in July 1836), "every branch of industry" he wrote, was "flourishing." Next month (December), it would reconvene to find "the whole country suffering intense pecuniary distress." (The timing itself seemed suspicious: Could Biddle foretell the future?) This impending crisis resulted, he explained, from the "mismanagement of the revenue." First, Congress had ordered that an enormous federal treasury surplus be distributed among the states. This simple task might have been done (indeed, had formerly been done by Biddle's bank) without the least disruption to financial markets; but Jackson's henchmen bungled the job, recklessly transferring money in and out of depositories "without reference to the wants or the business of the different sections of the union, the season of the year or the course of trade." To make matters worse, in August 1836 Jackson also had directed federal land offices to accept nothing but gold and silver in payment for land. The banks nearest land offices stopped making loans and scrambled to gather up specie; the resulting credit contraction triggered a wholesale suspension (said Biddle) "of commercial intercourse between the west and the Atlantic."[6] At the heart of Biddle's explanation lay a simple cautionary message: The people's favorites, carried into office on waves of hot air and popular fury, dare not be trusted to manage the credit machinery on which all modern prosperity depended. Lay the blame, then, not on the bank but on the bank war, on the destruction of the only fiscal agent (Biddle?) sufficiently endowed with expertise and insulated from political pressure to fulfill the delicate role of fiduciary czar.

These two kinds of narrative circulated freely in the years after 1837. In one, the servants of the people struggled to liberate their economic welfare from the hands of their ancient enemies, the propertied elites; in the other, ignorant demagogues pawed at the levers of power, lusting for advancement and heedless of the complicated systems they endangered. Neither story was true, of course, but neither story was wholly false. Contemporary analysts – and there were dozens of them spilling ink – toiled without ceasing to explain what had happened and prescribe a course of treatment guaranteed to bring

---

[6] Nicholas Biddle to John Quincy Adams, open letter reprinted in *Niles Register*, 17 Dec. 1836, 243–5.

about a cure. Still, no consensus emerged except for the troubling recognition that financial crises appeared to come out of nowhere – and nobody knew how to stop them or keep them from recurring. Had the loss of the national bank sparked an inflationary bubble? Or had the contraction of that bank's operations started a credit crunch? High tariffs might have been the trigger – or perhaps it was the lowering of tariffs that began in 1833. Hard money held the cure – or else inflationary paper emanating from the numberless banks made possible after 1837 by new "free-banking" laws in many states. The country clearly required either an independent treasury or a new national bank (at least nobody suggested both). Elected officials must play a larger role in economic regulation, or else they must withdraw altogether and let the markets operate freely, as they are wont to do in a state of nature.

Modern economists can prove that almost none of what contemporaries said was true about the causes of the "hard times" that followed the Panic of 1837. In 1969, using modern tools to analyze data from the early 1800s, Peter Temin discredited almost every claim put forth by contemporary observers. First, the boom of 1835–1836 owed nothing to the death of the Second Bank. Neither the sudden infusion of government deposits into "pet banks" in the states nor the absence of Biddle's restraining hand on the system of currency exchange contributed to the sharp increase of ready money. Rather, large imports of capital from England and the sudden Chinese preference for opium over silver in the Far East trade caused a very real increase in bank reserves in the United States. Second, the panic was not a response to any of President Jackson's financial policies. The Bank War had not caused the boom and so it could not be blamed when the bubble burst. Neither the distribution of the surplus nor the Specie Circular can be shown to have had the effects alleged. Finally, the whole five-year period of "hard times" that so scarred those who lived through it was nowhere near as deep and destructive (measured statistically) as they imagined. What at the time had produced widespread failures and business closures, unemployment, personal bankruptcies, suspensions of public works (several states defaulted on internal improvement bonds), and a sharp drop in commodity prices turned out to be, technically, "a deflation, as opposed to a decline in production."[7]

---

[7] Peter Temin, *The Jacksonian Economy* (New York: W. W. Norton, 1969), 23.

Of course, people in the past have no access to the wisdom (or pretensions) of later generations, so Temin's reassessments brought no comfort to antebellum Americans. Instead, they wrestled with the evidence before them and argued with each other and the experts of their day about the true nature of the market economy. Could it be trusted if left alone? Did it function on a national or global level, and did it deal fairly with all its participants? Did markets punish or reward dishonest, immoral, and deceitful behavior? If not, did the church or the state retain some obligation to do so instead? Could rising expectations be sustained along with equal opportunity and the promises of personal freedom that Americans claimed as a birthright? Finally, were periodic derangements such as the one just past the unavoidable price to be paid for rising prosperity through economic growth?

The return of panics and depressions with surprising regularity throughout the nineteenth century – in 1857, 1873, and 1893 (continuing in 1907, 1920, and ending with the "big one" in 1929) – gradually convinced Americans that business cycles were real. This is not to say that Adam Smith's promise was untrue: Free markets in a state of nature probably were automatic and self-regulating, and they certainly avoided the interest-group conflicts that erupted every time elected governments sought to shape or guide economic policies. But experienced up close in real time, market forces delivered incredible disruptions in the process of finding equilibrium – disruptions that economists now assure us are as natural as the seasons. Such periods of panic and depression – hard times, as they were called universally – focused everyone's attention on the inconstancy of economic growth, the unpredictability of capitalist enterprise, and the capricious distribution of losses and gains that accompanied the market revolution. For some, these periodic bouts of hard times may have bent (but did not break) their enthusiasm for the marvelous improvements that still, on the whole, marked the eight decades since the Revolution. For others, however, hard times were simply the lowest points in an oscillating downward path that seemed to usher in a new, unpopular regime, not of freedom, but of heartless markets and heartless men.

3

Heartless Markets, Heartless Men

Much of what people experienced with the rise of capitalist market relations derived from the depersonalization of transactions – from the rise of heartless markets and heartless men. In the pre-modern world, *who* you were had everything to do with how you were treated in public places: whether you received credit, merited trust, deserved poor relief, or belonged in a circle of "friendship." It was a hallmark of modern capitalist relations that transactions among individuals became routinized, institutionalized, and depersonalized, so that one could do business with strangers at a distance as readily as at home. In ways never intended (and largely unimagined at the time), the story of "marvelous improvements," discussed previously, radically transformed the social relations that early Americans once had assumed to be natural, desirable, and perhaps even immutable. The same developments that sustained enthusiastic narratives of prosperity and progress turned up in counternarratives of loss, frustration, and dislocation. Individuals seized opportunities for gain and advancement that embroiled them forever in market relations that undermined their places of comfort in earlier networks of family, community, and friendship. The maddening ambivalence of the experience of the market revolution in antebellum America lies not just in the existence of counternarratives but their coexistence with the narratives of progress, often running side by side, like unnatural harmonies, in the lives of individuals who could not reconcile their contradictions.

Nothing focused the attention of antebellum Americans on the nature of the market revolution quite like the suffering of men and women who

found themselves ruined by a reversal of fortunes. "Reversal of fortunes" –
the phrase itself implies a game-like quality, a roll of the dice; but coming
out of the revolutionary movement of the 1770s, Americans liked to see
themselves not as *fortuna's* playthings but as children of destiny, competent actors in a rational world. A man's fortune was supposed to bear
witness to his character, industry, and frugality, and his attention to
hearth and home. Nothing seemed more out of place in a popular,
self-governing republic than an economic system that scattered its benefits recklessly, rewarding and punishing with senseless caprice. The men
and women coming into the antebellum market revolution never had
lived in a world of truly objectified equality. They were accustomed to
contractual "justice" tempered with the "mercy" of discretion, friendship, loyalty, tradition, forbearance, and virtue. They still cherished the
notion that honest men and women deserved to earn a living, that
accidental misfortune should not produce ruin, that some advantages
were not to be taken if they authored great hardships on friends and
neighbors. But in the transition to capitalism that followed 1800, expectations such as these were sorely tried and often they were left unfulfilled.

FARMERS

Because they were (according to Jefferson) the "chosen people of God,"
begin with the plight of the yeomen farmers. In the ideal agrarian republic envisioned by nearly all the founders, a perfect citizenry comprised
independent farmers (with a smattering of artisans), proprietors in fee
simple, masters of their households, beholden to no man for bed and
board. Released from the grip of Britain's ruling aristocrats, Americans
imagined a nation of independent freeholders. Possessed of a fertile
continent (if you ignored rightful Indian claims) and clothed with an
equality that grew more insistent over time, the common American
farmer was cast as a central actor in the grand morality play that was
the United States. "What, then, is the American, this new man?" asked
Jean Hector St. John de Crèveceour. He was the yeoman who, together
with his bride, pursued that "first and great commandment, *Increase
and Multiply*" (George Washington's words).[1] Fee simple land tenure,

---

[1] J. Hector St. John de Crèvecoeur, *Letters from an American Farmer*, ed. Albert E.
Stone (New York: Penguin, 1981), 69; George Washington to Lafayette, July 25,
1785, quoted in John Lauritz Larson, *Internal Improvement* (Chapel Hill: University
of North Carolina Press, 2001), 14. Emphasis in the original.

honest labor, and incorruptible government close to home presumably guaranteed this agrarian idyll against all the evils of the Old World.

Riding this crest of optimistic ideology, common farmers all over the new United States plunged into the unsettled country. They walked to Kentucky – tens of thousands of them even while the Revolution raged. They trespassed recklessly on Indian lands as well as the pretensions of wealthy speculators in the Ohio Valley, the upland South, Maine, and upstate New York, staking claims on the ground to back up claims on the maps drawn after the Treaty of Paris. Both the Land Ordinance (1785) and the Northwest Ordinance (1787) had favored the pioneer farmers, promising fee simple deeds and guaranteed local self-government as soon as enough souls had filled the new country. Subsequent policies followed suit, trying to remove indigenous people and facilitate a transfer of the national domain from public to private hands. Never having gotten ahead of the pioneers on the southwestern frontier, Congress quickly welcomed Kentucky (1792) and Tennessee (1796) into the Union. Elsewhere, the new territorial processes applied, and after 1801 the government sold land for $2 per acre on four years' credit to all who applied. The object of all these policies was to fill the western country with sturdy white yeomen who would bring new states into the American Union.

The boom and bust that followed the War of 1812 exposed some of the dangers of pioneering in a rapidly expanding market system. Thousands of individuals wagered their energies on making new farms in undeveloped territory; perhaps an equal number gambled on the prospect of making fast money on the fluctuating value of land, labor, and produce under these conditions. When the Panic of 1819 slashed the values of cotton, wheat, and land itself, triggered foreclosures throughout the banking system, halved the wages of artisans and laborers and tossed thousands more out of work altogether, the hardship fell on the innocent and guilty alike. Unable to distinguish earnest settlers from "shameless" speculators, the federal government had no choice but to demand payment from all – or none – of its delinquent accounts. In states such as Kentucky, citizens begged to be rescued from the "paws of banks," and lawmakers tried to oblige with programs to stay the execution of debts until someone could distinguish wholesome victims from scoundrels.[2]

---

[2] Sandra F. VanBurkleo, "'The Paws of Banks': The Origins and Significance of Kentucky's Decision to Tax Federal Bankers, 1818–1820," *Journal of the Early Republic* 9 (1989): 457.

And yet the rule of law, the sanctity of contract, and the guarantee of equal opportunity for all in the economic marketplace made it virtually impossible to discriminate fairly and accurately among these hard-pressed citizens. Like their forefathers during the funding debates of 1791, this new generation found themselves unable to soften hard times without undermining markets altogether. Contract and mercy, equality and friendship, seemed to be hopelessly at odds.

Buying land and making new farms was not the only way the early yeoman found himself drawn into market relations. After 1790, American families that had thrived on semi-subsistence farms, sometimes for generations, found themselves confronted with new opportunities. Cities grew, exports recovered, and market demand for food and fiber promised to reward ambition. As transportation into the hinterland improved, farmers who may have sold butter and eggs, a few cattle or hogs, firewood, barrel staves, or a wagonload of surplus corn to pay taxes and balance their accounts found themselves tempted to grow more products for distant cash markets. Cash got farmers better terms on the storekeeper's books, and cash made it possible for country people to specialize in raising that which brought the best income while enjoying consumer discretion as they spent that income on a wide selection of goods made by somebody other than their friends and neighbors. Producing for the market typically increased farm income, but it also multiplied the risk to family welfare if the value of produce fell or the cost of consumer goods spiked – especially after local substitute sources gradually had disappeared. As the transportation revolution opened new lands deep in the interior, market farmers in the Hudson River Valley found their historical role as victuallers to New York City challenged by farmers upstate in the Genesee Valley. Such producers, who had once placed themselves directly in the path of progress, now howled in protest as government-assisted internal improvements brought in produce from distant frontiers at competitive prices. (In time, the upstarts themselves would be displaced by farmers in Ohio, Michigan, and Illinois, which sparked demands in upstate New York for fixed per-mile or "pro rata" railroad rates to preserve the advantage of proximity – and completely negate the point of improved transportation in the first place.)

In the shadows of rapidly growing cities such as New York, Philadelphia, Baltimore, and Boston, farmers sensibly turned their attention to supplying urban populations with things city folks could not provide themselves: fresh meat, vegetables, butter and eggs, firewood, and fodder for the livestock. None of these activities was new to semi-subsistence farmers; all had traded such goods at their neighborhood stores since the earliest days of settlement. But urban growth and the articulation of complex markets made what had once been ancillary industries increasingly the primary business of farms in hinterland regions that gained from propinquity of markets what they lacked in expansive frontier potential. One historian found a "butter belt" taking shape around Philadelphia in the decades after the Revolution. As the city expanded in size, and as cows disappeared from urban households, butter production on hinterland farms increased dramatically; in 1850, farms in several townships closest to the city yielded 1,000 pounds per year or more. Unfortunately (for rural household independence), this burst of income apparently fueled an equal rise in consumer expenditures, for additional cows, milkmaids, or capital equipment, but also for store-bought textiles, china tea sets, and other household luxuries. Wrote one student of this rural transition: "butter making enabled large numbers of rural people to participate in the early nineteenth-century American capitalist economy through the purchase of manufactured goods."[3]

After the Erie Canal came through, farmers in upstate New York also turned to dairy in a big way. At first, cheese brokers from the metropolis visited farms in the spring to contract in advance for the whole product of the summer season. In this way, farmers were encouraged to commit their own future labor to market production rather than family subsistence. Guaranteed a buyer for the season's cheeses, New York dairy farmers invested heavily in cows, pasture lands, equipment, and hired labor. Demand grew steadily, and with it regional prosperity. In the 1850s, overseas exports of cheese ballooned from 4 to 23 million pounds, which, at roughly 10 cents a pound (the farmer's price), pumped millions in cash back into the rural economy. The impact of the region was dramatic: Observers passing through noted many frame houses, barns, schools, and churches, few "very poor men," and a number of farmers driving "spring carriages and fine buggies."[4] Prosperity had

---

[3] Joan Jensen, *Loosening the Bonds: Mid-Atlantic Farm Women 1750–1850* (New Haven: Yale University Press, 1986), 93; map 210.

[4] Sally McMurry, *Transforming Rural Life: Dairying Families and Agricultural Change 1820–1885* (Baltimore: Johns Hopkins University Press, 1995), 60–1.

come through market specialization, but with it came dependence on those markets. As the export trade grew enormous, brokers faced tremendous exposure to losses if the cheese they contracted to buy turned out to be low quality, poorly cured, or spoiled in transit. To protect themselves, brokers switched to buying cheeses *after* they were made, which enabled them to take only superior products, dictate differential prices, and reject rancid cheeses. The change effectively handed back to the farmer risks the broker once had absorbed and put the buyer in position to dictate price; but by this time, these specialized farms could not readily go back to earlier ways. Who in the dairy business, for the sake of independence, was ready to return to the relative poverty of pre-export subsistence farming?

Putting-out systems pumped more cash into rural household economies, also with surprising long-term consequences. Making palm hats, weaving cloth, or binding shoes made it possible for rural households to augment their earnings without leaving the land or abandoning traditional strategies of farming. But when income from such manufacturing brought in most of the cash that was needed to balance the family's accounts, tensions in these households mounted as well. Independent yeomen, solid breadwinners all, found themselves unable to provide for their families unless their wives and children worked for the putting-out bosses. Rural independence eroded, debts mounted, and when hard times fell on such households, the sudden loss of cash wages, in addition to falling prices for country produce, easily ruined the yeoman's prospects. If such families escaped their debts and dropped out of the market economy, they slipped back into semi-subsistence obscurity, perhaps never again to gratify their rising expectations; if they sold the farm and moved to the city or industrial village, they gave up control of the means of production (which Marx soon would explain was the signal distinction between the capitalists and the proletariat).

Historians tracking these changes have argued about whether rural families dug their own graves or were driven into dependency by powerful outside forces. Detailed regional studies show that many eastern farmers tried to preserve the integrity of family operations and meet the expectations of ever-expanding networks of kin. Such men and women did not respond to the profit motive with naked greed, but they did put their oars in when market operations promised to serve (or preserve) the family economy. Out west on the antebellum frontier, self-sufficient ruffians such as Thomas Lincoln (Abe's father, who resented the sound of a neighbor's ax) tended to remove themselves voluntarily and pave the way for second-wave settlers for whom marketing the surplus constituted the whole reason for pioneering. Western community studies show that refugees from the market revolution did not long control the development of wilderness antebellum settlements.

ARTISANS

The most ardent, romantic agrarians among the revolutionary founders made room in their idealized republic for a requisite number of craftsmen, without whom no community could be called independent. Although Benjamin Franklin went to his grave convinced that profits in manufacturing were "pinch'd off the Backs and out of the Bellies" of the working poor, traditional artisans found a welcome place alongside the yeoman farmer in everyone's vision of the new United States.[5] Masters of their trades, owners of their tools, guardians of skill and knowledge, and pillars of their local communities, artisans qualified as independent (even if they owned no land) because they held a property in their occupation. But like all vested rights in the United States, the artisans' right to make a living with his skillful hands proved something of a paper shield against the slashing forces let loose by economic freedom.

There is irony aplenty in the artisans' tale, because one of the first consequences of liberation in the new United States was the final erosion of strict controls growing out of medieval guild traditions. American craftsmen, even in colonial times, had found it easy enough to enter a trade or a new community without securing any formal permission (the "freedom" of the city). A man's skill was affirmed more by his work than by certificates issued by his elders; apprentices often grew restless and bolted their indentures to set themselves up as master craftsmen in towns where no one was the wiser. (Read Franklin's account in his *Autobiography* of aborting his own apprenticeship, then compare it with the scandalous tales in Big Bill Otter's *History of My*

---

[5] Quoted in Drew R. McCoy, *The Elusive Republic: Political Economy in Jeffersonian America* (Chapel Hill: University of North Carolina Press, 1980), 57.

Own Times.[6]) Chronic supply-side shortages made it virtually impossible to suppress the ambitions of productive individuals, and this held true as well for craftsmen with a taste for innovation.

So it was that much of the energy that found its way into technological innovation and the rise of manufactures in America came from within the ranks of the artisans themselves. American conditions all but guaranteed to artisans a competence; if you chose to tinker and take a little risk, you could make a genuine fortune. Optimistic about their future, masters and journeymen joined together in new self-help societies, such as New York's General Society of Mechanics and Tradesmen (1785) or Providence's Association of Mechanics and Manufactures (1789). In addition to mutual assistance in times of crisis, these organizations promoted the mechanic arts, sponsored classes in science and natural philosophy, opened reading rooms, and stocked libraries with works on chemistry, metallurgy, mathematics, and political economy. In 1820, New York's General Society launched a tuition-free technical school, the Mechanics Institute; soon Philadelphia followed suit with the Franklin Institute. As late as the 1830s, many men who worked with their hands (and it was men, not women, who filled these ranks traditionally) welcomed new discoveries and gadgets as destined to relieve their physical labors and advance the standard of living for workmen and customers alike.

That said, the spirit of mutuality and "harmony of interests" among the leather apron set nevertheless started to crack soon after the Revolution. If few people saw the first steps toward industrialization as automatically ruining artisan republicanism, many did sense their vulnerability in the workshop hierarchy. Journeymen especially were moved to organize themselves and take a keen interest in preserving the customary rights and privileges known to brothers in their trade. Consider, for example, piece rates. In most crafts, journeymen were paid by the unit according to rates published in books that were intended to set the "just price" of skilled labor. In such a system, the price of labor reflected not just what the product was worth in the market but also what the craftsman required to maintain a respectable household. Enforcing these agreed-upon rates, and the

---

[6] See Benjamin Franklin, *Autobiography of Benjamin Franklin,* ed. Louis P. Mazur (1850; Boston: Bedford Books of St. Martin's Press, 1993); William Otter, Sen., *History of My Own Times,* ed. Richard B. Stott (1835; Ithaca: Cornell University Press, 1995).

underlying right to have such a common scale of wages, became a prime objective of new journeymen's organizations, because innovative manufacturers started looking for ways to cut down the wage bill. Nothing better exposed the conflict between traditional assumptions and new market forces than this defense of the just price of labor and the notion (whether quaint or audacious) that the skilled journeyman was "better able" than his employer "to decide upon the merit of his labor."[7]

Among the first working people to feel the pinch of changing times were journeyman printers, who in Philadelphia gathered themselves into the Franklin Typographical Society and in 1786 called a strike against their masters for refusing to pay the customary rate per day. Carpenters, tailors, and shoemakers all followed suit in the 1790s, especially in Philadelphia and New York, where market pressures surged. Sometimes they forced the masters to accept new terms or new books of prices; other times they did not. Shoemakers experienced a special foreboding because cheap shoes (known in the trade as "slop" lines) from Lynn, Massachusetts, flooded urban markets, forcing local artisans to cut corners, squeeze journeyman's rates, hire pieceworkers who worked at home, and exploit women (at less than half the cost) for much of the hand stitching. Shortly after the turn of the century, New York's Journeymen Cordwainers union came together in self-defense, and in 1808 they struck to protest collusion among their masters to employ nonmembers and "illegal" apprentices. Hoping to nip in the bud this kind of collective action, the masters in turn sued the union leaders for mounting a conspiracy against the trade *and* for infringing the inalienable right of nonmember workmen to make a living.

Both sides in the New York Journeyman Cordwainers' trial argued on behalf of liberty: for the masters, freedom to hire and fire and pay what they would; for the journeymen, freedom to defend the collective interests of "the trade" and prevent the abrogation of their property-in-skills by some new iron law of wages. Each side charged the other with conspiring to frustrate freedom; and in the process of arguing *for freedom*, both sides inadvertently discredited older notions of collective rights and community welfare. The masters, said the workmen, had

---

[7] Quoted in Sean Wilentz, *Chants Democratic: New York City and the Rise of the American Working Class, 1788–1850* (New York: Oxford University Press, 1984), 58.

sold out the trade to gratify their own acquisitiveness. They had turned their backs on the brotherhood. The workers, said the masters in return, sought to control their employers' property and dictate prices in markets where no man could survive paying more for labor than the going competitive rates. The New York court's inconclusive ruling in 1809 satisfied nobody; nevertheless, the cordwainers' trial clearly exposed all that was at stake in the battle for journeymen's rights. More strikes and more conspiracy trials would follow as Americans adjusted their love of liberty and their sense of justice to accommodate the new rules of the market revolution.

These changes in workplace tradition proved all the more devastating because they eroded the fundamental hope that skilled men would become their own masters. It was this promise that rendered the artisans comparable to the yeoman farmers as proper candidates for independent citizenship; their property in their occupations kept them from joining the working poor in abject dependency on others. Already by 1815, half of New York's journeymen were thirty years of age, and one in four was forty or more.[8] They all lived in rented dwellings, usually with their wives, and at least half listed four dependents or more. Combining the earnings of wives and children, these working-class families eked out a living and stood, at the end of life, no closer to prosperity or even a "competence" than before they started their journey. The culture as yet had no words to legitimize their station, but in truth they already were the proletariat. Through the 1820s and 1830s, their ranks swelled even more as four out of five master craftsmen fell from independent viability and signed on as hired hands in the "bastard workshops" that employed all those journeymen. Whatever value labor in these shops added accrued to the rising entrepreneurs – or to the consumers who snapped up goods at lower prices in competitive markets. Either way, the offspring of such bastard workshops could expect to inherit nothing – and over time, they would assume an attitude toward their employers that suited such a condition.

The very concept of labor's right to enjoy the fruits of its industry began to lose credibility in the first decades of the nineteenth century. Traditional thinking long had held that labor alone increased the value of natural materials in God's creation. The farmer's effort turned a seed

---

[8] Wilentz, *Chants Democratic*, 49; see Table 7 on 402.

into marketable wheat, or a calf into a full-grown cow. The butcher's blade turned the cow into meat, the tanner's skill transformed its hide into leather, and the cordwainer's artistry further processed it into shoes. All other charges amounted to rent or taxes imposed on the working poor who alone *created* wealth. In aristocratic Old World societies, such taxes had been commonplace, but they never were much respected in the more egalitarian communities of colonial North America. As a result, American workers – masters and journeymen alike – came out of the Revolution steeped in the labor theory of value, confident that the reward of "industry" belonged to those who worked, and certain that self-government ensured that no idle class of parasites would steal it away.

By the decade of the 1820s, however, competitive market forces were driving a wedge between masters and journeymen. In the bastard workshop, masters performed entrepreneurial and supervisory roles, often out of sight of the workforce altogether. They grew rich while workers grew desperate, and laborers began to see capitalistic employers as a new class of parasites – like the rent-collecting landlords of old. Capital's technical contributions to economic growth (savings, investment, and innovation) seemed terribly abstract; but the transfer of wealth that resulted when masters seized the whole gain and paid back in wages the least amount that the market would bear – this was a concrete fact that sparked the artisans' campaign against the forces of the market revolution.

Theoretical critics of social inequality abounded, reaching back to eighteenth-century radicals such as Thomas Paine and represented in the 1820s by Riccardian political economists such as Daniel Raymond and free-thinking utopians such as Frances (Fanny) Wright and Robert Owen. But some of the most compelling attacks on emerging market relations came straight from the mouths of the workers themselves. One of these voices belonged to Langton Byllesby, a printer born in 1789, who grew up with the bastard workshop in Philadelphia and New York. Like many small masters of his generation, Byllesby first gained and then lost his independence as a master printer during the tumultuous first two decades of the new century. Out of work in New York in the mid-1820s, he put his thoughts on paper *(Observations on the Sources and Effects of Unequal Wealth)*, trying to see how, in a free republic, the fruits of labor could accrue to almost anybody *but* the "producer." He blamed the veneration of private property and the invention of money and banking, which gave rise to speculative markets. In these markets, merchant-capitalists adopted new methods of production that siphoned off profits while increasing the suffering of the masses. Competition (he correctly surmised) was the heartless driver of these market forces, and republican liberty could not survive where the rights of property, the manipulation of credit, and the adoption of labor-saving machinery were allowed to crush "the labouring classes with resourceless distress."[9]

Such an early and articulate denunciation of the wage labor system suggests that relatively untutored victims already could see what Marx would detail a generation later. Dozens of other voices joined this chorus, filling the columns of working-class papers that sprang up in manufacturing centers all over the United States. Political liberty, natural rights, and economic independence seemed inextricably linked to each other. In New York, handloom weaver John Ferral proclaimed that the "accumulation of the wealth of society in the hands of a few individuals" was "subversive of the rights of men." New England carpenter Seth Luther denounced "those who toil not . . . but who are nevertheless clothed in purple and fine linen and fare sumptuously every day."[10] Touching a nerve that in twenty years would spark a vicious debate about slave and free labor, Langton Byllesby denounced any system where men were compelled to work while others claimed the proceeds; it was, he said, "the very essence of slavery."[11] Propelled by these angry voices, protest movements erupted everywhere. In Philadelphia, for example, in 1827 a shoemaker named William Heighton helped organize the nation's first citywide General Trade Union and launched the *Mechanic's Free Press*. By 1835, similar General Trade Unions existed in thirteen cities from Boston to Cincinnati.[12] Strikes and partisan political campaigns followed on behalf of the ten-hour day, the rights of working men, and the labor theory of value.

In 1829 in New York, while a sharp recession pressed hard on the resident journeymen, masters talked about lengthening the workday

[9] Langton Byllesby, *Observations on the Sources and Effects of Unequal Wealth* (orig. 1826; rpt. New York: Russell & Russell, 1961), 90.

[10] Quoted in Walter Licht, *Industrializing America: The Nineteenth Century* (Baltimore: Johns Hopkins University Press, 1995), 55.

[11] Byllesby, *Observations*, 50.

[12] Licht, *Industrializing America*, 53.

(but not wages) to keep up their profits. The working community exploded in protest, giving a firebrand machinist, Thomas Skidmore, a platform for venting his anger at the emerging market system. A self-educated artisan-tinkerer, Skidmore had steeped himself in radical thought reaching back to the eighteenth century and pieced together an agrarian denunciation of private property. *All* ownership claims, he snarled, violated the laws of nature and Creation: "Why not sell the winds of heaven, that man might not breathe without a price? Why not sell the light of the sun, that a man should not see without making another rich?"[13] Proposing to seize and redistribute all private property – and give full civil rights for Indians, Negroes, and women – Skidmore's vision far outdistanced the sentiments of most ordinary journeymen; but his anger at the system did not.

Strikes, protests, and organized resistance to the evolution of the bastard workshop continued apace, reaching a peak in 1836, as sharply rising prices ruined the purchasing power of whatever wages journeymen managed to command. Looking back, it is easy to see the common problem that confronted all these working men's movements: competitive pressure in trades undergoing industrialization. But workers in the 1830s did not understand that the brotherhood of the shop was disappearing for good, or that industrial capitalism would eliminate most of their agency in the disposition of their labor. Some critics, like Byllesby and Skidmore, instinctively found the heart of the problem, but the energies and hopes of many others were diverted toward other formulations. People with money and the leisure to be philosophical, such as Fanny Wright and Robert Owen, indulged fantasies of utopian worlds brought about by new approaches to education and social organization; but their message was clouded by commitments to free love and pantaloons, gender and racial equality, and contempt for religion. Another torrent of advice came from evangelical Christians, such as Arthur and Lewis Tappen, who urged laborers to discipline their own habits (especially drunkenness) and adopt frugal middle-class values. Self-help campaigns, including many by the new General Trade Unions, pushed education in science and the mechanic arts as a way of re-empowering the workers. Finally, theories of money and banking reform spattered the public discourse, drawing critical

---

[13] Quoted in Wilentz, *Chants Democratic*, 185.

attention to "red herring" claims for hard money or the elimination of bank credit. Credible manifestos from all such reformers built upon the same evidence of poverty and dislocation, but the solutions proffered were incompatible if not completely contradictory.

Confronted with such a bewildering array of explanations, the urban workers at the heart of the trade union movement never settled on a single analysis of their problems or a prescription for relief. Still enamored of the promise of self-government, and close enough to their mercantilist forefathers to assume that government controlled the economy, most workers thought there was a logical path to justice through political action. Accordingly, the General Trade Union movement often spawned local working men's parties who put up candidates and sometimes even got them elected. But what were they to do in office? No major party really campaigned against the free-market system, and the specific reforms on the table more often than not *increased* economic "freedom" and thereby accelerated the market revolution. Professional political organizers (a class of specialists just born in the 1820s) coveted the votes of working people and angled to coopt their support. As the Democratic Party of Andrew Jackson matured, the visible presence of employers in whatever other party fielded candidates tended to swing workers into the ranks of the Democrats. Jackson's spectacular war against the Second Bank of the United States helped solidify his reputation (not altogether deserved) as a friend of the working man.

In the end, the persistent rising and falling of individual fortunes, the swirl of opportunities that abounded in good years, and the hopes that individuals harbored for seizing the main chance "one of these days" made it hard for small masters and skilled journeymen to embrace truly radical, class-based alternatives to the petty capitalist market economy they saw before them. The idea of liberation resonated more deeply than did concepts of worker solidarity or class struggle. Freedom and prosperity, they thought, came from liberty, not regimentation and control. Furthermore, as more Americans found apparently safe niches in this new market economy – whether by way of education, temperance, evangelical piety, or just a lucky entrepreneurial break – they joined the chorus of voices celebrating progress rather than decline. The Panic of 1837 temporarily crushed the revolt of American journeymen, and by the time they recovered enough to agitate again in their own behalf, the ideology of artisan republicanism was nearly gone, replaced by new hymns to "free labor" that connected liberty not to the ancient traditions of the workshop, but to individual freedom to collect such wages as were offered – wages denied to black slaves in bondage.

FACTORY WORKERS

Factory workers present a special case in the rise of market relations in the early United States. Nobody in early America relished the creation of a dependent working class. Even in the Old World, working for wages was thought to be a temporary situation except for the classes of people already stuck at the margins of society: women, children, orphans, paupers, servants, and slaves. Proponents of American manufacturing, starting with Alexander Hamilton in the 1790s, always emphasized their intention to employ only "surplus" hands (that is, women and children) and not to steal men away from their independent farms and workshops. In 1817, Hezekiah Niles praised the enterprise of a Baltimore textile manufacturer for hiring one hundred "little girls" and a few women who otherwise earned nothing; such initiative, he concluded, transformed a "useless substance into pure gold."[14] In this way, factory production – first primarily in textile production, but spreading slowly into other industries where steam power or mechanization promised economies of scale – crept into American life.

Samuel Slater, who introduced water spinning to southern New England, saw the recruitment of workers as one of his most important challenges. Unfamiliar with the ways of the factory, Pawtucket's first child "operatives" abandoned their stations whenever their parents needed them for some other service at home. Slater tried to counteract this by hiring the heads of households as well, moving entire families into newly minted factory villages, where all things flowed from the wages paid by Slater. Until competitive pressures rendered it unsustainable, Slater held on to farm land and livestock to keep the men busy, while their "dependents" performed the real work of the textile mills. Still, Slater's control of the purse strings unavoidably encroached on domestic relations. Factory foremen, not husbands and fathers, now commanded the actions of women and children without whose income

[14] Hezekiah Niles, *Niles Register*, 7 June 1817, quoted in Seth Rockman, *Scraping By* (Johns Hopkins University Press, 2008), 39.

the "head" of the household enjoyed no sustenance. Slater's brother John added a strong sense of Christian evangelism to this paternalistic business model, and the second generation of Slaters sought refuge in "fancy goods" products, where price competition remained less severe. Nevertheless, from the 1830s on, competitive pressures required the Slaters to pay close attention to controlling the wage bill. Vestiges of family autonomy for workers gradually fell away, and factory operatives found themselves wholly dependent with no claim to a house, an occupation, or a little scrap of land.

Perhaps more disappointing than the plight of the rural villagers who cast their lots with the cotton mills was the experience of thousands of "factory girls" who went to work at Lowell. Frances Cabot Lowell and his imitators shared a deep revulsion toward the degraded factory operatives they saw mired in hopeless squalor in places like Manchester, England. By design, Lowell hoped to import Britain's factory system without reproducing its laboring class. To this end, the corporations at Lowell recruited young unmarried girls from New England's dying countryside, paid them good wages, housed them in chaperoned boarding houses (locked tight at 10 P.M. to ensure the girls' safety and "virtue"), and provided them wholesome outlets for their fragments of leisure time. Factory work would fill the awkward years between coming of age and marriage (roughly four to six years before age twenty-two, although some girls entered the mills as early as age thirteen). Such employment soaked up the labor of hands that were "surplus" in rural households while generating a cash income to augment the family treasury, pay off the mortgage, or fatten the marriage purses of the women themselves. Above all, factory work for these women was *supposed* to be a temporary pause, a station on the way to their "real" life's work as wives and mothers. In this way, so the mill barons hoped, cotton factories might tap the economic potential of industrialization while the army of workers melted without a trace back into surrounding pre-industrial communities.

At first, some young women found the Lowell option appealing. Vermont teenager Sally Rice gladly turned her back on her father's "Rocky farm only 2 or 3 cows" in what she called "that wilderness."[15]

---

[15] Thomas Dublin, ed., *Farm to Factory: Women's Letters, 1830–1860* (2nd ed., New York: Columbia University Press, 1993), 20–1.

Parents sometimes disapproved, but surviving letters suggest that the girls themselves found mill work preferable to "working out" (as domestic servants) or teaching school. The confinement of the boarding houses chafed a bit, but others found the freedom to shop, attend lectures, and go to religious services exhilarating. Unfortunately, over time, market forces squeezed the profit margins that made these "perks" and high wages possible. Employers at Lowell stretched the workday to thirteen hours in summer (eleven in winter), sped up the machinery, doubled or tripled the number of machines tended by a single operative, and chipped away at wages as well. Charges for room and board increased. Conditions in the factory deteriorated, and as operatives' health began to suffer, companies moved to deflect the expenses (and criticism) associated with illness. Dissatisfaction grew more prevalent as women worked year after year, supporting themselves but "laying up" nothing toward their long-term objectives of marriage and independence.

Competition, the owners insisted, forced these changes in the work life at Lowell. Competition – a pressure emanating from where? – seemed to close off the freedom of entrepreneurs to do right by their workforce. The primary force behind deteriorating conditions showed no face or origin, or so the owners said. Some working women did not buy it. Complaining in 1848 that she had never "worked so hard" in her life, Mary Paul penned this skeptical analysis: "The companies pretend they are losing immense sums every *day* and therefore they are obliged to lessen the wages, but this seems perfectly absurd to me for they are constantly making *repairs* and it seems to me that this would not be if there were really any danger of their being obliged to *stop* the mills."[16] Paul identified a fundamental irony of capitalist enterprise: Under pressure, successful entrepreneurs often increased capital investment while suppressing wages and ramping up production. Capitalists might protest that they had no choice, but to labor, these actions seemed voluntary, intentional, and mean.

Although employers admitted no personal fault when market forces squeezed their workers, they expected nothing less from their operatives than individual loyalty and top performance. Confronted with rumors of a 25 percent cut in wages in early 1834, some eight hundred

---

[16] Ibid., 129. Emphasis in the original.

Lowell women staged a "turn out" that caught managers somewhat off guard. The strike quickly collapsed, but the patina of benevolent paternalism at Lowell faded. A much bigger strike followed in 1836, this time protesting an increase in boarding house rates. Because markets happened to be booming at the time, the mill barons chose to rescind the new charges, but the nationwide panic of 1837 brought massive layoffs and the hard times that followed into the 1840s effectively crushed any organized protests by Lowell's female operatives. Taking advantage of worker dependency, owners launched another speed-up, in some cases quadrupling the number of machines tended and running them significantly faster. In 1845, women protested once again, launching the Lowell Female Labor Reform Association to campaign for the ten-hour day. This too came to naught.

Throughout the decades of the 1840s and 1850s, the social experiments at Lowell and elsewhere melted away; in their place emerged familiar factory scenes throughout New England's textile towns. More operatives moved to the cities with their families, crowding into cheap flats no longer policed by the owners of the mills. Women stayed in factory work longer, they married somewhat later, and they tended to marry other urban workers. They seldom returned to bucolic New England farms. Their adventure in independence matured into a complete *dependence* on wages they could not control, earned for work they could not guarantee, but which they needed to purchase necessities of life that did not cease or diminish when "hard times" struck the industry.

In 1840 Orestes Brownson published a scathing indictment of the textile bosses: They reduced independent men and women to pathetic creatures "hurrying in all directions," whipped by the sound of the factory bell like slaves before the lash. "Wages is a cunning device of the devil," he thundered, "for the benefit of tender consciences, who would retain all the advantages of the slave system, without the expense, trouble and odium of being slave-holders."[17] This was an early shot in a bitter debate that would explode in a later decade between the advocates of free (wage) labor and defenders of black slavery in the South, but the argument also could backfire. Writing in *The Lowell Offering*, a literary magazine written by mill workers

---

[17] Orestes Brownson, "The Laboring Classes," *Boston Quarterly Review*, July 1840, 370.

and published with the assent of the employers, a reader identifying herself as "A Factory Girl" took horrible offense that Brownson would "slander" young women "who generally come from quiet homes, where their minds and manners have been formed under the eyes of the worthy sons of the Pilgrims, and their virtuous partners, and who return again to become the wives of the free intelligent yeomanry of New England, and the mothers of quite a proportion of our future republicans."[18] This already was fiction, not fact, but nobody wished to admit the obvious for industrial New England: The *"proletarii"* (Brownson's word) had arrived.

Eventually the mills abandoned all pretence of concern for freeborn republicans or social engineering. With the sharp spike in immigration to the United States in the 1840s, factory towns filled with foreign-born families clamoring for the bottom rung of a modern ladder of social and economic class. Coincidentally, by the 1850s the factory itself had outgrown its original home in the textile industry. Large-scale production facilities filled with power machines tended by dozens or hundreds of wage-earning operatives could be found by 1860 making shoes, nails, firearms, clocks, clothing, farm equipment, and machinery itself. Industrialization had come to stay.

WOMEN

The story of textile operatives may be the most familiar, but it is hardly the only example of market relations disrupting the lives of women. In many ways, less transparent – and more insidious – market forces cracked open the sealed container that was the pre-industrial family unit and placed at the disposal of outside employers control over the women and children once thought to be wards of – practically the property of – male heads of households. The legal doctrine of coverture *(femme covert)* long had dissolved the civil identity of women into that of their male protectors: The primary justification for men's control over the bodies and property of women lay in their patriarchal role as defenders of these dependents. Market forces, such as they were in the eighteen century and before, surely pressed on the household unit, and

---

[18] A Factory Girl, "Factory Girls," *Lowell Offering* I: 2 (1840), rpt. Benita Eisler, ed., *The Lowell Offering: Writings by New England Mill Women, 1840–1845* (1977; paper ed. New York: W. W. Norton, 1998), 188.

European social historians now question how effectively dependents were shielded from disruptive winds of commerce; nevertheless, in theory, would-be masters reached inside the family *only* with the consent of the paterfamilias.

Not just practice but also public discourse started to change in the United States as soon as Hamilton singled out women as underemployed resources that might be harnessed to build up manufacturing. We have already seen how putting-out systems invaded the sanctity of early American households, fostering dependence on cash and reorienting household priorities to suit the needs of the marketplace. Female shoe binders, dairy maids, and the makers of palm hats all found themselves marching to the beat of the market's drum, whatever the rhythms of country life once promised. The women of Lynn started out helping their shoemaker husbands fulfill their contracts; but as the shoe bosses tightened their grip on the business, more women were hired directly for outwork and later brought into the central factories. Outworkers in textiles saw their niches invaded by constant mechanization. Rural dairymaids saw once ancillary operations grow into full-blown enterprises that redefined the nature of the farm itself. In each case, the entering wedge involved taking advantage of what had once been the unpaid labor of women in the household.

For young women in early America, work outside the home often meant work inside the homes of others. Although Americans resented any hint of servile status (native-born domestics preferred to be called "helps"), domestic service presented a ready avenue to earnings for young, unmarried women. Their numbers swelled along with the pretensions of the wealthier urban households; in Boston, for example, at mid-century fully 60 percent of working women worked as domestics.[19] Immigrants dominated overwhelmingly: In New York in 1855, 74 percent of all servants were young Irish women; another 14 percent were German, 3 percent were black, and 4 percent native-born.[20] Servants "lived in" with their employers, which severely curtailed both their freedom and their leisure, but it did help to stretch their meager wages of $6 or $7 per month (about half what a woman

---

[19] Thomas Dublin, *Transforming Women's Work: New England Lives in the Industrial Revolution* (Ithaca: Cornell University Press, 1994), 157.

[20] Christine Stansell, *City of Women: Sex and Class in New York 1789–1860* (New York: Alfred A. Knopf, 1982), 156–7.

made at Lowell). Chores included cooking and cleaning, hauling water, emptying slop jars, and dumping wastes – much of it work young women had been doing for their mothers at home and would later do for husbands and children in households of their own. As the decades passed and the "culture of domesticity" inflated the expectations of urban mistresses, serving girls clung to their place as cash employees rather than servile persons and resisted the efforts of ladies to mentor or improve their character. On the contrary, according to Dr. William Sanger, who studied New York prostitutes in the 1850s, quite a number of girls "in service" worked the streets at night.

Another third of all working women plied their needles in the garment trade, especially in New York, where after 1820 the ready-made clothing industry grew exponentially. Following the example of shoemakers, ambitious merchant-tailors used their skilled journeymen to cut out the garments, then sent the pieces out to women at home, who stitched them together for pennies a piece. Women first gained a foothold sewing vests and pantaloons, but over time they took up shirts and other clothing also. One good cutter could supply hundreds of outworkers, and by the late 1840s, one mammoth firm, Lewis and Hanford of New York, employed four thousand pairs of hands. Such "sweated" labor, because it took place at home, could be integrated into family schedules and made use of assistance from children who working mothers could not leave untended. Conducted this way, the garment trade required little capital and thus attracted a flood of small competitors, each clamoring to undersell the other. The booming expansion of the cotton South boosted demand for ready-made slave clothing, as did the western trade in sturdy work clothes opened up by the Erie Canal.

Outwork in the needle trade paid even worse than domestic service: At 7 cents a shirt, Boston women earned between 50 cents and $1 per week![21] Outwork was undependable because garment bosses cut back employment at the first sign of softening demand. Finally, women faced outright fraud when bosses refused to pay them at all or docked their wages for imagined shortcomings in the work. In New York in 1853, at a time when $600 was thought to be the minimum subsistence for a

---

[21] Jane H. Pease and William H. Pease, *Ladies, Women, and Wenches: Choice and Constraint in Antebellum Charleston and Boston* (Chapel Hill: University of North Carolina Press, 1990), 46.

family of four, needlewomen working full-time (which never happened) could make at best $91 per year. Outworker's wages stayed so low in part because the city was awash in workers – refugees from the rural countryside as well as German and Irish immigrants. But garment bosses never had much choice either: The free play of market forces depressed the price of this mass-produced clothing until there was practically no profit left. As Horace Greeley observed (without fully understanding the import of what he was writing), "if they were compelled to pay living wages for their work, they must stop altogether."[22]

Regardless of where they worked, wage-earning women suffered a special disadvantage as the market revolution transformed American households. New market forces engendered work in profoundly different ways. Men's work now was done outside the home, in public, and was compensated with wages paid in cash. Its value now bore a number. Traditional women's work – housework – seemed to become less visible because it carried no price and commanded no cash reward. As a result, married women came to be seen as living in leisure sustained by the wages of their husbands. Such an assumption helped justify paying women half as much as men even for doing similar jobs; but it bore no relation to reality for the vast majority of working-class households, where men's income (if a man was around) was undependable and where women had no choice but to work or starve. The cash demands of urban life drove women into the market performing tasks with no "market value" – cooking, sewing, cleaning, and nursing children. Meanwhile, their own children scratched for income, hawking baked potatoes or hot corn, running errands, doing odd jobs, or stealing produce from vendors' carts.

Finally, as women negotiated the winds of exploitation in antebellum free-labor markets, the logic of the cash nexus made the sex trade tragically attractive. Prostitutes never escaped moral censure – if anything, Victorian mores were raising the wall of separation between virtuous women and whores. But especially in urban settings, women who had to subject themselves to wage work anyway – whose households offered no sanctuary, nor husbands protection, nor children comfort – these women sometimes found that the sex trade returned a better income, more personal freedom, and little more degradation

[22] Quoted in Stansell, *City of Women*, 113; see 108–11 for wage rates.

than they confronted in occupations that earned only pennies by comparison. By 1830, New York had gained a reputation as second only to New Orleans as the city for illicit sex. Everything about the city drew crowds of strangers, fortune seekers, young men with grand ideas, and women in search of excitement (or at least independence). Contemporary estimates suggest that something between fifteen hundred and ten thousand women serviced the New York sex trade.[23] Some lived in first-class brothels in the Fifth Ward west of Broadway, where nearby theaters attracted out-of-town "gentlemen." A far larger number worked the seedier district near Five Points or walked the streets, independent "entrepreneurs" in the strictest sense of the word. Few of these women worked full-time in the sex trade. Many had been married, with families, driven by the loss of a male provider to seek quick profits in sexual commerce. Most of them served time in low-paid female trades or domestic service. (Oddly, women who sewed umbrellas seemed especially prone to prostitution.[24]) Middle-class moralists and reformers wrung their hands at this epidemic of spoliation, but working women may have seen it as a shrewd and sensible response to forces beyond their control. Heartless markets and heartless men.

PERSONS AT THE MARGINS

One of the defining characteristics of free markets was their capacity to strip away the importance of non-economic variables (such as friendship, family name, or birthplace) in the conduct of transactions. In theory, a job was a job, a product was a product, and it mattered little what kind of person did the work. But such generic neutrality did not always prevail. When women began sewing vests and pantaloons just as handily as male tailors, the market responded by paying only half the prevailing male wage – because social conventions allowed the differential. In time, as immigrant men moved into the "sweated" trades, the lower pay scale applied to them as well, with the odd result that convictions about the value of women's labor eventually depressed men's wages as well. Similar ironies surrounded the condition of

[23] Patricia Cline Cohen, *The Murder of Helen Jewett* (New York: Random House, 1998), 71–2.
[24] Timothy J. Gilfoyle, *City of Eros: New York City, Prostitution, and the Commercialization of Sex, 1790–1920* (New York: W. W. Norton, 1992), 61.

various marginal individuals who existed outside the "normal" containers of public and private life.

Free blacks, for example, differed from slaves precisely because they got paid wages, yet no successful performance in paid occupations could lift the restrictions that accompanied race. In the North after the Revolution, state-by-state emancipation gradually transformed slaves into free persons. Roughly fifty thousand African Americans inhabited the northern states in 1790 (more than half enslaved in New York and New Jersey).[25] Emancipation came first where blacks were least numerous and where employers sought increased flexibility in managing their capital and their wage bill. These first emancipations were not driven by the kind of prejudice against bound labor that later gained popularity among employers; indeed, as late as the 1820s, commentators North and South openly touted the advantages of enslaved factory hands ("they are more *docile*, more constant, and *cheaper*").[26] Antislavery in the North did not imply much sympathy for racial integration, and freedom almost always brought declining social conditions. Massachusetts feared the persistence of free blacks and contemplated legal exclusion. States where slavery lingered well into the nineteenth century (New York freed its last slaves in 1827) saw hostilities toward free blacks increase in direct proportion to their numbers. Blacks found themselves crowded into segregated neighborhoods, where any legal rights they might enjoy were truncated by resistance from hostile neighbors.

Most free blacks found employment at the very bottom of the laboring classes. In rural New Jersey, persons freed by the gradual emancipation law typically stayed in the households of white farmers or hired themselves out on long contracts that represented a kind of waged peonage. Other freed men worked as day laborers, ditch diggers, and woodcutters and worked at construction sites or on the waterfront, usually (but not always) at wages below their white counterparts. Skilled artisans among the former slaves often found themselves driven

---

[25] James Oliver Horton and Lois E. Horton, *In Hope of Liberty: Culture, Community, and Protest among Northern Free Blacks, 1700–1860* (New York: Oxford University Press, 1997), 81.

[26] Thomas P. Jones, *An Address on the Progress of Manufactures and Internal Improvements . . . Delivered in the Hall of the Franklin Institute, November 6, 1827* (Philadelphia: Judah Dobson, 1827), quoted in Rockman, *Scraping By*, 43. Emphasis in the original.

from their trades no matter what their talent or industry. In some places, white workers walked off the job if black laborers tried to sign on. Blacks worked as porters, coachmen, cooks, or barbers; in New York the chore of emptying tubs of human waste from urban neighborhoods was reserved especially for them. Some found niches in service to their own community, vending groceries, making clothing, or running oyster bars and taverns. Most cities denied them licenses to operate hacks, cabs, or pushcarts. Black women found work keeping house, sewing, or dressing hair. There was no shortage of ability or ambition among free blacks in the North, yet the cash market failed to neutralize the non-economic variables. Free blacks lost their economic standing, according to one Philadelphia report, "on account of the unrelenting prejudice against their color."[27] To make matters worse, by the 1850s white Irish laborers crowded blacks out of what had become their traditional employments. In the deep South, where slavery was not endangered and where the white master class found it useful to play black craftsmen against skilled white workmen, free blacks sometimes fared better; but even there it was not their true market value but their exploitability on racial grounds that opened the niches they managed to fill.

For the indigenous people of North America, the impact of market forces came early – at least a century before most white persons experienced discomfort – and ended in a cruel trick of racist dishonesty. The introduction of attractive European goods (blankets, edge tools, cooking pots, and brandy) that could be had in exchange for the roughest of forest produce (namely, deer skins and beaver pelts) upended the balance of hunting, gathering, and patch agriculture that had sustained native people for generations. Whether useful or intoxicating, trade goods focused the work of Indian men on hunting for the market; at the same time, guns sold to each village band set off an arms race among their neighbors. As soon as the Cherokees acquired guns in large numbers (as early as the 1690s, according to one careful scholar), they began a steady transition from a "stable, hunting-gathering-farming society with a subsistence economy" to a "mobile, free-trade, market economy with heavy reliance on European trade goods and alliances."[28] In other words, long before Anglo-American families

---

[27] Ibid., 117.
[28] William G. McLoughlin, *Cherokee Renascence in the New Republic* (Princeton: Princeton University Press, 1986), 4.

experienced market dependency, Native Americans found themselves virtually enslaved to goods they could neither give up nor make for themselves. Furthermore, in exchange for cessions of land, the Indians entered into solemn written "contracts" (treaties) that proved binding on them but not on the Americans who freely and repeatedly ignored their obligations. Markets determined the Indians' role during colonization, but market instruments brought them no protection nor could market-based behavior save them from whites who relentlessly pursued their own economic liberty on Indian lands.

Despite abundant evidence throughout the seventeenth and eighteenth centuries, colonial whites steadfastly refused to acknowledge the existence of Indian farming – partly because it was done by women, not by men, and partly because, according to the European "law of nations," if the Indians did not farm, then Europeans could take their land. Early colonists shared an almost universal assumption that indigenous people would "recede" as Anglo-American settlement advanced. Nevertheless, at the founding of the Republic, with the natives numerous and strong, American leaders chose to affirm Indian rights rather than spark an all-out war for control of the interior. As a result, American authorities after 1789 could not displace the Indians except for cause (such as violence or indigence) or by the voluntary sale of lands that everyone agreed they owned. Official legal positions notwithstanding, the people followed their own reasoning: If Indians roamed free pursuing wild animals, built no barns, plowed no fields, erected no fences, and did not *use* their property according to "enlightened" expectations, whites could fairly drive them off, extort them in trade, and swindle them out of their lands through all kinds of dishonest dealing. The justification for dispossession lay in their failure to embrace civilization – to settle down, abandon the hunt, raise export crops, manufacture cloth, and drive African slaves to do their work without wages. To such as this the good Lord would not leave the riches of a continent.

But what if the Indians reformed? What if they embraced the injunction to civilize themselves and take up the white man's ways? Behold the Cherokees, who after 1815 faced encroaching frontiersmen from all directions and decided not to fight but to accept the encouragement of government to give up Indian ways. Crowded now into less than half of their earlier homeland (northwestern Georgia, western North

Carolina, and eastern Tennessee), the Cherokees traded what whites called their "surplus" lands for farm equipment, tools, clothing, and education in the arts of rural industry and market production. They developed a written language (an extraordinary feat of accommodation), wrote a constitution, and developed ways of government based not on tribal custom, but on written law, judicial procedure, and the rights of private property. They fenced in farms, raised cotton and wheat for the export market, bought (and beat) slaves like their white neighbors – in short, by the middle 1820s, some of them managed to transform themselves into plausible copies of successful frontier planters. Confronted with this evidence of acculturation, in 1828 the government of Georgia proclaimed its sovereignty over Cherokee lands, voided all Cherokee laws and legal claims, and set about stealing everything of value the Cherokees had collected. Why? Because "civilized" resident Indians might never give up their lands to whites, and that was unacceptable to freedom-loving white Americans. Georgia's action was ruled illegal by the U.S. Supreme Court, but nobody stopped "the people" from having their way.

Across the continent and through the decades into the 1870s, Indians who clung to their "savage" ways found themselves condemned, swindled, and forcibly removed while those groups or individuals who chose to accommodate and "whiten" their behavior just as surely were excluded on racial grounds. Indians apparently could not become white. The confusion of changing values could be seen in the self-serving rhetoric of American frontiersmen who raged against banks, merchants, and speculators while at the same time faulting Indians for yearning to perpetuate pre-market values and subsistence strategies. Whites said that the Indians clung to "savage" ways on purpose and thus forfeited their place in a modernizing world, but clearly it was race, not behavior, that set them outside the rules of the game. (In 1887, the Dawes Act finally dissolved the remaining foundation of the Indians' tribal nations – their common land holdings. The federal government distributed Indian property in allotments to individuals, and invited market-savvy sharpsters to finish the job of cheating Indians out of what had been their native country.)

Immigrants who came to the United States, especially after 1820, confronted the hard face of a market economy without the moderating influence of home and family traditions. Most newcomers came from the British Isles or the German principalities. If they had a trade, they crowded into manufacturing cities such as New York, Philadelphia, and Boston, or else they took up niches in ethnic enclaves in Pennsylvania, the southern backcountry, and the Ohio River Valley. Cincinnati, St. Louis, and Milwaukee collected large populations of skilled German immigrants in the two decades before the Civil War. Newcomers without skills filled out teams of common laborers; Irish "navvies" (a nickname earned building navigation works in England) built the roads and canals and worked on boats that brought the market revolution deep into the American interior. The rate of immigration rose significantly from 1820 to 1844, then spiked dramatically until 1857: Three million arrived in the single ten-year period from 1845 to 1855, mostly Irish fleeing the potato famine but also Germans escaping unrest surrounding the European revolutions of 1848.[29]

Whether driven by starvation or drawn by a thirst for opportunity, immigrants tended to seize whatever the market held out to them, which made them less inclined than their native-born counterparts to protest commercialization or romanticize a lost golden age. The timing of their arrival often coincided precisely with rising pressures in American markets (especially manufacturing), so that capitalist employers confronted with disgruntled native-born workers found it tempting enough to replace their force with immigrants – sometimes at lower wages. Not surprisingly, real and perceived competition for jobs made scarce by changing technology or "hard times" encouraged hostility along lines of racial and ethnic identity, so that by the 1840s people began to calculate their "whiteness." Recent cultural historians have argued that whiteness was the marker that distinguished legacy Americans from those who had recently arrived or were excluded from the start on racial grounds. The resulting social tensions pitted the logic of the market, which in theory cared only that the work got done and cheaply, against popular notions about who was entitled to the fruits of American material success. Over time, a process of cultural negotiation admitted the Germans, Norwegians, and even the Irish (grudgingly) into the ranks of white people, in the process investing ever more social importance in the color lines that separated Africans and Indians from everybody else. In the meantime, conflicts rooted in changing social

[29] Wattenberg, ed., *Statistical History*, 106.

relations caused by the market revolution easily acquired ethnic and racial dimensions that tended to obscure the character of new class relations brought about by industrialization.

During the Jacksonian era, new class relations stood out most sharply in the largest cities. There the lure of cash wages attracted a steady stream of country youths, Irishmen, free blacks, single women, and other emancipated characters to whom the market revolution offered money, amusements, and unsupervised freedom to indulge themselves in ways they never had considered when they were swaddled in family relations. Master craftsmen turned apprentices out of their attic rooms and left them to find for themselves both bed and board. Young women in service probably lived in their employer's house, but when they went out, they went out with money in hand and no chaperon. Young men serving as clerks, filling the middle ranks of a bustling business community, lived alone in boarding houses, paid cash for food and drink, laundry, and entertainment – and learned that almost anything they wanted was for sale in New York City. Their coarser brothers, day laborers, lived similar lives in shabbier surroundings, mixing it up with the sailors and waterfront hands, the least respectable class in port cities. Women in the needle trades, married or not, when they *had* work set their own hours and satisfied material needs (however meagerly) by spending their hard-won wages. What characterized all of these people was their status as "masterless" persons – young people no longer tucked in their parents' homes and not yet engaged in making homes for families of their own.

In former times, all such persons had been bound to the care of guardian-employers who vouched for the needs of their bodies *and* their souls. By the 1830s, however, big cities such as New York and Philadelphia swarmed with youngsters without a past, without connections, without property or any stake in "respectable" society. The terms of their employment covered labor alone, leaving them free to spend their leisure and their earnings any way they saw fit: cock-fighting, prize-fighting, theatrical shows, gambling dens, saloons, oyster houses, dancehalls, brothels, and minstrel shows, and "model artist" exhibitions (where women posed as fine art figures, nearly naked, all the time). Such youths formed gangs and amused each other picking fights, setting fires, and smashing windows and furniture in brothels and saloons. Their "sprees" often resulted in physical injury, sometimes gang rape, and, once in a while, murder. Typically drenched in alcohol, members of this urban subculture helped define a class of persons in pursuit of disgraceful, not respectable, living. New York developed a notorious "sporting culture" in the 1830s. Erotic literature circulated freely, commercializing sex and rendering the trappings of marriage (wife, house, and children) wholly uninteresting to the Bowery "B'hoys" and "Gals" or their slightly wealthier "dandy" sporting friends in the theater district. Keeping the peace eventually required hiring professional police and legislating standards for public behavior; meanwhile, moral and religious reformers rent their garments over the sinful bravado on display all around them.

There is nothing about capitalist relations that required the embrace of debauchery, but everything about the cash nexus emphasized fleeting, anonymous transactions, in private life as in business. There is nothing about capitalist relations that required racial exclusion for Indians and African Americans, but neither did anything discourage it or foster any spirit of integration. Persons on the margins, racial outcasts, and masterless men and women – easily exploited, challenged by their "betters" to develop self-control, but given no good reason to believe doing so would make them any happier – such were the social artifacts of the spread of the wage labor system and market relations by the end of the Jacksonian era. Respectable middle-class Americans were appalled, but they focused remedial attention on the sins and sinners, not the system, and instead of modifying "heartless" markets for the sake of social improvement, they built prisons and asylums in which to incarcerate the victims of the rise of the market economy.

SOUTHERN VARIATIONS

It is tempting to see the plantation South as lying outside the reach of the market revolution for most of the antebellum period. The master-slave relationship evolved not just as an economic connection but a social and cultural framework as deeply embedded in the planters' expectations as were the customary rights of yeoman farmers or traditional master craftsmen. In much of the South by the time of the Revolution, the tobacco economy had been in decline so long that many people in Virginia and Maryland entertained the idea – like their northern contemporaries – that slavery would expire in the new United States. In 1782, Virginia passed a private manumission law, and over the next two decades many leaders in the founding generation (most famously George Washington) used their last will and testament to free their slaves. Others scaled back their labor force, liberated family favorites, and openly discussed schemes of gradual emancipation. But in the deep South – especially South Carolina and Georgia – white men had only begun to enrich themselves using bound black labor, and these planters mounted a stubborn resistance to antislavery impulses. It was also in the deep South that the rise of the cotton culture breathed new life into the slave labor system and grafted it onto the promise of liberty and equality for newly minted American citizens.

Growing cotton in most of the South had not been practicable until 1793, when the invention of the cotton gin made it possible to separate seeds from the fibers of the short-staple upland cotton that grew so well across the region. Many hands labored to break this bottleneck; Eli Whitney took the credit, but his machine was quickly copied and widely modified. What mattered more was the explosive spread of the cotton culture across upland South Carolina and Georgia and out into Indian country in what would become the states of Tennessee, Alabama, and Mississippi. Building a fortune in the United States by growing cotton with slave labor was made possible, of course, by industrial textile production in England that generated rising demand. In this sense, the market revolution served as prime mover for the spread of slave-based agriculture in the southern United States. But nineteenth-century staple crop production for export did not differ markedly from colonial production of commodities such as sugar, rice, and tobacco, a fact that gives credence to claims (then and now) that the southern economy followed a divergent course – perhaps even a contradictory course – to that unfolding in the North.

Following Marx's claim that slave labor was incompatible with the capitalist system of production, some historians have focused our attention on paternalistic social and cultural conventions that did make southern life different. Never simply workers, slaves were also the wards of their owners, wholly dependent human property whose every care fell to the master as a result of his ownership claim. Economic decisions made by slaveholders never reflected simple market calculations but always were clouded by obligations inherent in the master-slave relationship. At the same time, the influence of the market revolution can be seen impinging on systems of slave-based production in three important ways. First, emerging market forces in the presence of slave labor encouraged southerners to invest more social significance in race as a marker of who could exercise economic freedom. Second, market developments on the fringes of the plantation system, especially in cities and towns, greatly enlarged the practice of leasing and hiring slaves, which made such human property much more flexible (and hence more valuable) to masters who were not big planters. Finally, market considerations – and the emerging ideology that respected them as natural forces that could not be denied – made it possible for masters to renege on the obligations that supposedly defined their paternalist identities. Some masters undoubtedly viewed their slaves as dependent members of a large organic household. Others just as clearly saw them as investment instruments, a handy way to store a little surplus capital. Whether the resulting economic system remained pre-capitalist or merged into a variant of the modern market-based enterprise system, the market revolution could not go unnoticed in the Old South.

The plight of skilled artisans in the South, for example, was markedly different because of the presence of skilled slave craftsmen who provided the same goods and services that white artisans sold for cash. In cities such as Richmond, Charleston, and Savannah, poorly paid black artisans, slave and free, kept wages depressed for independent white workers and probably discouraged or delayed the kind of innovations that up north produced the bastard workshop. Customers could play black carpenters, blacksmiths, or tailors off against their white counterparts until they found what they wanted at the right price (white artisans denounced slave workmen as a "curse upon our working interest").[30] Of course, white workers, skilled and unskilled, refused to share workspace and social roles with black people, bound or free. As a result, race – not slave status – came to divide the southern working class more completely than did ethnicity or any other factor in the North. Certain trades were virtually monopolized by African American labor (such as boatmen and domestic servants), while wealthy people comforted the white working poor with the notion that their "whiteness" itself was a kind of property.

---

[30] Ira Berlin, *Slaves without Masters: The Free Negro in the Antebellum South* (New York: Pantheon, 1974), 229.

This increased investment in racial discrimination can be seen in new laws as the antebellum era progressed, reversing the expansion of private manumissions and requiring newly freed slaves to vacate the state to enjoy their freedom. Black codes further circumscribed the activities of blacks (not just slaves), and the tolerance of private fraternization across the color line (including marriages) steadily decayed over time. Similarly, definitions of who was black and who was not grew much tighter until an Arkansas judge in 1857 proclaimed the infamous "one drop" rule that placed individuals with any admixture of African blood beyond the pale of the ruling race. The vast majority of free blacks worked as farmhands or day laborers, and the stigma thus attached to menial tasks degraded the work ethic just at a time that the market revolution would have tapped it to mobilize wage workers. Instead, planters preached to their poor white neighbors that all must police the color line because that alone kept black people "in their place." Even though planters shared little of the fruits of the cotton culture with their poor white neighbors, they kept them aligned with the master class. Everyone "knew" that the wealth came not through hard work or innovation, but through the ownership of slaves. The interests of the planters were the interests of all: If they lost control, an army of angry blacks surely would rise up to wreak vengeance on all white people.

In the end, this emphasis on white solidarity did nothing to protect the interests of white artisans in the Old South. One student of manufacturing in Georgia found two disturbing trends squeezing the fortunes of skilled craftsmen. First, in the 1820s and 1830s, cheap mass-produced goods from the North – especially shoes and ready-made clothing – flooded southern markets and introduced the same downward pressure on prices that drove small producers out of business in New York. Second, by the 1840s, bulky manufactures that were less easily imported, such as furniture, saddles, and wagons, were being produced in small manufacturing firms that practiced the same division of labor and rationalization of production techniques found in northern bastard workshops. In short, while the planter class distracted lower-class whites with talk of racial privilege and servile insurrection, they pursued their own advantage as consumers in the market revolution to help eat the ground out from under traditional small producers to whom they often spoke of loyalty.

One of the hallmarks of the free-labor system brought on by the market revolution was the reduction of labor relations to a simple cash transaction. Employers paid for hours worked, after which further obligations for either party dissolved. This free-labor system allowed entrepreneurs to sail very close to the wind in rapidly changing markets. Slavery created quite the opposite situation: Masters paid the overhead for all of their workers, regardless of when or how they were used. Accordingly, the southern economy ought to have been sluggish and unresponsive because of this high fixed cost of labor. On the whole, this was true, but its importance was softened by the second major impact of the market revolution in the South: a flexible lease-hire system for redeploying the labor of slaves.

Since the founding of the Republic, southern states, public works projects, and turnpike corporations had been hiring slaves to help clear rivers, build roads, and dig canals. Similarly, plantation masters sometimes leased out their hands, especially skilled artisans, for temporary service in nearby towns, on riverboats, and even in industry. The slave Gabriel, who plotted a rebellion in Richmond, worked as an artisan for wages. The Buffalo Forge in rural Virginia routinely augmented its workforce with hired hands and often leased for the entire year. Cities such as Charleston and Savannah teamed with wage-earning slaves who lived on their own, paid their own keep, and delivered to their masters (at the end of the week, month, or year) the balance of their income. This possibility of leasing out bondsmen made it possible for widows, urban professionals, and other middle-class whites to own slaves they did not need for full-time agricultural employment. At the same time, it gave lessees control of a workforce they did not have to retain if markets turned against them. Parties to these arrangements thought like calculating entrepreneurs, not benevolent guardians, exhibiting a bourgeois sensibility that undercut their claims to be paternalistic. Finally, it piled up abundant evidence of the capability of blacks to perfect their trades, conduct their own business, fulfill obligations, and perform in every other way the things expected of free (white) persons.

However smoothly it worked in practice (and it worked smoothly much of the time), the business of leasing and hiring slaves, paying them wages, and letting them live on their own as if they were free cut deep into the cultural lies that sustained black slavery in the first place.

Slaves were slaves, masters said, because they would not work for wages – but they worked for wages quite successfully. Slaves were "children" who could not provide their own bed and board, except when they did for the master's convenience. Slaves could not enter into contracts, yet they dutifully collected and remitted the master's due. Slaves were chattel, property, not people in the way whites were people; but we find them in the antebellum South saving their earnings to buy a wedding ring, Christmas presents, or the freedom of a loved one. How could the absurd claims of the master class, to own and control the body and soul of persons they called slaves, survive all these contradictions that openly mocked the stories that masters told to justify their possessions. These contradictions helped transform a social structure based on slavery into a caste system focused on race instead of status or property law. These shifting foundations for American slavery may not have been caused by the market revolution alone, but the lure of economic advantage in the emerging market economy encouraged masters to rethink their economic interests and social obligations in ways that paralleled ambitious capitalists in the North.

Finally, the calculating ways of the market economy can be seen over time encroaching on the ways slaveholders talked about their business, managed their workforce, and re-imagined their own expectations. One study of antebellum slaveholders (not just plantation owners) found that young southern men sought to buy slaves as the key to material advancement. Old tobacco farmers such as Thomas Jefferson might wring their hands over the ancestral "burden" of slavery and agonize about holding a "wolf by the ears," but young men in the new Southwest craved land and slaves as the most certain instruments of capital gain. The best stock for a young man is "negro Stock," advised a Louisianan in 1818: "Negroes will yield a much larger income than any Bank dividend." Thirty years later, a Texan advised his young nephew to "Get as many young negro women as you can, Get as many cows as you can," and come to Texas, "the greatest country for an increase I ever saw."[31] Ambitious slaveholders routinely recorded slave, livestock, and commodity prices in the same calculating language: "Money market very tight evry [sic] Where – negros have fallen

---

[31] Quoted in James Oakes, *The Ruling Race: A History of American Slaveholders* (New York: Alfred A. Knopf, 1982), 73–4.

from $1200 to 8 & 900 'men' – Pork prime $11." A slave "that wouldn't bring over $300, seven years ago will fetch $1000 cash, quick, this year . . . but now, hogs, they ain't worth so much as they used to be."[32] Particularly among younger men who owned ten slaves or less, it was this language of material ambition, not traditional paternalism, that characterized their communications.

Changing conditions and market pressures gave rise to advice literature on how best to rationalize the management of slaveholders' "factories in the fields." Opinions differed on whether positive incentives or forceful punishment worked best in the long run. Experience proved that respectful treatment, special privileges, and even cash incentives mobilized black workers effectively, but critics worried that any relaxations of the master's threat of violence encouraged rebelliousness and undermined the culture of subordination on which slavery depended. Some planters adopted time disciplines similar to those used in northern cotton mills, ringing bells to punctuate the workday in strict regimentation. Rational cost/benefit analysis sometimes favored improving slave quarters and rations: One South Carolinian thought whitewashed cabins made slaves breed more prolifically. On the other hand, short-term economizing and even mistreatment might pay off better in times of falling prices. Market pressures – especially debts brought on by collapsing markets – became an unassailable excuse for selling slaves and breaking up their families no matter how committed the master might be to the benevolent care of his "people." (Harriet Beecher Stowe wove this dilemma into the narrative of *Uncle Tom's Cabin* to prove that good men could not ameliorate a wicked institution.) In the 1850s, forty years after everyone had denounced the African slave trade, some slaveholders called for reopening the trade before spiking prices threatened to bar the next generation from buying a stake in the master class.

Regardless of the contradictions and cultural baggage that swirled around the master-slave relationship, the fundamental cash transaction that made one man the property of another could not help but focus attention on the logic of capitalist markets. A painstaking study of the antebellum New Orleans slave market shows how the fixing of a price inscribed on the body of the slave not his or her value as a human

---

[32] Ibid. 170–1.

being, but a balance sheet of inputs and outputs, projected on an unknown future, against which all parties bid. Nothing (not even killing) so completely dehumanized the slave. Buyers and sellers, like their counterparts in livestock markets, grew wary of each other's tricks and tried to calculate their odds of being cheated in these brutal transactions. Buying slaves made manifest the hopes and dreams of purchasers, turned their wives into "ladies" and themselves into "patriarchs," made them money and advanced their social standing. Buying blacks made white men "fully white."[33]

By the eve of the Civil War, the persistence of slavery in the United States had become unacceptable to many, yet the claims of African Americans to the promise of American liberty had grown more tenuous, not less, over the decades. Across the states, North and South, the rights of blacks had been so thoroughly circumscribed by an ideology of racial exclusion and degradation that even Abraham Lincoln – no friend of slavery, to be sure – felt moved to deny any sympathy with genuine racial equality. Fending off charges of promoting "amalgamation" (interracial sex) and social equality, put forth by Stephen Douglas in the first of their famous debates, Lincoln clarified his own position: "I agree with Judge Douglas [that the Negro] is not my equal in many respects – certainly not in color, perhaps not in moral or intellectual endowment. But in the right to eat the bread, without the leave of anybody else, which his own hand earns, *he is my equal and Judge Douglas's equal, and the equal of every living man.*"[34] It is a mark of the impact of the market revolution on the South that all the tragic complexities accompanying slavery and the systems that sustained it now came down to this: that American freedom consisted only of the right to earn wages.

THE ENTREPRENEURS

Not even entrepreneurs, heroes of the capitalist system, were spared the discouraging effects of the market revolution. Easily condemned as the "heartless men" of the new era, entrepreneurs endured their own

---

[33] Walter Johnson, *Soul by Soul: Life inside the Antebellum Slave Market* (Cambridge, MA: Harvard University Press, 1999), 116.

[34] Abraham Lincoln, First Debate, Ottawa, Illinois, 21 August 1858, in *The Lincoln-Douglas Debates,* ed. Harold Holzer (New York: Harper-Collins, 1993), 63. Emphasis in the original.

rough handling by heartless markets over which they exercised truly little control. As free agents – the independent actors most responsible for innovative products and processes – they of all people ought to have been close to the reins of power during this transition to free-market capitalism. Yet in practice, entrepreneurs found control of the new system as elusive as anyone else. Early entrepreneurs rode the capitalist tiger, bareback if you will, without stirrups for balance or spurs to intimidate the beast. More often than not, the experience ended not in wealth and power, but in failure.

The first challenge of the market revolution involved placing a positive value on risk and innovation. Pre-modern social and economic values celebrated static, traditional relations (regardless of whether these actually obtained any longer). As we have seen, the American colonial experience had loosened  traditions even before the Revolution. High deman obility, and rapid growth eroded the restrai , government, and even family patriarchs. I s of economic free agents had fallen substa merican Revolution enshrined the twin virtue fter the Revolution, this guarantee of liberty trepreneurship, producing a dramatic release market economy.

Favorable trends notw did not immediately welcome risk without discomfort. Early economic legislation in the states and in Congress, for example, often saw the advocates of banking, industry, internal improvements, or commercial innovations begging for protection from loss or from competition that might frustrate their enterprises. Early business partnerships and corporations (the Charles River Bridge, for example, or the Boston Associates at Waltham) tapped the status of community elites to bolster the legitimacy of innovations and minimize the appearance of reckless greed. Internal improvement promotions, such the New York Inland Lock Navigation companies, the Pennsylvania Society for Promoting the Improvement of Roads and Inland Navigation, and the Potomac Canal wrapped the spirit of innovation in the cloak of civic leadership and denied they were pushing risky businesses. Gentleman entrepreneurs in the early Republic held fast to the social entitlements that shielded elites from raw market forces even while they pried open the economic system that such forces controlled. Consider, for example, the case of Henry Lee.

Infatuated with grandiose visions for Matildaville, his boom-town speculation at the Great Falls of the Potomac, "Light Horse Harry" cheated many of Virginia's leading families. Eventually they all cut him loose, but Lee insisted right up to the day he was thrown in debtors' prison that his "friends" had no business imprisoning one of their own for frauds and deceptions unbecoming of a "gentleman."[35]

One reason risky business was discouraged in pre-modern social systems derived from the assumption that the social order was best preserved when all households were guaranteed a living, if not of their own making than through the charity of their community. Misfortune, it was thought, could strike anyone, and the best defense against arbitrary ruin was a promise of mutual support. Such communities expelled needy strangers but agreed to take care of "their own." Men who failed were rehabilitated by whatever means possible. When debtors were punished, it was not for suffering misfortune but for angling to defraud their creditors. The taking of extraordinary risks was confined (in theory) to men of sufficient estate that they could suffer loss without injuring the rest of the community. Recall, for example, the moralistic lectures delivered in 1819 condemning reckless borrowing, greed, and high living (remember the $50 plum cakes?). According to those old values, proper businessmen ought to know better than to endanger the foundations of public credit, while most of the other victims had no business borrowing money and grasping for riches beyond their station.

Two assumptions had to change before a modern credit-based capitalist economy could take shape in such a culture. First, debt itself had to be recast, not as evidence of folly and indulgence, but as a legitimate burden of entrepreneurship. Second, independent households could not be guaranteed a subsistence in communities where banks and businesses failed and workers got laid off as a result of market forces. In this new game, the entrepreneur who traded on credit did not endanger the public welfare but rather advanced it. Individuals thrown down by a turn in the market deserved more sympathy than censure. Insolvent debtors belonged not in jail or the poor house but out there working for somebody else, for wages, perhaps to buy back their independence. Their

[35] Charles Royster, *Light-Horse Harry Lee & the Legacy of the American Revolution* (New York: Cambridge University Press, 1981), 181.

wives and children deserved, not a living at public expense, but whatever earnings they could add to the household income. In other words, debt itself had to lose the stigma that for generations had made it shameful. At the same time, poverty, long thought of as misfortune, started to *acquire* a stigma as evidence of weakness or vice, a refusal to scramble for wages in the new free-market economy. To that end, antebellum American lawmakers struggled to remodel systems of poor relief and to establish bankruptcy protections that might relieve failed entrepreneurs without creating an entitlement for families whose wages they no longer paid.

Failure marked the stories of antebellum entrepreneurs far more often and more indelibly than thumbnail sketches of their successes lead us to suspect. The biography of any one of the famous inventors contains a dozen false starts for every advance toward fame and fortune. A new study of Samuel Colt and his extended family reveals an almost unrelenting tale of failure in the bizarre career of one entrepreneur universally remembered for outstanding success. Individuals gained and lost tens, even hundreds of thousands of dollars – spectacular fortunes in terms of real money at the time. Some repaired their estates and returned to the ranks of the fortunate; many never did. Business cycles – most famously the panics in 1819, 1837, and 1857 – tossed hundreds of fledgling capitalists into economic oblivion, but the fortunes of others turned on the loss of a sale, a government contract, or a single speculation, which might occur at any time in any year. Failure stalked the ambitious relentlessly, which probably explains why many small masters and frustrated journeymen grimly endured privation in the bastard workshops of Jacksonian America: Things could always be worse!

If they managed to avoid the winnowing fork of business cycles and panics, successful entrepreneurs seldom found a way to lock in their gains in this open, competitive system. Each innovation engendered a dozen imitations, at least one of which yielded incremental competitive advantages. Patent laws tried to postpone the inevitable crush of competition, but technology changed so quickly in the nineteenth century that legal protection seldom prevented the development of rival machines that raised productivity or lowered costs. It may have been unmet demand that stimulated brand-new inventions, but once new production techniques became commonplace, markets quickly were glutted with goods. The resulting downward spiral of prices favored consumers but threatened to ruin producers who could not reduce their inputs. Firms in low-capital industries such as ready-made garments constantly fought off new rivals who managed to squeeze from their workers just a little bit more. Alternatively, textile factories with huge investments in capital equipment struggled to protect their market share and prevent the loss of shrinking profit margins. Angry textile operatives at Lowell might wonder why factory owners who could build new machines could not raise women's wages instead, but the owners correctly perceived that wages increased the expense of production while capital investments improved productivity for the next round of competition.

Those who survived these games of competition learned to resist any effort to hold them responsible for the welfare of workers, families, and communities. The most successful competitors paid no attention to social costs or consequences. This too was an adaptation, for not many entrepreneurs took so narrow a view at the beginning of the century. Samuel Slater, for instance, organized his early textile villages with an eye to sustaining whole communities of working people. The downward pressures of competition, however, forced him, and later his sons, to compromise this holistic strategy and attend to the bottom line. The managers of Lowell-style factories jettisoned the chaperon system, leaving wages – and wages alone – to determine the welfare of workers and the neighborhoods in which they lived. Even as late as the 1850s, Samuel Colt built a model manufacturing town, Coltsville, designed for worker welfare and comfort as well as efficiency and economy; but such sentiments quickly disappeared in the next generation. In the South, entrepreneurial slaveholders dropped their paternalistic masks and bought, sold, nurtured, or punished their hands according to naked self-interest. After all, in the market system described by Adam Smith, self-interest alone would produce the most satisfactory outcomes. Other motives were liable to distort supply and demand and disturb the equilibrium toward which "nature" inevitably tended. Before Charles Darwin even published the theory of evolution that would be perverted into a harsh sociology, the principal tenets of "social Darwinism" – laissez-faire and survival of the fittest – could be seen taking root in the economic culture of mid-nineteenth-century America.

For young people, especially the sons of the middling classes, the market economy presented a world of opportunity littered all over with the evidence of failure. Finding a good situation, acquiring a living, comfort, security, wife, family, and respectability, rewarded those who could thread the eye of a very small needle. Permanent success seemed especially elusive; a few false steps, however, resulted in consignment to the wage-earning class, whose comfort remained forever contingent on the success of somebody else. By the 1830s, those youths who resisted the temptations of New York's "sporting" society strove to keep themselves on the straight and narrow path. They pored over self-help books and listened to evangelical sermons intended for their guidance. Industry and frugality, as in former times, loomed large in all of this advice, but so too did new injunctions to defer all kinds of gratifications – especially courtship, sex, and marriage – until one's *economic* success had earned him the right to enjoy the fruits of adult life. The modern concept of adolescence (and adolescent angst) was born of this subtle change in the expectations of the life cycle. Procreation (even in marriage) became not the automatic consequence of human relations, but an act of private indulgence, the virtue of which could be measured in terms of the stock of resources laid up by expectant parents. (Oddly enough, the injunction to limit fertility was coupled with the criminalization of masturbation and birth control, forcing sexually mature individuals to choose between celibacy and ruin.) Middle-class values of self-control, hard work, and chastity, shored up with piety and temperance, became by the 1850s the standards for admission into the ranks of polite society; they marked for some a bright line between acceptable behavior and the self-destructive ways of the working poor.

When the sectional crisis finally resolved itself into the Civil War, heartless markets and heartless men had transformed American society, most profoundly in the North but in the South as well, in ways that prepared it for the heavy industrialization and rise of big business that would come in the next generation. A republic of yeoman farmers, tradesmen, and shopkeepers had been refashioned so that farmers functioned more as agrarian capitalists, tradesmen had been sorted into managers and workers, and a growing army of clerks and commercial functionaries stood ready to fill white-collar jobs in large bureaucratic firms that already were forming in the rapidly integrating railroad industry. A face-to-face world was fast dissolving into an integrated, national, commercialized, consumer society. Once comfortably embedded in relatively small communities governed by personal relations that were colored by kinship, friendship, and familiarity, Americans now moved restlessly in and out of pluralistic cities and towns, conducted business with strangers at home and abroad, and felt themselves increasingly powerless to shape the world in which they lived. The promise of American liberty that once encompassed a host of social, political, and economic expectations had been distilled (to nobody's satisfaction) into a free-labor ideology that equated freedom with wages and the *hope* of owning property, but very little else – not property itself, not independence, not self-sufficiency, not even self-defense. The great puzzle, already engaged by commentators in Jacksonian America, and argued ever since by historians, economists, and custodians of political heritage, is this: How had this come about? Who had authorized the transformation? How could such a free people find themselves staring at a future that none of them ever had envisioned, let alone intended to bring into being?

4

How Can We Explain It?

How then to explain this market revolution in the early United States? Never simply a matter of historical curiosity, the rise of the market economy triggered ideological claims that linked freedom with market-based capitalism so completely that later apologists scarcely could believe they were not the same thing. As a result, histories of the new United States have been shaped from the beginning by conflicting interpretive objectives: One side wants to naturalize the market revolution and celebrate the outcome as what ought to be; the other catalogs the losses of security and independence experienced by so many and argues that something must have gone terribly wrong. Because the new American Republic was the product of intentional founders, because its design was supposed to yield a "new order for the ages," what followed literally begged for a normative reading.

As the antebellum sectional conflict degenerated toward war, Americans began to see how interpretations of the founding experience could justify different conceptions of the nation. Regional trajectories clearly diverged: One perpetuated staple crop agrarian ways first perfected in the Chesapeake before Independence, the other embraced forms of commercial and industrial modernization once considered alien by some persons in the founding era, regardless of where they lived or whether they owned slaves. Both sides, South and North, insisted they were living out the promise of the American Revolution, and in important ways, they were. When they finally took up arms over slavery, Union, and "state's rights," they also fought over what stories would be offered up in the future to measure the triumph (or perversion) of their grand national experiment.

THEORETICAL FOUNDATIONS

It is the central conceit of the capitalist system that it springs from a state of nature. The progress of "civilization," according to Enlightenment thinkers, was the natural consequence of free human beings following their instincts unencumbered by corrupt restrictions. The argument itself derived from the scientific efforts to discern nature's laws as they applied to the universe, plants, animals, and human society. The question framed in the minds of learned Scots such as David Hume, Francis Hutcheson, and Adam Smith guaranteed an upward trajectory: What was the cause of the opulence of civilized people contrasted with the brutal poverty of what they called "savages"? Had the question been posed by those "savages" on the receiving end of European colonization, the answer may have focused on theft and exploitation. In the minds of Scottish common-sense philosophers, however, both the outcome and the process were pleasing.

Because he is universally cited as the father of capitalist political economy, let Adam Smith speak for the community of scholars who introduced us to the engines of modern progress. The first cause of the wealth of nations, Smith argued, was the improvement in "productive powers" resulting from a division of labor. Specialization and careful attention to each discrete task increased human productivity several orders of magnitude over what obtained in communities of hunters and gatherers. This "improvement" resulted, Smith explained, not from "human wisdom" but a "propensity in human nature ... to truck, barter, and exchange one thing for another."[1] Here Smith has introduced the fundamental assumption that guides all the rest of his arguments: Human nature – not culture, wisdom, or reason – directs social evolution.

Guided by this assumption, Smith ascribed to human nature everything he saw that did not manifest a proximate cause or an intervening

---

[1] Adam Smith, *An Inquiry into the Nature and Causes of the Wealth of Nations*, ed. Kathryn Sutherland (orig. 1776; New York: Oxford University Press, 1993), 21.

meddlesome hand. The use of money "naturally" arose as a convenience in barter and exchange. The value of things could be measured by
the labor that one expended to acquire them, producing "natural prices"
that found handy reflections in the nominal prices in money that became
affixed to goods in the marketplace. As society advanced, land was
carved up into private property and some individuals accumulated stocks
of wealth beyond what they needed for subsistence. This gave rise to rent
and capital. As soon as capital stock had accumulated in people's hands,
some of them would "naturally employ it in setting to work industrious
people, whom they supply with materials and subsistence, in order to
make a profit from the sale of their work." Behold the capitalist and the
worker, the concepts of profit and wages, arising without any author
from the very nature of the human experience.[2]

For hundreds of pages in *The Wealth of Nations*, Smith constructed
his conjectural system out of things that he "knew" to be true in eighteenth-century Britain. Consumers, he posited, always would angle to
buy at the lowest price, while vendors just as ardently sought the opposite. Workmen naturally desired high wages and lighter work; employers
necessarily strove to command the most labor for the least expenditure
in wages. Both sides conspired to advance their own interests (although
capitalists, being few in number and better connected in their communities, typically enjoyed more success than did laborers). Competition
naturally depressed prices, which in turn pressed downward on wages;
but wages could not fall below a certain level or the working class would
fail to reproduce. At virtually every step in this dynamic network of
exchanges and transactions, individuals were tempted to interfere to
advance their own interest or protect some inefficiency that competition
naturally endangered; yet everything truly was regulated best by letting
nature be. Every individual by nature conducted his business in a way
that yielded its greatest possible value, and by intending his own gain
only, he was "led by an invisible hand to promote an end [the general
welfare] which was no part of his intention."[3]

Smith ably described all the pieces of the market revolution that was
taking shape in Britain in the eighteenth century, but more importantly
he explained these changes as the triumph of nature over human

---

[2] Ibid., 11, 21, 45, 48.
[3] Ibid., 291–2.

confusion. Every custom or tradition that fixed prices or wages, limited worker mobility or entrepreneurial freedom, closed fields to entry, or propped up existing vested interests – even "corn laws" that guaranteed a nation's food supply in time of war – all these were the products of mistaken analysis and selfish interjections of policy designed to corrupt the economic system in the interests of a few against the many. Smith posited a rarefied "nature" for human beings that permitted (if it did not intend) his readers to believe that government always was wrong and largely unneeded.

Fresh off a rebellion against British controls that favored the interests of the Empire over those of the American periphery, colonists understandably seized upon Smith's arguments against all policy restraints. What they did not see as clearly was the necessary framework of law and social order that regulated life in contemporary Britain – a framework rooted in culture, not raw competition. (Smith probably meant to explain as much in his "planned third volume" on law.[4]) Near the end of Book IV of *The Wealth of Nations*, Smith promised that an "obvious and simple system of natural liberty" would follow the removal of preference or restraint: "Every man, as long as he does not violate the laws of justice, is left perfectly free to pursue his own interest in his own way."[5] Such a promise appealed to Americans engaged (they thought) in forging a more perfect world order, but the conditional factor that Smith assumed as a constant – respect for the "laws of justice" – referred precisely to the framework of law, custom, and tradition against which many Americans chafed. While British entrepreneurs struggled for another generation to enlarge their freedom under British law, the American bourgeoisie claimed it at once as the promise of the American Revolution.

Smith himself did not live to see what kind of society grew out of unfettered competition; but by the middle of the nineteenth century, when Karl Marx sat down in the British Museum to answer the same kinds of questions, his query was informed by a much different scene around him. Industrialization had brought forth a rising, landless

---

[4] See Warren J. Samuels and Steven G. Medema, "Freeing Smith from the 'Free Market': On the Misperception of Adam Smith on the Economic Role of Government," *History of Political Economy* 37 (2005): 221.

[5] Ibid., 391.

proletariat in Europe and urban America, a class of persons without property or any access to a living except through wages offered by the capitalist class. No less convinced than Smith that natural laws guided history's inevitable march, Marx identified a new prime mover for the progress of civilization: the class struggle over control of the means of production. Where Smith claimed it was our natural tendency to "truck and barter" that gave rise to the capitalist system, Marx argued that the system resulted from the capitalists' intentional campaign to monopolize private property. Converting all relationships to a "callous cash payment," the capitalist system transformed simple inequality into "naked, shameless, direct, brutal exploitation."[6] Smith's imaginary "Natural Man," argued Marx, had no counterpart in history; real persons never lived outside of time, place, and custom. In barely a hundred years, the bourgeois capitalist system had stripped "nine-tenths" of the population of their common claim on the world's property. In doing so, it also relieved the individual of all his natural and essential ties to genuine human communities.[7] Despair, however, was not Marx's message: The relentless, selfish demands of the bourgeoisie inevitably would beat down the working class until it rose up en masse, seized political power, abolished private property, and unmasked the lies about freedom that sustained bourgeois society. Thus liberated, he predicted (somewhat romantically), the proletariat would usher in a golden age of communism.

Marx's golden age has not materialized, but the importance of his work lies in his stinging critique of capitalist ways, not as expressions of human nature, but as instruments of privilege by which one class exercised power over another. Workers around the industrialized world responded to Marx's (and others') radical analysis by demanding rights and protections, either through collective actions in the workplace or through political movements that threatened the sanctity of private property. Marx himself saw little point in ameliorating social conditions in the bourgeois regime: Soon enough it would be swept off the world-historical stage. For real men and women, however, the hardships of industrialization proved debilitating here and now, so that

---

[6] Karl Marx, *The Communist Manifesto* (1848), in *The Portable Karl Marx*, ed. Eugene Kamenka (New York: Viking Penguin, 1983), 206.

[7] Marx, *Grundrisse* (1857), in *Portable Karl Marx*, ed. Kamenka, 376.

the radical critique often fueled a class struggle to *reform* the capitalist system, regardless of whatever utopian visions "history" might promise in some distant future. Throughout the second half of the nineteenth century and most of the century that followed, these visions of a communist or capitalist future structured political and economic conflict wherever the market economy took root.

ANTEBELLUM AMERICAN VOICES

Marx survives in the twenty-first century as the most famous critic of capitalism largely because of what happened in Europe and Russia long after his publication in 1848 of *The Communist Manifesto*. But before the English-speaking world met Karl Marx, other radicals had fixed on private property and absolute economic freedom as the probable causes of working-class distress. Recall, for example, Langton Byllesby, the Pennsylvania printer, who in 1826 published *Observations on the Sources and Effects of Unequal Wealth*. Building on America's scriptural text, the Declaration of Independence, Byllesby began with the assumption that everyone entitled to life and liberty was obliged to permit the same to others. Therefore, no man's "pursuit of happiness" should infringe on the rights of others to pursue happiness.[8] Labor produced all real value, but wealth could be gained by controlling the labor of others (through ownership of land, equipment, and natural resources) and skimming a portion off as profit. Such control of the means of production – property – deprived other men of access to the source of all wealth and thus infringed on their pursuit of life, liberty, and happiness.

Like nearly all political economists, Byllesby ransacked history to explain how private property, the rise of money, credit, and interest, and the application of labor-saving machinery all had encouraged unjust accumulation by those who contributed nothing through labor. Counting all sorts of intermediaries, bankers, clerks, lawyers, and government functionaries among the parasitic classes, Byllesby wondered how the "trafficker, or merchant," could claim a larger proportion of wealth than the workman who produced it: It "stumbles the mind to

---

[8] Langton Byllesby, *Observations on the Sources and Effects of Unequal Wealth* (orig. 1826; rpt. New York: Russell & Russell, 1961), 26–7.

conceive, and is wholly irreconcilable with equal natural rights." Turning back on wealthy Americans their excuse for taking land away from Indians, he quoted President James Monroe: "no tribe or people have a right to withhold from the wants of others more [property] than is necessary for their own support and comfort."⁹ Accordingly, he offered communitarian association as the true solution to the inequality of wealth: Return the ownership of property to people in common, distribute to each according to the value of his labor, and eliminate instruments such as money and banks that made it possible to hoard the surplus and lock it away from others. Byllesby appended to his volume a long account of George Rapp's Harmonie Society and Robert Owen's New Lanark, two among many utopian experiments that in his day held out promise for genuine reform.

Home-grown American radicals as well as intellectual utopians (many arriving from Europe) shared a common alarm at what seemed like a shockingly negative consequence of just one generation's experience with widespread economic freedom. Those with roots in the left-wing democratic politics tended, like Byllesby, to locate the fault among the business classes, but few of them recognized the causal connection between liberty itself and the market revolution. Outside of working-class movements in the largest cities, attacks on private property failed to appeal to rural, agricultural majorities, who indeed possessed a little capital of their own. Consequently, truly radical solutions mostly were confined to utopian communities. Critiques of the market revolution easily got lost in the general democratizing rhetoric that focused on eliminating privilege and government corruption – narrowly targeted to neutralize specific predatory agents such as banks or corporations. This is why the money question drained off the political energy of urban workingmen's parties. If killing the "monster bank" (as Andrew Jackson promised to do) solved the problem *and* preserved individual economic liberty, nothing could be more appealing. Before surrendering the right to strive and gain – and *keep* the property so acquired – the vast majority of early Americans wanted to be sure the older enemies of freedom and independence (aristocrats, government favorites, and corrupt public officials) truly had been vanquished.

---

⁹ Ibid., 62, 41.

A second feature made the Smithian promise especially attractive to early Americans: It described an automatic, self-regulating mechanism guaranteed to minimize corruption, maximize opportunity, and allocate resources in the most efficient manner. To Americans who yearned, like Jefferson, for little government close to home, Smithian markets promised to arbitrate conflicts that otherwise would mire everyone in interest-group politics. It is telling that intentional schemes for *promoting* business interests fared just about as poorly in early America as pro-labor movements and other proposals to *impede* the progress of the market revolution. Henry Clay's "American System," for example, first articulated as a program in 1819, tried to package national banking, land sales, protective tariffs, and internal improvements in an interlocking program of development that would stimulate national wealth and integrate the disparate sectors within the American economy. Andrew Jackson's widespread popularity rested, in part, on his refusal to endorse such intentional development and his promise, instead, to maximize the freedom of individual Americans to go about their business, make new farms and plantations, and seek their fortunes however they chose without interference from the hand of government.

The presence – and resurgence – of slavery further enhanced white Americans' commitment to freedom, even as the market revolution started profoundly to modify its meaning. As we have seen, the labor perceived as most degrading in the early United States was that done by unfree blacks. Chief among the disabilities that stigmatized the slaves in the minds of white contemporaries was their total lack of personal and private freedom – to come and go, live where they chose, marry whom they wished, and control the welfare of their offspring. Even while they labored to restrict many of these choices for the free blacks among them, whites invested more and more in their own sense of racial superiority as they quarreled over freeing the slaves. Race marked these victims of forced labor and commodification, and white Americans placed them beyond the pale of ordinary citizenship; this in turn made the legal rights and freedoms of northern white workers seem profound in spite of their declining economic power. In the 1840s, German, Irish, and French Canadian immigrants began flooding the ranks of the North's urban workforce, and while they were not technically "people of color," the habit of racial marginalization made it tempting for native-born Americans to lump them together with blacks as better suited to industrial dependency than the children of the Founding Fathers.

Not everyone, of course, missed the ironies attending "free labor" in a world of slavery. Freedom implied a degree of control over one's own destiny in history, a certain autonomy or capacity to act independently of the will of another. In this sense, "freedom" stood to lose a great deal as capitalist employers secured more control over the lives and livings of their workers, an encroachment workers recognized from the beginning. For example, when the New York Supreme Court convicted striking journeymen of illegally restraining trade, an 1836 handbill proclaimed: "The Freemen of the North are now on a level with the slaves of the South! With no other privilege than laboring that drones may fatten on your life-blood."[10] A popular antebellum schoolbook, Lindley Murray's *English Reader* (called by Abraham Lincoln the "best schoolbook ever put in the hands of an American youth"), juxtaposed "liberty" with "servile compliance," the latter a condition in which the victim "forfeited every privilege" of his natural condition (note the transitive verb employed) and ended as an "absolute dependent on the world." Preoccupied with securing his own essential agency, the fledgling capitalist forcefully rejected employee complaints, shifting blame for working-class dependency – as Americans had done from the beginning with African slaves – onto the inherently flawed character of the undeserving poor.[11]

Writing in the depths of the depression that followed the Panic of 1837, Orestes Brownson agonized over the plight of factory workers who retained, of the wealth they produced, a smaller portion "than it costs the master to feed, clothe, and lodge his slave." Refusing free-labor apologists the high moral ground, Brownson called for war against both slavery *and* free labor, adding that even immediate emancipation would do the slave little good: "He would be a slave still, although with the title and cares of a freeman." Wage slavery sounded "honester" than slavery, but in substance it was probably "more

---

[10] Quoted in Sean Wilentz, *Chants Democratic: New York City and the Rise of the American Working Class, 1788–1850* (New York: Oxford University Press, 1984), 417.

[11] See François Furstenberg, "Beyond Freedom and Slavery: Autonomy, Virtue, and Resistance in Early American Political Discourse," *Journal of American History* 89 (2003): 1295–1331, quotations at 1308–9.

profitable to the master." Free labor, he concluded somewhat omi-
nously, "would supplant slavery, and be sustained – for a time."[12]

One man's bizarre interpretation of the market revolution may have
done more than any other to solidify the northern commitment to free
labor and market capitalism. In 1850, George Fitzhugh of Virginia
published a little essay called "Slavery Justified." Carefully picking
his words for maximum inflammatory impact, he opened with an
all-out assault on bourgeois freedom: "Liberty and equality are new
things under the sun," he proclaimed. Only France and the northern
states had "fully and fairly tried the experiment." And that experiment
had failed. Upending Adam Smith's assumptions, Fitzhugh argued that
human beings by nature oppressed and destroyed whomever they
could. To check this impulse, government existed in every human tribe
and culture, but political economists since Smith had discredited
restraining institutions in order to release "Free Competition." The
resulting "struggle to better one's condition, to pull others down or
supplant them," was, in Fitzhugh's mind, "the great organic law of free
society." By contrast, he portrayed the southern farm as the "beau ideal
of Communism." A slave consumed "more than the master," never
worried about unemployment, married when he pleased (knowing
"he will have to work no more with a family than without one"). Well
fed, well clad, warm, and happy, slaves experienced "no rivalry, no
competition." Nor was there "war between master and slave" because
their interests, however unequal, harmonized perfectly: "Nature com-
pels master and slave to be friends; nature makes employers and free
laborers enemies."[13]

Here, and in two more book-length diatribes, Fitzhugh poured hot
coals of abuse on the claims of liberal free-labor civilization while he
celebrated a paternalistic romance of southern bondage. Liberty without property, he claimed in *Cannibals All* (1856), was no freedom at
all; on the other hand, "the negro slaves of the South" were the "hap-
piest, and, in some sense, the freest people in the world." So essential
was slavery to the welfare of the weaker members of society that

---

[12] Orestes Brownson, "The Laboring Classes," *Boston Quarterly Review*, July 1840,
370–1.
[13] A Southerner [George Fitzhugh], *Slavery Justified* (Fredericksburg, VA: Recorder
Printing Office, 1850), 3–4, 10.

Fitzhugh finally prescribed it for most white people as well as blacks: "nineteen out of every twenty individuals have 'a natural and inalienable right' to be taken care of and protected, to have guardians, trustees, husbands, or masters; in other words, they have a natural and inalienable right to be slaves."[14]

Fitzhugh's "sociology for the South" amounted to a caricature of the kind of conjectural history made famous by men like Adam Smith, but his shots at the masters of the factories and his portraits of the dismal fate of free labor rang true enough to turn what might have been laughter into seething rage as northern abolitionists tried to counter this pro-slavery propaganda. Coupled with the equally critical sentiments of northerners (like Brownson), this critique of free labor might have yielded some adjustment to the powers of employers or rights of working people. But obsessed as they were with the legal abomination of chattel slavery per se – and insulted by outrageous portraits of happy, well-fed slaves proffered by Fitzhugh and others – northern leaders by the 1850s could not absorb any hint of criticism. Instead, they redoubled their efforts to demonstrate the "harmony of interests" that united farmers, merchants, manufacturers, and workers in the common pursuit of progress within the framework of the market revolution. At the same time, radicals were forced to choose between sounding like lunatic defenders of African slavery or endorsing the liberal promise that freedom (and a chance to get hold of the brass ring) was infinitely better than bondage.

Henry Clay as well as anybody spoke for the moderate friends of the market revolution in the antebellum United States. More politician than political economist (he was the perennial "Whig" candidate for president even before there was a Whig Party), Clay pursued a common-sense approach to the rising capitalist system because it generated wealth and seemed destined to dominate the world in which he lived. Rather than mourn the passing of artisan traditions or moon over magnolia fairytales of southern life and labor, Clay tried to look conditions square in the face and do what seemed most likely to reward his countrymen (and himself). Leaning heavily on the writings of Philadelphia economist Mathew Carey, Clay thought prosperity and

---

[14] George Fitzhugh, *Cannibals All! Or, Slaves without Masters*, ed. C. Vann Woodward (orig. 1856; Cambridge, MA: Belknap Press, 1960), 21, 18, 69.

national independence were best secured through the development of a vigorous home market. Consequently, he favored tariff protection for manufacturers but mounted no quarrel with the market economy itself. A slaveholder from Kentucky, he nevertheless favored gradual emancipation because he did not see slavery meshing neatly with the emerging free-labor system. He pressed for a national developmental program, the American System, because he had more confidence than most Jackson Democrats that government could intervene successfully to balance, promote, and referee the games of competition in the marketplace.

Clay later drew aid and comfort from Henry C. Carey, son of Mathew Carey, and an even more ardent protectionist than his father. The younger Carey focused his analysis on the harmony of interests *inside* the domestic economy as the central antidote to the poverty and class struggle that marked the British free-trade system. For Carey, the logic seemed transparent and irrefutable: Produce consumed at home rewarded farmers with incomes they could spend on local goods and services. Wages paid by employers allowed laborers to purchase their sustenance, while local capitalists plowed their profits back into productive capacity. Good wages encouraged working-class consumption, driving up revenues for farmers and capitalists alike. In short, there was no natural conflict of interest between labor and capital or producers and consumers; rather, all parties in a healthy market economy should benefit from a fundamental harmony of interests.

How could Carey's assertions be true, given the apparent class struggle and constant downward pressure on wages and profits experienced since the 1820s? The answer, he argued, lay in foreign trade by which other countries siphoned off the wealth of American producers, transferring it to foreign merchants and capitalists who invested in their own economy, not the United States. Free trade – always promoted by wealthy exporting nations – perpetuated colonial dependency and prevented both economic growth and self-government in less-developed economies. By 1847, Carey had worked out his theory *(The Past, the Present, and the Future)*, and in 1852 he published a detailed historical account *(Harmony of Interests, Agricultural, Manufacturing, and Commercial)* of how high tariffs in the United States had fostered every episode of general prosperity. Tariff reductions, on the other hand, inevitably produced falling wages, unemployment, crashing commodities prices, and all the attendant social disorder now excused by conventional wisdom as the inescapable cost of progress. But conventional wisdom was wrong, Carey argued: David Ricardo and Thomas Malthus – the theorists most responsible for gloomy pronouncements about "iron laws" and starvation wages – misinterpreted Adam Smith by confusing the impulse to truck and barter at home with freedom to steal from abroad through trade. Substituting the "Golden Rule" (do unto others as you would have them do unto you) for the "ignorant selfishness" at the center of the British system, Carey looked to the realization in America of "perfect self-government" and an economic system "the tendency of which was that of elevating while equalizing the condition of man throughout the world."[15]

Modern economists find little to commend in Henry Carey's analysis, refuting as it did both Ricardo and Malthus, and misreading Adam Smith as an advocate of *national* liberalism only. But late antebellum Americans found his analysis far more compelling than radical frontal attacks on private property, outrageous defenses of chattel slavery, or the dark, cynical conclusion that middle-class prosperity could be had only at the cost of rising poverty and social despair. One review of Carey's 1847 treatise praised it for consigning both Malthus and Ricardo to the "limbo of 'false facts.'" Carey's work combined "more points of value" than the reviewer ever had read, and he ventured to predict that it would "eventually occupy the first rank ... as a 'primary treatise' on the wealth and economy of nations."[16] Assuring his readers that a harmony of interests was inherent in the capitalist system, Carey promised free-born Americans that they *could* have freedom and prosperity both, as long as they took steps to protect themselves from predatory exploitation by the "Manchester liberals" who controlled Great Britain.

REVISIONISTS AT PLAY

The battle over slavery – its abolition, containment, or extension to all the states – eventually overwhelmed all other conversations

---

[15] Henry C. Carey, *The Harmony of Interests, Agricultural, Manufacturing, and Commercial* (orig. 1852; Philadelphia: Henry Carey Baird, 1868), iii, 228–9.

[16] *The American Review: A Whig Journal Devoted to Politics and Literature*, 2: 5 (November 1848), in American Periodical Series Online, 544.

concerning the health and future of the United States. Although the resulting Civil War in no way *caused* the market revolution, the Union victory in that contest marked its triumph by finally discrediting rival claims on the principles of liberty, equality, and independence. As the sectional crisis mounted, northern critics of southern "Slave Power" augmented their attack on the slave labor system with uncritical defenses of commercial values, wage labor, and the fundamental virtue of free-market forces. Southern "fire-eaters" in turn charged the North with conspiring to reinterpret the Constitution, to hijack republican values and deploy them perversely in an unholy bourgeois campaign to perfect class dominion and universalize wage slavery. At stake on one side were the rights of freeborn citizens to follow their own ambitions, neither hindered nor molested by interlocking networks of banks, corporations, or government officials. At stake on the other was the whole promise of modernization that required an interlocking web of practices and institutions, specializations and dependencies, private values and public policies. As a result, the death struggle for the soul of the Union, while built around the problem of slavery, in effect became a proxy war as well about the market revolution and the final incorporation – or possible rejection – of bourgeois values and institutions in the core definition of American freedom. Contrary to most expectations, the victorious Union did not disable "Manchester liberalism" but embraced much of its spirit as the true meaning of the American experiment.

Slavery itself, of course, stemmed from the colonial experience and had been central to the exploitative regimes of eighteenth-century Atlantic empires. The *problem* of slavery, the one that would threaten the American Union, derived from contradictory expectations coming out of the Revolution. At the time of the founding, slavery existed in all of the colonies, but it was not central to everybody's happiness. Many patriots found it embarrassing to demand their own freedom while perpetuating African slavery. People associated slavery with the imperial past, not with the promise of a republican future. (In the Declaration of Independence, Thomas Jefferson blamed it squarely on British tyrants.) In those northern states where blacks were few in number and slave labor insignificant, emancipations followed soon after Independence.

Even in the heart of the Chesapeake tobacco country (although not in Georgia or South Carolina), planters openly debated how to reduce their reliance on slavery. As a result, most people north and south imagined a day, however distant, when freedom might crowd out slavery – and probably the blacks as well. True, the new Constitution of 1787 protected slavery in the states where it existed; but northerners *believed*, and many southerners *said*, this was a temporary accommodation.

Cotton changed all that in the first decades of the nineteenth century. The spread of the cotton culture across Georgia, Alabama, Mississippi, Louisiana, and into eastern Texas fixed in the southern imagination a renewed sense that liberty and riches came to those who commanded slave labor. Even Virginia's ambivalent master class found that their children's welfare depended on enlarging, not reducing, slavery's domain. As a result, what had been a dissenting pro-slavery view in the 1780s took center stage once again in the culture of the antebellum southern states. "Fortunately" for all white Americans, the structure of the federal Union – with its emphasis on states' rights and strictly limited national power – made it possible for some states to cherish slavery while others purged their economies of unfree hands. Southern voices on the national scene might still apologize for their "peculiar institution," but southern material and cultural interests grew ever-more dependent on a racial caste system and bound labor. Until his death in 1826, Jefferson eloquently agonized over the slave-holder's dilemma, urging (perversely) the widespread dispersal of blacks to the West in order somehow to hasten the day when they all would vacate the country.

One central assumption sustained the culture of compromise that nourished the antebellum Union: There was no compelling need to impose a uniform racial or labor regime throughout the United States. Having abolished slavery in their own jurisdictions, northerners felt little urge to liberate slaves elsewhere, and nobody guaranteed free blacks anything like equal rights. But gradually the friends of progress and modernization – that is, the market revolution – found themselves in need of more interstate integration, uniformity, and positive accommodations (such as credit, banks, protective tariffs, and internal improvements) in order to erect the bourgeois networks that made the economy grow. Cotton exports bank-rolled the modernization of the North (bringing in cash to pay for canals and railroads) while northern business leaders begged for government support for policies and institutions that cotton planters found appalling. More ironically, profits from the market revolution in the hands of evangelical idealists (such as Arthur and Lewis Tappan) fostered moral reform campaigns that soon were denouncing the crime of slavery as un-Christian and un-American as well.

Throughout the 1830s, while southern dependence on slavery deepened, abolitionist extremists, generously financed by newly rich merchants in New York and New England, took advantage of mass communications, improved transportation, and expanding commercial intercourse to heap abuse on the slaveholding class and stir up rebellion among their bondsmen. This produced a prickly sectional consciousness that, by the time of the war with Mexico in 1846, caused people who might not have cared about slavery to question the intentions of the shrillest voices on either side. Paranoid masters conjured up lurid scenes of servile insurrection, spurred on by cynical abolitionists who seemed ready to welcome a sea of blood if it yielded emancipation. Equally fearful "free-soilers" (northern agriculturists who resented both slavery and black people) believed the lords of the lash would not rest until they had planted their unholy system on every acre of unsettled land, and then all over the northern states. The free-labor North thought slavery degraded work and undermined the values required to support wage-based economic growth. Slaveholders feared fanatical capitalists who spent their fortunes campaigning to capture federal power and overthrow the planters who crouched behind shields of local sovereignty and states' rights.

In this way, the uncompromising enemies of slavery locked horns with its desperate defenders in the final decade of the antebellum period. Their attention fixed on the glaring final steps of each other's paranoid logic, during the 1850s they laid waste to the middle ground in which older notions of American liberty had flourished – capacious notions that once embraced republican artisans, yeoman farmers, country shopkeepers, coastal merchants, local magistrates, lawyers, planters, and gentleman politicians (including many of the Founding Fathers). Disintegration and local autonomy had made it possible, year after year, for politicians to embrace compromise positions that honored the rights of Americans to disagree on matters of race, religion, social structure, and cultural values, as long as nobody took advantage of the acquiescence of others. But compromise rested on confidence, and by the time that the war with Mexico forced Congress to deal with slavery in the West, sectional confidence had expired.

The turning point arrived in the early spring of 1850. A deadlocked Thirty-First Congress had quarreled fruitlessly for days, unable to organize itself or even elect a doorkeeper without tripping on the problem of slavery. The aging Henry Clay introduced in the Senate a package of resolutions intended to reconcile all the points of contention that were poisoning political discourse. Having lived forty years at the center of congressional politics, Clay sought "to settle and adjust, amicably," as Congress had done before, the particular issues arising out of the problem of slavery. Peace and harmony rested on procedural fairness and mutual concessions; Clay blamed the present crisis on an excess of "passion" and "party spirit." Both sides he accused of revising the historical agreements on which peace and the Union depended. The South now demanded the extension of slavery into new territories, while the North would bar it by the raw force of majority will. The Constitution, thought Clay, sustained neither action. "No earthly power," he promised, would ever make him vote "to spread slavery over territory where it does not exist"; conversely, nothing could touch the right of sovereign states (including new states) to deal with slavery as their citizens saw fit. Even where Congress possessed unquestioned authority to act – against slavery in the District of Columbia, for instance – Clay discouraged it as "unneighborly," not in the spirit of "fraternal connection existing between all parts of this Confederacy." The historical Union was a neighborhood of friends in which the North and South had prospered together, giving and taking, approaching each other like husband and wife, "forbearing, conceding," and living together "in happiness and peace."[17]

Clay gave perfect voice to the tradition that had kept the Union going in spite of mounting disappointments as a second generation came to understand that they would never agree about the problem of slavery. The traditional solution required both parties not to care too much how the other half lived, but this had grown more difficult

---

[17] U.S. Congress, *Congressional Globe*, 31 Cong., 1st Sess. (5–6 Feb. 1850), *Appendix*, 115–27, quotations at 115–16, 123, 127.

for two parallel reasons. First, the powerful forces of the market revolution now required integration of American commerce and economic life. Second, leading abolitionist extremists sprang from the ranks of the bourgeois elites, and these individuals conflated their moral and religious values with their economic aspirations. The market revolution made some people very rich, and some of those people made war upon slavery. Friends of decentralization, local autonomy, states rights – and the slave labor system – found it hard by 1850 not to connect those dots and feel themselves threatened by revisionist forces that would redefine the national Union.

John C. Calhoun – once a partner with Clay in promoting the American System, but since 1825 a fierce advocate of southern interests and local sovereignty – made a final appearance in the Senate to refute Clay's interpretation of political tradition and expose the startling truth of what it was that "endangered the Union." His explanation (read by another while the dying Calhoun rested grimly on a cot) must have chilled the crowded chamber. What endangered the Union, he said, was the rise to power of a northern majority able to seize total control of the national government, destroying the "equilibrium which existed when the Government commenced." Had this shift in the balance of power come about naturally, nobody could quarrel, but it had not, said Calhoun: "It was caused by the legislation of this Government, which was appointed as the common agent of all, and charged with the protection of the interests and security of all." A quick revisionist tour through national history revealed three intentional campaigns (1) to exclude the South from common territories, (2) to gather riches for northern improvement with tariffs that fell most severely on exporting planters, and (3) to usurp for the federal government absolute supremacy over the states in every situation, directly contradicting the original intentions of the Founding Fathers. Faced now with the towering wealth, population, and political preponderance of the free-labor states, the South could not feel safe in the Union without explicit guarantees for the rights of slaveholders and the supremacy of white people, everywhere and forever.[18]

---

[18] U.S. Congress, *Congressional Globe*, 31st Cong., 1st Sess. (4 Mar. 1850), 451–5, quotations at 451.

Calhoun's memory stood history on its head. Most Americans (including Clay) believed the southern states had dominated Washington since the election of Thomas Jefferson. If anything, the compromise tradition had acceded to southern demands even as the cotton revolution re-energized their commitment to the slave labor system. Now they were told that the South had been cheated every step of the way by northerners hostile to slavery. In Calhoun's retrospective view, abolitionist extremists must have governed the North from day one. All pretence of accommodation had been calculated and dishonest. Clay's appeal to the compromise tradition became laughable in Calhoun's view: one more suicidal acquiescence to the grand designs of fanatics who intended all along to rob the planter class and foster race war. Nothing but surrender to radical southern demands could prevent dissolution of the Union.

Such an ultimatum moved all kinds of northerners, who may not have sympathized much with slaves or the abolitionists, to draw their own line in the sand and reject terms of Union little better than the original Articles of Confederation. Calhoun's story denounced the character of national progress to date and stripped from the booming, thriving majority population of the North all hope of improvement in the future. Whatever quarrels people had with the free-market capitalist system, almost nobody north of the Ohio River wished to replace it with the racial police state and sham democracy they saw in the cotton South. Just as abolitionist extremists drove southern moderates into the arms of men like Calhoun, southern intransigents forced northern voters to embrace as congruent and inseparable commitments to personal liberty, free labor, progress, popular democracy, and free-soil access to the western territories – plus immediate emancipation and all aspects of what we have been calling the market revolution. And while most northerners in 1850 still hoped to resist this conflation of traditional republican values with market forces and racial equality, some seized the moment to advance precisely such an assessment, proudly standing Calhoun's twisted history on its feet once again.

On March 11, 1850, New York Senator William Seward eloquently met Calhoun's challenge – and in the process laid the first planks in the platform of a sectional Republican Party that would elect Abraham Lincoln and trigger the Civil War. He agreed with Calhoun about this: The longstanding habit of legislative compromise was "radically wrong and essentially vicious." Despite the "nearly unbroken ascendency of the slave states under the Constitution," the North had outstripped the South in population growth, wealth, innovation, and every other measure of modern prosperity. The public domain was a gift to mankind from "the Creator of the universe." The Constitution had devoted that domain "to union, to justice, to defence [sic], to welfare, and to liberty"; furthermore, a "higher law than the Constitution" bound them to "the same noble purposes." The Constitution never intended to perpetuate slavery: The framers had found slavery existing "and they left it only because they could not remove it." Now, sixty years later, no modern Christian state believed in slavery because it contradicted key elements of a great nation: "security of natural rights, the diffusion of knowledge, and the freedom of industry." Slavery was doomed, according to Seward, and he did not really care whether the planters thought that endangered the Union. *Slavery* endangered the Union, and slavery "must give way, and will give way, to the salutary instructions of economy, and to the ripening influence of humanity." Even so, Seward would not countenance violence against the "slave power" because, whatever Congress decided, emancipation was "inevitable" and "near."[19]

Where was the ground for compromise? If African slavery, white supremacy, local autonomy, and plantation agriculture had been true objectives of the Constitution, then everything about the progress of the northern states indeed endangered the Union. But if slavery was morally wrong and historically out of step with the march of civilization, then clearly its extension into new country – perhaps even its continued existence in the southern states – contradicted the course of history and the designs of God. Remarkably enough, after they had glimpsed these apocalyptic choices, in what we call the Compromise of 1850 members of Congress and most of the American people chose to retreat and paper over the conflict once again. Henry Clay went to his grave (in 1852) believing that cooler heads had prevailed and the Union was preserved. But the center could not hold, because the fundamental premise of the original compact – to agree to disagree about slavery – no longer satisfied the requirements of either side.

---

[19] U.S. Congress, *Congressional Globe*, 31st Cong., 1st Sess. (11 Mar. 1850), *Appendix*, 260–9, quotations at 262–3, 265, 268.

Abraham Lincoln was no abolitionist, but he ardently believed that slavery was wrong and incompatible with freedom. By the time he rose to prominence in Republican Party politics, the center had been battered to pieces by the fight over "free" California and various Pacific railroads, the crisis over "Bleeding Kansas," the persistent insult of the fugitive slave law, the Supreme Court's Dred Scott decision, and John Brown's murderous raids at Potawatomi, Kansas and Harpers Ferry. In his Senate campaign against Stephen Douglas, Lincoln carefully had charted a moderate but firmly antislavery position focused on nonextension. Like Seward, he urged no violent assaults on the South's peculiar institution, but also like Seward, he believed that slavery was destined to fail. "A house divided against itself cannot stand," he quoted scripture to the Illinois State Republican Convention. The Union could not endure "half slave and half free." Either the opponents of slavery would arrest it or its advocates would "put it forward" until it was lawful in all the states.[20] Two years later, when Lincoln was elected president, these words were used to label him a "black abolitionist," bent on eradicating slavery at whatever cost to the South. There was no real chance that he intended to emancipate the slaves, but Lincoln's intentions were entirely beside the point. He was elected by a northern majority without a single slaveholding state's vote: He might intend no harm to the South, but he could destroy it if he chose.

On December 20, 1860, a special convention in South Carolina voted to sever the state's ties with the Union. Borrowing the framework introduced in Calhoun's Senate valedictory in 1850, the delegates explained themselves as victims of a forceful and intentional campaign by northern interests to capture the federal government and subjugate the slaveholding states. The result was a renewed state of colonization, and no one among these delegates believed that their ancestors "intended to establish over their posterity, exactly the same sort of Government [consolidated, absolute, arbitrary] they had overthrown." A grand experiment in popular sovereignty and mutual accommodation had failed. "Time and the progress of things" had destroyed the "identity of feelings, interests, and institutions" that bound the original Union. Now the natural tendency to "plunder and oppress" (whenever

[20] Abraham Lincoln, "House Divided Speech," Springfield IL, 16 June 1858, quoted in David Herbert Donald, *Lincoln* (New York: Simon and Shuster, 1995), 206.

plunder and oppression were achievable) placed the South in the grip of a limitless "sectional despotism." The original "fraternity of feeling" had turned into hate because the new northern culture had become so aggressive and intolerant. Southerners renounced all aggressive intentions; they were content that all nations "should be satisfied with their [own] institutions." But the modernizing North would have none of it:

If they prefer a system of industry, in which capital and labor are in perpetual conflict – and chronic starvation keeps down the natural increase of population – and a man is worked out in eight years – and the law ordains that children shall be worked only ten hours a day – and the saber and the bayonet are the instruments of order – be it so. It is their affair, not ours. We prefer, however, our system of industry, by which labor and capital are identified in interest, and starvation is unknown, and abundance crowns the land. . . . All we demand of other peoples is to be left alone, to work out our own high destinies.[21]

Equal parts Fitzhugh and Calhoun, South Carolina's declaration marked the final polarization from which there was no peaceful recourse. (Interestingly enough, what South Carolina charged in 1860 was exactly what economist Walt W. Rostow identified a century later as a necessary precondition to economic modernization: the capture of power by bourgeois elites willing to disable traditional values and institutions that prevented the free play of market forces in a global capitalist economy.[22])

NOTHING BUT FREEDOM

"Nothing but freedom," wrote historian Eric Foner, summing up the gift of emancipation to African Americans after the Civil War. In almost perverse fulfillment of George Fitzhugh's worst nightmare, the Union triumph discredited all values and obligations that ever had been used to bolster the claims of "benevolent" masters. Paternalism, common or collective rights, community responsibility, benevolent hierarchy – everything was jettisoned that had derived from earlier republican visions and been bent by the planters into service to the

---

[21] South Carolina Secession Declaration, 24 Dec. 1860, found at http://history.furman.edu/~benson/docs/scdebates3.htm, accessed 30 July 2008, quotations at 3–4, 6.
[22] Walt W. Rostow, *The Stages of Economic Growth: A Non-Communist Manifesto* (orig. 1960; 2nd ed., Cambridge, UK: Cambridge University Press, 1971), 167.

"Lost Cause." Whatever broader commitments antislavery leaders may have pledged to moral reform, social justice, and racial equality, the achievement of their central objective – the end of chattel slavery – took the wind out of everybody's sails. Lincoln's wartime consensus had formed behind the narrowest of goals: to put down the rebellion. Emancipation was accepted (barely) as a stratagem of victory by a people little interested in remodeling the moral or racial assumptions they brought with them into the war. The way the northern majority saw it, slavery was the problem, freedom was the answer, and freedom had carried the day.

By the end of the Civil War, and certainly after the adoption of the Thirteenth, Fourteenth, and Fifteenth Amendments to the Constitution, all vestiges of bondage inherited from earlier times – the bondage of slaves, indentured servants, apprentices, wives, and children – effectively were gone. Most had been replaced gradually by contracts "freely joined" between parties presumed to be equal (whatever was the practical reality). The last vestige of traditional bondage – chattel slavery – was destroyed by the emancipation of the southern workforce, driving African Americans into a free-labor market that was stacked against them in every conceivable way. Nevertheless, the Union victory brought a popular certainty that virtue had triumphed over evil, that freedom had prevailed against anachronistic slavery. Northern society, because it won the normative struggle over who represented the intentions of the founders, stood vindicated now as the natural heir to the American Revolution. Whatever yearning remained for that security once enjoyed by individuals embedded in complex (hierarchical) social relations, nothing like it survived – except on the lips of the unvanquished sons and daughters of the Confederacy.

This abolition of bondage inadvertently established its rhetorical opposite – contractual freedom – as the only effective meaning of American liberty and equality. Swept away with the dishonest claims of the southern slaveholders was a complex package of rights and privileges that had been on the minds of early Americans before the antebellum market revolution: rights rooted in those older sentiments – to a "competency," a "living wage," the property implicit in mastering a trade, a "fair return" for an annual crop, community relief in the face of adversity. These found no place in the political economy that prevailed after the Civil War. All had been reduced, by the market revolution, to cash transactions unencumbered by history, benevolence, feeling, or the old-fashioned sense of justice with which Adam Smith himself had qualified the work of the "invisible hand."

In the period right after the war – belittled by Mark Twain as a gilded, not a golden, age – belief in a struggle for survival crowded out older commitments to common rights, a harmony of interests, or the universal goal of happiness. The language was borrowed from Charles Darwin (*On the Origin of Species* came out in 1859), but the sentiments owed nothing to Darwin's scientific speculations. At the center of Darwin's theory of evolution lay the engine of competition – survival of the fittest in a natural environment that was drenched in the blood of contesting creatures. Although Darwin himself did not connect this competition with "progress," his admirers did so immediately, and social theorists in England and America quickly adapted what they thought were Darwin's insights into a sociological framework that naturalized and justified the heartless competition that marked industrial economies. Suddenly the "dog-eat-dog" ethic with which George Fitzhugh had embarrassed northern free-labor spokesmen acquired the imprimatur of "natural law." The ruthless pursuit of self-interest – what Henry Carey had disdained as "ignorant selfishness" – became the driving force that perfected civilization, just as it shaped the perfection of the natural world.

The leading architect of social Darwinism was England's Herbert Spencer, but the same arguments fell from the lips of many Americans in the three decades that followed the Civil War. William Graham Sumner at Yale spoke most eloquently for American social Darwinists. "Let it be understood," he wrote, "that we cannot go outside this alternative: liberty, inequality, survival of the fittest; not-liberty, equality, survival of the unfittest." All efforts to bring about equality inexorably produced "retrogression." Every person deserved a chance, but not a competency or living: "Let every man be sober, industrious, prudent, and wise, and bring up his children to be so likewise, and poverty will be abolished in a few generations."[23] Social conditions, Sumner concluded, resulted from natural laws that no man could alter or deny. The social conditions of the Gilded Age – desperate poverty,

---

[23] Quoted in Sidney Fine, *Laissez Faire and the General Welfare State* (Ann Arbor: University of Michigan Press, 1956), 82–3.

declining income, frequent unemployment, child labor, unsafe conditions, hideous crowding in filthy slums – all this, according to theory, was destined to be, ought to be, and could not be otherwise. Reform and amelioration were illusions that could have no lasting effect on the natural order of things. The collective experiment in popular self-government that began with the Revolution of 1776 had come to this: survival of the fittest in a savage environment where the "rights of man" had dwindled to a tenuous claim on a pitiful wage.

American businessmen found much to celebrate in these Darwinian axioms. With equality discarded by nature and liberty restricted to property rights, business and industry abandoned all pretense of concern for the social consequences of enterprise. Independence now implied not freedom from the tyranny of others (something "all men" could enjoy), but final victory in the bloody struggle for survival in the marketplace (by definition, a prize for the powerful few). The industrial transformation that followed 1865 dwarfed every antebellum experience by several orders of magnitude. Railroads and heavy industries gave birth to giant companies, sometimes owned and controlled by single individuals (such as Andrew Carnegie and John D. Rockefeller) whose will shaped the fortunes of thousands almost as completely as any slaveholder master controlled his slaves' fortunes. Darwinian theory explained why social conditions were never the fault of the entrepreneurs, even while they labored to evade competition, fix prices and wages, cheat each other and their consumers, break unions, blacklist employees, secure tariff protection (the odd exception to their strictly liberal orientation), and bring the money supply back to the gold standard. Their libertarian posturing further reified the automatic marketplace as a thing by nature incorruptible.

The close association of natural law with God's laws brought many Christian pulpits into line with the capitalists' thinking. For example, New York clergyman Henry Ward Beecher credited God alone with causing the "great to be great and the little to be little." No man, he believed, suffered from poverty unless it was "more than his fault – unless it be his *sin*."[24] The triumph of this business point of view in jurisprudence, social science, and even popular religion made it almost impossible for opponents to ground their complaints in moral or

---

[24] Ibid. 118–19. Emphasis in the original.

historical principles that were not already discounted by advocates of laissez-faire. Critical voices did abound in Gilded Age America, some mixing arguments from deep in the republican tradition with radical theories (domestic and imported) about workers' rights, class solidarity, monetary theory, cooperation, tax reform, and the public seizure of private property. The Patrons of Husbandry (the Grange), for example, begged for a fair return on agricultural products in markets not distorted by railroad corporations. Granger rhetoric recalled the organic rights of yeomen and artisans to civil equality and a competent living. The Knights of Labor, organized in 1869, revived the "producerist" language of the antebellum era in an effort to gather under one umbrella all men and women who worked for a living. However traditional their claims, such critics sounded quaint in the 1870s, and they found themselves blocked by the newly enlarged, sacred rights of capital – that is, private property.

How then to explain this market revolution in the early United States? How do we best describe a zebra? Is it a black horse with white stripes, or a white horse with black? The modern industrial capitalist system, born of the antebellum market revolution, did generate "marvelous improvements." It sparked astonishing inventions, delivered material prosperity, and sustained a booming population, not in Malthusian squalor but in a relative comfort that was (and is) the envy of people in less prosperous parts of the world. At the same time, the regime of "heartless markets and heartless men" wreaked havoc on the hopes and dreams of ordinary people who endured it, some of whom did not live to see the benefits "in the long run." Market forces ripped control of material conditions out of the hands of traditional authorities – husbands and fathers, masters, community leaders, great landlords, even popular elected officials. As economic historian Karl Polanyi noticed decades ago, most people over the last five centuries have perceived this elevation of autonomous markets to be morally wrong and socially disruptive, even if they came to appreciate its material advantages.[25]

---

[25] Karl Polanyi, *The Great Transformation: The Political and Economic Origins of Our Time* (orig. 1944; 2nd ed., Boston: Beacon Press, 1957), see chapters 4–6.

Something unprecedented happened between the American Revolution and the Civil War, because of which the means of production were transformed forever. Social, family, and even sexual relations were reconfigured. Wealth piled up and was distributed according to new and unpopular criteria. Something changed that was not the expected result of American revolutionary republicanism, of popular self-government, of constitutionalism and the rule of law, or of liberty and independence. Americans alive during those eight decades believed in that grand political experiment for which they were famous throughout the world, and this is why they were so quick to look to politics for causes of whatever went on in their world. But those same Americans endured something else – what we have called the market revolution – that changed the nature of material life, reallocated power and influence, and finally redefined such essential terms as freedom, equality, liberty, and property. America's founders thought the key to prosperity was widespread freedom for independent households, but after the market revolution, independence and autonomy for most people stood at odds with the complex systems that delivered material riches. People did welcome prosperity, but very few had seen the price they would pay in terms of social and political agency.

Contrary to enlightenment theorists at the time (and modernization apologists today), what Americans experienced between the Revolution and the Civil War was not the relentless unfolding of some natural order. These developments required the exercise of power by some at the expense of others, but the cast of characters will not resolve itself neatly into simple dichotomies: the worthy against the licentious; aristocrats versus "the people"; producers and parasites; honest men and rogues. Much of this was unexpected, but it was not wholly unwelcomed by a self-created nation whose citizens enjoyed more genuine freedom than anybody else on the planet to embrace or reject its advance. As in any revolution, some embraced it completely, some struggled to resist, and a great many kept their heads down waiting to see where it would end. Americans wrestle still with how to account for why a self-governing people got such surprising, ambivalent, and unintended consequences from a purposeful effort to invent an ideal world. At the same time, the friends and beneficiaries of the capitalist system continue in the twenty-first century to promote it as a certain cure for the burden of scarcity that Marx identified long ago as the curse of human history. And so the struggle to control the means of production continues among nations of the world, among the classes inside those nations, and within the expectations of conflicted individuals who persist in trying to enjoy community *and* autonomy, equality *and* liberty, prosperity *and* independence.

Epilogue: Panic! 2008

Déjà vu *All over Again*

The Panic of 2008 struck while I was finishing this book. During the third week of September, networks of short-term credit that fed the cash needs of banks, brokerages, and large corporations started to freeze up. Declining value of capital assets was forcing lending institutions to call in loans and reduce their exposure, setting off the familiar downward spiral that makes investors panic. Markets recoiled in surprise, and confidence – that mysterious, invisible energy that keeps all financial bodies snug in their proper orbits – began to evaporate.

In the late twentieth century, capitalists worldwide had come to believe that institutional firewalls, sophisticated central banks, and modern regulatory regimes had consigned this nightmare scenario to the dustbin of historical fantasies – but here it was in the autumn of 2008 spinning madly out of control. Giant banks defaulted, stock markets shuddered, and financial institutions refused to lend to each other for fear that the morning news would report further bankruptcies. Thriving industries found it impossible to sell the commercial paper (very short-term loans) that allowed them to pay for materials and parts or meet their weekly payrolls. Money markets seized up. The interest rate on United States Treasury Bills, thought to be the last safe haven for cash, fell to zero. (In effect, investors were *paying* the treasury to keep their money.) By late September, had there still been windows that opened onto Wall Street, rich, young MBAs might have been falling like rain. The Dow Jones index at the New York Stock

Exchange, which had been flying high above 14,000 just one year before, plunged toward the low 8,000s. Treasury Secretary Henry Paulson and Federal Reserve Chair Ben Bernanke huddled with President George W. Bush, desperate to craft emergency actions that might avert what people were starting to call a global financial "meltdown."

If the credit "freeze" and its consequent "meltdown" (in times like these, metaphors get mangled) came on suddenly, its cause was neither precipitous nor mysterious. For over a decade, in a coordinated effort to sustain an overripe real estate boom, banks and mortgage brokers had hustled marginal customers into dicey, no-money-down, adjustable "subprime" contracts that concealed the inevitable costs of property taxes, insurance, and built-in payment adjustments that borrowers were told either would never come or would be offset by the increased value of their home. Mortgages, people said, were the key to the American Dream, and "Uncle Sam" just wanted all Americans to claim their piece of what President Bush liked to call "the ownership society."[1]

Alas, in 2007, the American housing market softened, as everyone knew it must. Across the country, home prices stopped rising and then began declining as record inventories of unsold properties clogged the listings of realtors everywhere. Sluggish sales depressed the value of homes not on the market, and such downward assessments triggered adjustments that suddenly boosted peoples' monthly payments by 20, 30, even 50 percent. Struggling borrowers fell behind, incurred late fees, and earned credit demerits that left them ineligible for the refinancing that lenders had promised would make their original contracts affordable. Once upon a time, when banks were local institutions, bankers might have sat down with their customers, restructured their debts, and set things on a slow but steady road to recovery. But these days, secondary markets had swept up these mortgages and sold them a dozen different ways such that the link between the debt and tangible property behind it had become almost unrecoverable.

These defaulters had not lost their jobs or suffered any other economic misfortune. The willful miscalculations of the lenders had set up the risky situation, and it was their subsequent response to the turn of the market that sparked the subprime crisis. No one was more

---

[1] See Zachary Karabell, "End of the 'Ownership Society,'" *Newsweek*, 20 Oct. 2008, 39–40.

surprised than the borrowers to learn that the same personal financial condition that had earned them approval a few months before now was declared untenable. Banks dumped foreclosed properties on falling markets and prices declined more steeply, forcing further adjustments on millions of contracts that threw hundreds of thousands more into foreclosure, pushing prices down again. By the summer of 2008, analysts despaired of assigning a market value to securities derived from mortgages on homes that had no selling price – because they could not be sold.

This full-blown crisis in the housing sector took down the global financial system because these mortgages made up the base of a pyramid of securities (derivatives) that were bought and sold many times over until everybody's capital assets to some degree depended on the value of American homes. The underlying properties had long since disappeared through "slicing and dicing" (as they said on the "Street"), so no investors knew whether the paper they held stood for real or fictitious value. Fear replaced confidence in all these instruments, and as everybody ran for cover, interbank lending started to freeze. Then it came to light that a trendy new product – the "credit default swap" – had dragged insurance companies into this speculators' nightmare. These clever instruments helped banks flout existing reserve requirements by turning liabilities into assets through the purchase of default insurance. Their liquidity restored, banks could lend again and again, while exposure mounted on the books of underwriters. (Wall Street investment banks Bear Stearns and Lehman Brothers each had loaned their capital stock thirty-five times over![2]) Since 1999, banks and insurance companies had been trading these "swaps" as well as the paper they supposedly protected. Every transaction yielded a profit. And who believed that modern financial corporations, stuffed with Ivy League MBAs and padded and restrained as they had been since the New Deal, could fail?

But fail they did. Bear Stearns ($400 billion) fell in March. The treasury forced Bear Stearns' sale to JP Morgan Chase, wiping out about 90 percent of shareholder value. Then in July came the crisis at Fannie Mae and Freddie Mac – two government-backed firms that

---

[2] Andy Serwer and Allan Sloan, "How Financial Madness Overtook Wall Street," *Time,* 18 Sept. 2008, http://www.time.com/time/printout/08816,1842123,00, accessed 7 Oct. 2008.

guaranteed over $5 trillion in American mortgages. Authorized by Congress to intervene, but only if necessary, Treasury Secretary Paulson seized control of both firms on September 7. One week later, a bankrupt Lehman Brothers came begging. Paulson turned them away empty-handed, and an equally shaky Merrill Lynch quickly sold itself to Bank of America for dimes on the dollar. Twenty-four hours later, the treasury learned that insurance giant AIG needed $14 billion *tomorrow* and maybe tens of billions more in the week ahead to collateralize its credit default swaps. Paulson loaned AIG $85 billion, installed a new CEO, and took an 80 percent stake in the company. Simultaneously, terrified depositors started a ten-day, $16 billion run on Seattle-based Washington Mutual, an enormous thrift ($307 billion) that was deeply involved in the California real estate market. On September 25, federal regulators seized the bank and sold its accounts to JP Morgan Chase for $1.9 billion – the largest single bank failure in United States history. Another giant, Wachovia, avoided bankruptcy by first selling part of its operations to Citibank and four days later merging wholesale with Wells Fargo, leaving guests at both weddings hopelessly confused.[3]

One by one, financial analysts began to acknowledge that nearly thirty years of deregulation had left the system dangerously vulnerable. Touted by Ronald Reagan specifically to cripple the hand of government and dismantle the New Deal, the gospel of deregulation had been credited (on questionable warrant) with causing the long recovery from the 1970s oil crisis, the collapse of Soviet communism, and the explosive economic growth of the 1990s. At the policy helm had sat "The Oracle," Alan Greenspan, a free-market fundamentalist (once a follower of Ayn Rand's "objectivist" creed) and chair of the Federal Reserve from 1987 to 2006. Greenspan hated government interference and praised the very subprime mortgage contracts that caused the present panic. He served four presidents – Reagan, George H. W. Bush, Bill Clinton, and George W. Bush – and his wisdom supposedly transcended mere partisan considerations.

---

[3] Ibid.; Daniel Gross, "The Captain of the Street," *Newsweek*, 29 Sept. 2008, 25–9; National Public Radio (NPR), *All Things Considered*, 26 Sept. 2008, http://www. npr.org/templates/story/story.php?storyId=95105093, accessed 28 Sept. 2008; Matthew Philips, "The Monster That Ate Wall Street," *Newsweek*, 6 Oct. 2008, 46–7, accessed 28 Sept. 2008.

Cheap food, easy credit, imported oil, and lower taxes – these were declared to be the answer almost regardless of what was the question. In 1999, near the end of Bill Clinton's second term, Democrats fought with Republicans over who got credit for repealing Glass-Steagall – the last fragment of that New Deal wall of separation that had kept Wall Street's hands out of ordinary people's rainy-day savings in local commercial banks. Senator Phil Gramm, a Texas Republican, proudly declared our final emancipation from the backward and superstitious rules laid down in the wake of the Great Depression, and George W. Bush rolled into office in 2001 determined to cut the taxes on wealthy Americans with which Bill Clinton at least had balanced the federal budget while he fanned the fires of reckless growth.

In retrospect, there always were signs of trouble ahead, and as the Panic of 2008 unfolded, pundits began to recall events that should have given them pause. Perhaps most unfortunate was the refusal to regulate derivatives and credit default swaps, once called "time bombs" by billionaire capitalist Warren Buffett. All three of the current experts now calling for controls (Bernanke, Paulson, and Securities and Exchange Commission [SEC] Chair Christopher Cox) testified against regulation in 2005 and 2006.[4] Instead, Bush ordered the SEC to back off and let Wall Street's "Masters of the Universe" work their magic. The administration even tried to privatize Social Security, hoping to place billions of old-age pension dollars at the brokers' disposal. Having promised an entire generation of Americans that New Deal "liberalism" was a tragic mistake – that regulation was bad, taxes were worse, and free traders could do no wrong – neither political party had the guts to admit there might be a wolf at the door.

Now the architects of deregulation found themselves peering into an abyss last seen by Herbert Hoover's treasury secretary, Andrew W. Mellon, in 1929. Despite a month of frantic interventions by Secretary Paulson, the game refused to stabilize. On September 17 and 18, short-term lending froze nearly solid – in the words of National Public Radio analyst Adam Davidson, "America's economy almost died."[5] Over the weekend, Paulson slapped together a three-page request for a shocking $700 billion to buy

---

[4] See http://www.propublica.org/article/top-regulators-once-opposed-regulation-of-derivatives, accessed 28 Oct. 2008.

[5] NPR, *All Things Considered*, 26 Sept. 2008, http://www.npr.org/templates/story/story.php?storyId=95099470, accessed 28 Sept. 2008.

up the faulty securities that lay at the bottom of this mess. Members of Congress recoiled in horror: Senator Jim Bunning (Republican from Kentucky) denounced this "financial socialism" as "un-American." The next week, lawmakers grilled Paulson and Fed Chair Bernanke, accusing them of pandering to Wall Street and refusing to believe their warnings of total disaster. On September 24, President Bush finally put in his oar, telling the country "our entire economy is in danger."[6]

Political response to the Bush administration's emergency proposals highlights our enduring historical misunderstanding of the market revolution in America. Two gilt-edged economic experts, Paulson, capitalist extraordinaire and long-time CEO of Goldman Sachs, and Bernanke, an academic student of the Great Depression and how to prevent its recurrence, both Republicans, both Bush appointees, showed up on Capital Hill, hat in hand, asking for help to prevent the implosion of finance capitalism – an event that surely would trigger massive layoffs, business failures, and a global depression at least as severe as that of the 1930s. With national elections not six weeks away, everybody kept one eye on the voters; but what was the right thing to do? Congressional leaders in both parties struck cooperative poses, although the Democrats insisted on inserting into the "Paulson Plan" various safeguards as well as punitive rhetoric condemning the salaries of Wall Street executives, whose nine-figure incomes defied comprehension. Pandering to angry constituents, House Republicans toyed with the hope of voting "no," forcing a Democratic Congress to pass the bailout without them so they could run for reelection *against* the fruits of their own deregulation. The presidential candidates, senators John McCain and Barack Obama, rushed back to Washington, where their presence only complicated things. Everybody huddled at a special White House summit Thursday afternoon, hoping to seal the deal and show the country how sophisticated statesmen handled themselves in a crisis. It was not to be.

Even as designated spokespeople "leaked" news of an imminent agreement, the deal unraveled. At the afternoon White House conference, House Minority Leader John Boehner (Republican from Ohio) introduced a rival proposal, apparently blessed by John McCain,

---

[6] NPR, *Morning Edition*, 25 Sept. 2008, http://www.npr.org/templates/story/story. php?storyId=95026089, accessed 28 Sept. 2008.

that other principals found unacceptable. Renegade Republicans broke ranks and ran for the nearest media microphones. The Paulson Plan was a socialist conspiracy, they cried; nothing less than creeping nationalization. Nervous Democrats piled on: billions to bail out Wall Street, they shouted, but nothing for the people! Senator Bunning delivered this obituary: "the free market for all intents and purposes is dead in America." Virginia Congressman Eric Cantor repeated on Friday a misapprehension about American history that is shared by nearly everybody in Washington: "We've always had a free market in this country. It has worked. It will work again." (Former SEC Chair William Donaldson, the aggressive watchdog earlier curbed by President Bush, missed the historical mark in the opposite direction when he told NPR's Robert Siegel that America has always had the "gold standard of regulation."[7]) Tense negotiations supposedly progressed throughout the weekend, while everyone up for reelection (468 members altogether) nervously monitored the phones. Monday morning, 228 U.S. representatives stunned the nation by voting against the emergency bill. The Dow plunged over 777 points that afternoon (it would fall another 2,000 in the weeks ahead).

They had nothing to sell but fear itself, and fear was selling like hotcakes during the first few days of October. The public response to the whole fiasco had been visceral, nasty, and wildly uninformed. Talk show hosts on radio and television exhausted themselves whipping into a frenzy both hired pundits and the "ordinary people" who called in to vent about bankers, brokers, and congressmen – "fat cats" all, who lied and cheated and stole from us every chance they got. Calls and emails to members of Congress were said to be running one hundred to one against Paulson's "bailout" plan. Out on "Main Street," consensus quickly formed: To hell with the bankers, let the market crush them all.

Raw anger had taken over the public discourse, and although on Friday, October 3, Congress finally passed a modified version of the Paulson Plan, economic experts now confronted a hydra-headed

<hr />

[7] Ibid., 24 Sept. 2008, http://www.npr.org/templates/story/story.php?storyId=94973418, accessed 28 Sept. 2008; NPR, *All Things Considered*, 26 Sept. 2008, http://www.npr.org/templates/story/story.php?storyId=95118212, accessed 28 Sept. 2008; ibid., 22 Oct. 2008, http://www.npr.org/templates/story/story.php?storyId=95995010, accessed 28 Sept. 2008.

monster: paralyzed financial institutions at home, panicked reactions by governments abroad, capital markets gyrating wildly (mostly down), rising threats of imminent layoffs, and a political dialogue in the United States hopelessly poisoned by charges of socialism, communism, cronyism, and every other "ism" people could think of. Even with billions in hand, Paulson's bailout had no immediate effect because it required, for implementation, that somebody sort out the mortgage paper and assign plausible values, precisely what the bankers and analysts already could not do. European governments (less hobbled by ideological nonsense) seized control of their own tottering financial structures, forcing Paulson to reverse his initial position and pump billions directly into American banks, making shareholders of the American people. This "partial nationalization" of financial services, nearly unthinkable in terms of popular American rhetoric, was endorsed by experts from almost every quarter. (Economists at the University of Chicago, the bastion of free-market fundamentalism, approved, as did an entire panel of fifteen experts who sent comments to the World Bank on October 9.[8])

The Paulson Plan may not have been the best thing for Congress to pass in late September 2008, and honorable experts sharply disagreed about the details; but loose talk of socialism and the death of market freedom contributed nothing to resolving the crisis. Senator Bunning probably entertained informed misgivings about the legislation, but his actions energized the likes of Indiana Congressman Mike Pence, who urged his fellow ideologues to stand firm: "Duty is ours, outcomes belong to God."[9] Like the pitiful imposter in *The Wizard of Oz*, an aging Alan Greenspan shuffled into the Capitol October 23 and admitted his "shocked disbelief" at the turn of events: "I made a mistake in presuming that the self-interests of organizations, specifically banks and others . . . were best capable of protecting their own shareholders and their equity in the firms." It was an honorable confession that acknowledged (however grudgingly) the central flaw in the gospel of deregulation. As *Newsweek* columnist Fareed Zakaria put it days

---

[8] NPR, *Day to Day*, 9 Oct. 2008, http://www.npr.org/templates/story/story.php?story Id=95557342; NPR, *Morning Edition*, 14 Oct. 2008, http://www.npr.org/templates/story/story.php?storyId=95683563, accessed 23 Oct. 2008.

[9] http://www.mikepence.house.gov/news/DocumentSingle.aspx?DocumentID=103922, accessed 21 Oct. 2008.

before the *opéra bouffe* of September 25 and 26: "This crisis should put an end to false debates about government versus markets. Governments create markets, and markets can exist only with regulation. If you want to be truly free of regulation, try Haiti or Somalia. The real trick is to craft good regulations that allow markets to work well."[10] Verified by history a hundred times, Zakaria's point was so compelling, how could anyone doubt it? And yet we found ourselves locked in a bizarre situation where the titans of American capitalism were trying desperately to stop "the people" from slitting the throat of the capitalist system on which those people utterly depend. Andrew Jackson, your war against the Monster Bank endures!

It was true in the antebellum era, as it is true at the beginning of the twenty-first century, that the enemies of government, not just the friends of private business, helped shackle the public hand in modern market systems. In the absence of state regulations, of course, markets will structure interactions in a capitalist system; but actual capitalists always have recognized the need for rules and institutions to guide and referee competitive behavior. Entrepreneurs seek freedom only when it serves their interests. During the original market revolution in America, the public welfare often was challenged by freedom-loving entrepreneurs; yet it was not the Whigs (ostensibly the party of the capitalist class) but the Jackson Democrats who canonized the doctrine of laissez-faire. Perfecting their appeal to the voters by promising never to impinge on their freedom, Jacksonians made war upon governance itself and set up a deceptive contest for power in which private rights and economic interests appeared to be the same when clearly they were not. Convinced by ideology that governance was unnecessary, a people empowered by their Revolution to set the agenda and govern themselves on behalf of the common good chose instead to dismantle the state.

In the resulting vacuum, America's nineteenth-century entrepreneurs understandably wrote their own rules and imposed order to suit their comfort and convenience. Their objectives were more pragmatic than ideological. Living as they did in a real, not fictitious, universe, businesspeople tended to be more flexible in adjusting to changing conditions in the market and society around them. Libertarian ideologues, on the

---

[10] Fareed Zakaria, "Big Government to the Rescue," *Newsweek,* 29 Sept. 2008, 22–3.

other hand, ensconced in academic departments, on the benches of the judiciary, and at the offices of political campaign machines, found the lure of theoretical models irresistible – intellectually rewarding because of their elegance, and, in the case of popular political campaigns, profoundly effective. In the American historical experience, politicians since Jackson have achieved phenomenal success by denouncing the complexities of governance and exciting latent fears that somebody else might use government to gain the upper hand. The threat of corruption may well have been legitimate, but the promise that disabling government would keep people from harm was then – and is now – simply untrue. Furthermore, nothing proved more useful for concealing an unholy alliance between governors and special interests than a cloak of indignation sewn up with the rhetoric of freedom and private rights.

The success of this Jacksonian formula has left us a political culture in the United States, perhaps unique in the industrialized world, where candidates advocating workers' rights and social welfare programs collect a following among elites and the educated middle class only to be thrashed at the polls by the desperate masses who oppose all efforts to regulate business or tax the rich on their own behalf. Given the choice, of course, even honest entrepreneurs prefer minimal government as long as they can get the regulations they *require* by less conspicuous means; but at times, this cynical strategy has left business dangerously exposed to the short-sighted animosities of persons in power who do not understand the systems on which their prosperity depends. In short, wealthy capitalists routinely pursue their economic interests, but the common people remain enthralled by politicians conjuring imaginary threats to their basic personal freedoms. This is not a logical phenomenon but a historical tradition deeply rooted in the market revolution and the popular politics of the age of Jackson. The tradition reflects badly on reckless capitalists but even more damningly on political adventurers who would rather inflame the ill-informed mob than exercise the stewardship of power and resources that voters placed in their hands.

What the Panic of 2008 demonstrates clearly is that the problems of the market revolution, which so preoccupied Americans in the early nineteenth century, remain central features of modernization at the start of the twenty-first. Americans long since have made peace with their abject dependency on a complex, consumer-driven, capitalistic market economy, and the capitalists, in self-defense, will right the system and restore a modicum of comfort and security. The panic merely exposes the depth of our otherwise invisible dependency. Meanwhile, around the world, the capitalist system is still introducing its transformational forces in places once held in colonial bondage or dismissed as hopelessly "underdeveloped." This process, now called globalization, has been guided by the World Bank and the International Monetary Fund – the former dedicated to alleviating poverty through development, the latter charged with stabilizing worldwide financial markets – both constructed after World War II precisely for the purpose of preventing the worst hardships that accompanied modernization. For over thirty years, the World Bank and the IMF charted an admirably pragmatic course through the perilous waters of the Cold War era, despite powerful efforts of the Soviets and the Americans to absorb every problem of third-world development into their own game of cosmic animosity.

In the 1980s, with the return of "Manchester liberalism" (relabeled "fiscal conservatism" by Ronald Reagan in America and Margaret Thatcher in Great Britain), a strident commitment to abstract principles restored the ruthless fidelity to "heartless markets and heartless men" first seen in the 1830s and perfected in the late nineteenth century Gilded Age. According to Joseph Stiglitz, chief economist for the World Bank from 1997 to 2001 and winner of the 2001 Noble Prize for economics, a rigid fixation on free-market models and the interests of the richest nations and their central banks, at the expense of field observations and humane considerations, resulted in punishing levels of unemployment and deflation in post-Soviet Russia and its satellites as well as in post-colonial societies such as Indonesia that were struggling to throw off a century of imperialism followed by corrupt strongman rule and the worst examples of "crony capitalism." Globalization itself, argues Stiglitz, "is neither good or bad." It has "the *power* to do enormous good," and for countries such as China that have embraced it "*under their own terms,* at their own pace, it has been an enormous benefit."[11] But since the 1980s, under the IMF's "one-size-fits-all" mandates, the world's poor have lost jobs, agricultural markets, food and fuel subsidies, health care, and access to education, ordered by the

[11] Joseph Stiglitz, *Globalization and Its Discontents* (New York: W. W. Norton, 2002), 9–22, quotation at 20 [italics original].

finance ministers of the wealthiest countries (all of which still subsidize *their* farmers) to "discipline" third-world regimes.

Globalization has succeeded by the twenty-first century in making nearly everyone on earth susceptible to market forces and the fickle ups and downs of international financial speculations. And despite assurances from western leaders, local populations in many less prosperous and powerful countries are receiving this global advance of capitalism with precisely the same suspicion and ambivalence we saw among early American farmers, artisans, and factory workers. At stake, according to the friends of globalization, is the economic growth on which depends all hope for relieving the desperate privation of billions of very poor people. At stake, according to its critics, is all semblance of independence, local autonomy or self-determination, cultural integrity, and protection from the howling winds of economic turmoil. Billions of people worldwide wondered anew whether markets truly are global or whether western capitalism, born of imperialism, remained the hegemonic tool of its masters. Reforms *always* seemed to open other people's banks and markets to exploitation by outsiders, while the "inevitable" suffering *never* fell on western societies. With the Panic of 2008, the hypocrisy finally has peaked: In their anguished concern for the jobs and the welfare of western consumers, custodians of the global marketplace seem to have acknowledged that what was good for the Indonesian goose is not, in fact, good for the American gander.

At the heart of the capitalist ideology lies the claim, laid down by Adam Smith and distorted into absolute dogma by later libertarian disciples, that markets answer to the laws of nature. Like all other natural laws, we are told, these market forces cannot be escaped, repealed, nor amended. Supply and demand are no less binding than the laws of gravity or mechanics. We might not like them, but we dare not flout them because nature will not be denied. But in many respects, starting in the nineteenth century, what we like to call progress has derived from a steady assault on precisely those laws of nature once thought to be immutable. Early railroads were said to "annihilate" space and time. With the advent of aviation, we suspended gravity and gave ourselves flight. We redirect rivers to transform deserts and block out the tides to defend our coastal installations from "forces of nature." The city of New Orleans, which lies below sea level, has been destroyed many times in three hundred years; and yet we rebuild. We now create organisms that do not – nay, cannot – exist in nature, in order to frustrate the natural actions of predators and prey in agricultural systems. We clone living creatures from single cells in defiance of reproductive laws. In the new Large Hadron Collider, physicists generate temperatures colder than any that obtain on earth or in deep space.

None of these achievements actually suspends the laws of nature, but all of them mock once popular convictions about what can or cannot be done in the world we inhabit. Time and again, human ingenuity has overturned what appeared to be limits fixed in nature. Why, then, do we cower whenever the friends of the capitalist system raise the shield of nature to defend the sovereignty of market forces? Most critics of modern markets do not question their obvious virtues: They generate wealth, increase human productivity, facilitate exchange, expand the stock of necessities on which human life depends, and reward creative innovation. But if clever contrivance can override gravity to keep aloft a jumbo jet, surely markets are susceptible to human management or improvement. Nobody argues that poverty is better than wealth, nor slavery better than freedom, nor blind tradition better than insight or innovation; but throughout history, human beings routinely have compromised absolute freedom in order to secure some protection against disaster. Capitalism alone among social and economic systems pretends that prosperity cannot be achieved without exposing the people to ruin. The only alternative, argue disciples, is a return to the conditions of want and misery such as prevailed in the seventeenth century.

Notwithstanding the positive impact of modern economic systems, what Marx called the terrible burden of scarcity has not been vanquished by prosperity through economic growth. For 250 years, advocates of the free-market capitalist system have insisted that simply producing more would eliminate the need to think about the distribution of wealth. Justice, equality of opportunity, satisfaction, "happiness" (the pursuit of which so captivated Thomas Jefferson) – all these objectives supposedly would come if we allowed ambitious and innovative persons to control the means of production. The capitalists would make such a generous economic pie that everyone could eat his fill no matter how much powerful individuals tried to monopolize the whole. Experience has shown this simply is not true. It *is* true that the rich have grown more rich (fabulously so) than they were in Adam Smith's day, and the prosperous are far more numerous than before; but the poor remain still more numerous than all the prosperous classes combined, and the desperately poor today outnumber the whole population of the earth in Adam Smith's day.

It was the mantra of the market revolution that any restraint on the agency of "economic man" necessarily killed the goose and stopped the flow of golden eggs on which prosperity depended. History will not verify the claim. Smith rescued "fortune" from the hands of the gods and lodged it "safely" in an automatic, self-regulating, natural market. It became clear in the nineteenth century that his confidence was overstated, but by then interested parties had learned that preaching laissez-faire allowed them to cloak their own manipulations, convincing the masses that nobody held the reins of economic power. Wealth piled up most quickly in the hands of ruthless entrepreneurs when regulations were removed, but so did social dependency as well as the burden of private failure and public disorder that necessarily fell as a charge upon the whole community – either in the form of welfare contributions or the cost of carting off the bodies. Joseph Schumpeter, one of the truly brilliant economists of modern times and a fond friend of the capitalist system, acknowledged as much half a century ago in *Capitalism, Socialism, and Democracy* (1942). By the early twentieth century, what business historian Alfred D. Chandler, Jr., called the "visible hand of management" had taken the edge off cutthroat competition while state and even federal regulations (sometimes welcomed by battle-weary businessmen) blunted the most egregious social abuses.[12]

Most Americans born after 1930 thought the New Deal forever had established a similar "visible hand of government" to stimulate faltering markets and check the power of naked greed on behalf of common sense and a modicum of justice. Experts agree it was the Second World War, not the alphabet soup of government programs, that brought an end to the Great Depression; but what was World War II if not an orgy

---

[12] Joseph Schumpeter, *Capitalism, Socialism, and Democracy* (New York: Harper and Brothers, 1942); Alfred D. Chandler, Jr., *The Visible Hand: The Managerial Revolution in American Business* (Cambridge, MA: Belknap Press, 1977).

of government hiring and spending that stimulated economic growth? Postwar Republicans, led by Dwight D. Eisenhower, sanctioned (reluctantly) a permanent state of war along with massive investments in public works in order to ward off the wolves of depression. Laissez-faire ideology took cover for a generation, nourished in exile by scholars such as Ludwig von Mises, Frederick Hayek, and the young Milton Friedman. In the 1980s, it returned with the "Reagan Revolution." Deregulation brought new consumer benefits through cutthroat competition; but, as it had in the late nineteenth century, cutthroat competition funneled wealth to the fiercest competitors while effective control of personal destiny declined for the horde of shoppers who made up the modern middle class. Finally, deregulation set the stage for rogue misbehavior by the "Masters of the Universe" who brought us in regular succession the "junk-bond" savings-and-loan scandals of the 1980s, the "dot-com" boom of the 1990s, and the subprime debacle that underlies the current Panic of 2008.

More portentous than all the immediate consequences of our modern commitment to heedless growth and Smithian assumptions is the ever-more-obvious fact that the present model cannot be sustained into the long-run future. At the moment, 305 million Americans (4.6 percent of the global whole) consume 33 percent of the world's resources. If half of all people laid claim to our standard of living, it would require two more identical planets to sustain them. Geographer Jared Diamond believes that to lift them all might increase consumption eleven times over – *assuming zero population growth!*[13] From that catastrophic demand on the planet Earth, deduct perhaps as much as half to account for technological mediation, but add back another factor (the dimension of which is yet unknowable) for the loss of productive capacities as fruitful lands succumb to desertification and capital assets (primarily seaboard cities) sink beneath the rising oceans – all thanks to climate change. Then factor in a rising population that cannot possibly stabilize at less than 10 billion. Any fourth grader can do the math. Whatever its past virtues, modernization cannot be

---

[13] Amy Cassara, "Ask EarthTrends: How Much of the World's Resource Consumption Occurs in Rich Countries?" World Resources Institute, 31 Aug. 2007, http:// www.earthtrends.wri.org/updates/node/236, accessed 30 Oct. 2008; Jared Diamond calculations from January 2007, quoted in Thomas L. Friedman, *Hot, Flat, and Crowded* (New York: Farrar, Straus, and Giroux, 2008), 66–7.

projected into any imaginable future without driving most of the world's population away from hope and back into slavery.

It is no credit to the utopian vision of America's extraordinary founders to accept the negative effects of the market revolution as the natural result of inexorable historical forces. That kind of thinking once characterized Old World scoffers who "knew" that monarchy alone reflected both divine inspiration and the natural social order. It was precisely this "dead hand" of history against which our ancestors staged their Revolution. If we agree with William Graham Sumner, the Gilded-Age rock-star of social Darwinism, that liberty and equality cannot coexist, then we must proclaim America a failure. To accept as "collateral damage" the worldwide dependency and exploitation that must result from feeding the rising expectations of twenty-first century Americans is to repudiate completely the liberal dreams on which this experiment was founded.

Likewise, it is no rebuke to the honest and honorable millions who for nearly two centuries embraced the market revolution, to conclude that its promises were incomplete – and perhaps unattainable. False gods appear in many guises, and history is littered with blueprints for ideal worlds that turned out not to work as predicted. The capitalist system ushered in by the market revolution during the nineteenth century brought phenomenal changes in the material conditions of human life, changes that have continued to spread around the world as a result of commerce and enterprise. But the original intent of the American founders was not limited to wealth accumulation; in fact, rank materialism gave John Adams reason to wonder whether his neighbors, "addicted to commerce" as they were, possessed "virtue enough" to sustain a republic.[14] Accumulation without distributive justice and sustainability stood at the center of the bill of indictment against the Old Regimes of early modern Europe; it was the promise of the age of democratic revolutions that such regimes would be swept away.

What truly captured the imagination of our ancestors was a vision of liberty that promised independence, a comfortable living, a high degree of freedom of action, no arbitrary barriers to individual advancement

---

[14] John Adams to Mercy Otis Warren, 16 April 1776, quoted in Drew R. McCoy, *The Elusive Republic* (Chapel Hill: University of North Carolina Press, 1980), 71.

(such as hereditary privilege), a respect for human dignity and the "rights of man," topped off by the hope of lasting peace born of a system of justice that undercut the most intractable incentives for war. This much historians can prove, and it flatly contradicts the self-serving claims of present-day market fundamentalists that success equals wealth and power. The market revolution in America grew out of the freedom and ambitions of the people, but it was neither the intended outcome of the Revolution nor was it wholly welcomed by the people once they recognized its features. History shows the American people once believed that liberty and prosperity traveled the same road; later on, they traded independence for personal riches and comfort. What history has not yet shown is whether widespread freedom, prosperity, *and* some kind of just equality can be forged with the tools of enterprise and self-determination that so inflamed the imaginations of our founders. Surely the utopian roots of the American Republic can sustain idealistic commitments to peace and justice, commitments no more risky or counterintuitive than, say, cloned sheep, particle physics, aviation, and space travel – or even a democratic, self-governing republic built on a continental scale, open to all people, and capable of modeling freedom to the world.

An Essay on the Sources

This study of the market revolution rests on a vast, extraordinary literature, produced over more than half a century and crossing the subdisciplines of business, economic, agricultural, and technological history; social and labor history; women's history; and studies of slavery and race. The titles selected for inclusion here represent works on which I have depended particularly and recent titles whose bibliographies will further guide the serious reader into the riches that lie below. It is my intention here to acknowledge freely my enormous debt to several generations of scholars without making any claim by this listing to have exhausted the relevant resources.

For an excellent point of entry into what happened in the decades covered in this book, start with *The Cambridge Economic History of the United States*, ed. Stanley L. Engerman and Robert E. Gallman, vol. I, *The Colonial Era* (1996) and vol. II, *The Long Nineteenth Century* (2000). An older excellent reference work is *The Encyclopedia of American Business History*, ed. Glenn Porter (1980). I relied often on Jeremy Atack, Peter Passell, and Susan Lee, *A New Economic View of American History*, 2nd ed. (1994). For a sweeping look at early American development from a geographer's perspective, see Donald W. Meinig, *The Shaping of America*, vol. I, *Atlantic America, 1492–1800* (1986) and vol. II, *Continental America, 1800–1867* (1993).

The colonial experience is introduced in John H. Elliott, *Empires of the Atlantic World* (2006); Alan Taylor, *American Colonies* (2001);

and two books by Jack P. Green, *Pursuits of Happiness* (1988) and *Peripheries and Centers* (1986). For the environmental impact of colonization see Alfred W. Crosby, *Ecological Imperialism*, 2nd ed. (2004); Virginia DeJohn Anderson, *Creatures of Empire* (2004); John F. Richards, *The Unending Frontier* (2003); and William Cronon, *Changes in the Land* (1983). For the colonial economy in particular, see Stephen Innes, *Creating the Commonwealth* (1995); David Hancock, *Citizens of the World: London Merchants and the Integration of the British Atlantic Community* (1995); John J. McCusker and Russell R. Menard, *The Economy of British North America* (1985); Charles H. Wilson, *England's Apprenticeship* (1965); and the classic study by Bernard Bailyn, *New England Merchants in the Seventeenth Century* (1955). For a handy introduction to politics in Georgian England, see Robert A. Smith, *Eighteenth-Century English Politics* (1972). For relevant aspects of the Atlantic slave trade, see Joseph E. Inikori, *Africans and the Industrial Revolution in England* (2002); Hugh Thomas, *The Slave Trade* (1997); and the essays collected in *The Atlantic Slave Trade: Effects on Economies, Societies, and Peoples in Africa, the Americas, and Europe*, ed. Joseph Inikori and Stanley L. Engerman (1992).

For the economic background to the coming of the American Revolution, see Joseph Ernst and Marc Egnal, "The Economic Development of the Thirteen Continental Colonies, 1720–1775," *William and Mary Quarterly*, 3rd. ser. 32 (1975): 192–222; and Marc Egnal, *A Mighty Empire: Origins of the American Revolution* (1988). Still useful are Jack M. Sosin, *Agents and Merchants: British Colonial Policy and the Origins of the American Revolution* (1965); and Oliver M. Dickerson, *The Navigation Acts and the American Revolution* (1951).

The literature on the American Revolution in general is enormous. Two works by Gordon S. Wood stand at the center of the field: *The Radicalism of the American Revolution* (1991) and *Creation of the American Republic* (1969). For differing views, see Timothy Breen, *The Marketplace of Revolution: How Consumers Shaped the American Revolution* (2004); Edward Countryman, *The American Revolution*, rev. ed. (2003); and Gary B. Nash, *Urban Crucible* (1979). For the confederation era, see Peter S. Onuf, *Origins of the Federal Republic* (1983); and Jack N. Rakove, *The Beginnings of National Politics* (1979).

For roots of the Constitution, see Max M. Edling, *Origins of the U.S. Constitution and the Making of the American State* (2003); Jack N. Rakove, *Original Meanings* (1996); Michael Lienesch, *A New Order for the Ages* (1988); the essays collected in Richard Beeman et al., eds., *Beyond Confederation* (1987); and Forrest McDonald, *Novus Ordo Seclorum: Intellectual Origins of the Constitution* (1985). Robin Einhorn, *American Taxation, American Slavery* (2006), focuses on taxation; Saul Cornell, *The Other Founders* (1999), rehabilitates the Anti-Federalists; Peter S. Onuf and Cathy Matson, *A Union of Interests* (1990), favors economic issues, as does Drew R. McCoy, *The Elusive Republic: Political Economy in Jeffersonian America* (1980).

Gerald R. Stourzh captures an often-missed side of his subject in *Alexander Hamilton and the Idea of Republican Government* (1970); but see also Forrest McDonald, *Alexander Hamilton: A Biography* (1982); and John Nelson, *Liberty and Property* (1987) on Hamilton's economic policies. For James Madison's pivotal experience, see Lance Banning, *The Sacred Fire of Liberty* (1995); and Drew R. McCoy, *The Last of the Fathers* (1989). Implementation of the new frame of government can be traced in Stanley Elkins and Eric McKitrick, *The Age of Federalism* (1993); while Richard K. Matthews, *The Radical Politics of Thomas Jefferson* (1984), gives access to the opposition. Two very recent works focus on the Jeffersonian Republicans and their relation to manufacturing: Lawrence Peskin, *The Manufacturing Revolution* (2007); and Andrew Shankman, *Crucible of American Democracy* (2004). The long and fascinating shadow of the Jefferson presidency is explored by various authors in Peter S. Onuf, ed., *Jeffersonian Legacies* (1993).

A number of excellent recent books survey the half-century after 1800. See Daniel Walker Howe, *What Hath God Wrought* (2007); Christopher Clark, *Social Change in America* (2006); Sean Wilentz, *The Rise of American Democracy* (2005); and Daniel Feller, *Jacksonian Promise* (1995). Two of the early scholars to place the market revolution at the center of the story were Charles E. Sellers, *The Market Revolution* (1991); and Harry Watson, *Liberty and Power* (1991). For earlier useful treatments of the period, see Edward Pessen, *Riches, Class, and Power before the Civil War* (1973); and Marvin Meyers, *The Jacksonian Persuasion* (1957).

The story of the rise of capitalism has fascinated historians for a generation, yielding an enormous outpouring of writing. For synthetic or historiographical discussions, see Scott Martin, ed., *Cultural Change and the Market Revolution* (2005); Naomi Lamoreaux, "Rethinking the Transition to Capitalism in the Early American Northeast," *Journal of American History* 90 (2003): 437–61; Joyce Appleby, "The Vexed Story of Capitalism Told by American Historians," *Journal of the Early Republic* 21 (2001): 1–18, and *Inheriting the Revolution* (2000); Richard Lyman Bushman, "Markets and Composite Farms in Early America," *William and Mary Quarterly*, 3rd ser. 55 (1998): 351–74; Paul Gilje, ed., *The Wages of Independence* (1997); Melvyn Stokes and Stephen Conway, eds., *The Market Revolution in America* (1996); Thomas L. Haskell and Richard F. Teichgraeber III , eds., *The Culture of the Market* (1993); Winifred Barr Rothenberg, *From Market-Places to a Market Economy* (1992); and James A. Henretta, *The Origins of American Capitalism* (1991). Still important in framing the issues are Elizabeth Fox-Genovese and Eugene Genovese, *Fruits of Merchant Capital* (1983); and Eric E. Williams, *Capitalism and Slavery* (1944).

Local and regional case studies include Martin Breugel, *Farm, Shop, Landing* (2002); Thomas S. Wermuth, "New York Farmers and the Market Revolution: Economic Behavior in the Mid-Hudson Valley, 1780–1830," *Journal of Social History* 32 (1998): 179–96; Alan Kulikoff, *The Agrarian Origins of American Capitalism* (1992); Christopher Clark, *The Roots of Rural Capitalism* (1990); Andrew R. L. Cayton and Peter S. Onuf, *The Midwest and the Nation* (1990); and Joyce Appleby, *Capitalism and a New Social Order* (1984). Useful introductions to antebellum economic thinkers can be found in Paul K. Conkin, *Prophets of Prosperity* (1980).

Studies of class and especially the articulation of an American working class include Simon Middleton and Billy G. Smith, eds., *Class Matters: Early North America and the Atlantic World* (2008); Douglas R. Egerton, "Slaves to the Marketplace: Economic Liberty and Black Rebelliousness in the Atlantic World," *Journal of the Early Republic* 26 (2006): 617–39; essays by Martin Breugel, Naomi Lamoreaux, Michale Zakim, Stephen Mihm, Douglas Egerton, and Walter Johnson in a special issue edited by Cathy Matson of *Journal of the Early Republic* 26 (2005): 515–652; a symposium on class featuring Seth

Rockman, Jennifer Goloboy, Andrew M. Schocket, and Christopher Clark, edited by Gary Kornblith, in *Journal of the Early Republic* 25 (2005): 523–64; Seth Rockman, "The Contours of Class in the Early Republic City," *Labor: Studies in Working-Class History of the Americas* 1 (2004): 91–107; Stephen P. Rice, *Minding the Machine: Languages of Class in Early Industrial America* (2004), Billy G. Smith, ed., *Down and Out in Early America* (2004); Carla G. Pestana and Sharon V. Salinger, eds., *Inequality in Early America* (1999); and Gary Kornblith, ed., *The Industrial Revolution in America* (1998). For access to the scholarship on prisons, asylums, and poor relief institutions, see Seth Rockman, *Welfare Reform in the Early Republic* (2003); and the classic by David J. Rothman, *The Discovery of the Asylum* (1971).

On money, banking, and finance, see Stephen Mihm, *A Nation of Counterfeiters: Capitalists, Con Men, and the Making of the United States* (2007); Richard Eugene Sylla, "Political Economy of Financial Development: Canada and the United States in the Mirror of the Other, 1790–1840," *Enterprise & Society*, 7 (Dec. 2006), 653–65; Robert E. Wright, *The First Wall Street* (2005), and *Wealth of Nations Rediscovered: Integration and Expansion in American Financial Markets, 1780–1850* (2002); Charles R. Geisst, *Wall Street: A History*, rev. ed. (2004); two excellent detailed works by Howard Bodenhorn, *State Banking in Early America* (2003) and *A History of Banking in Antebellum America* (2000); and the very dependable *American Public Finance and Financial Services, 1700–1815* by Edwin J. Perkins (1994). Still useful are the technically focused *Origins of Central Banking in the United States*, by Richard H. Timberlake, Jr. (1978); and the dated but politically rich *Banks and Politics in America From the Revolution to the Civil War*, by Bray Hammond (1957).

Legal innovations shaping the market revolution can be seen in Christopher Tomlins, *Law, Labor, and Ideology in the Early American Republic* (1993); William J. Novak, *The People's Welfare* (1996); Morton Horwitz, *The Transformation of American Law* (1977); and famously in J. Willard Hurst, *Law and the Conditions of Freedom* (1956). The evolution of English into American law can be seen in A. G. Roeber, *Faithful Magistrates and Republican Lawyers: Creators of Virginia Legal Culture 1680–1810* (1981). The evolution of American corporations is discussed in Andrew Schocket, *Founding*

Corporate Power in Early National Philadelphia (2007); Pauline Maier, "The Revolutionary Origins of the American Corporation," *William and Mary Quarterly,* 3rd ser. 50 (1993): 51–84; and Oscar Handlin and Mary Flug Handlin, *Commonwealth* (1969). Municipal corporate development is the subject of Hendrick Hartog, *Public Property and Private Power* (1983). For the pivotal Charles River Bridge case, see Stanley I. Kutler, *Privilege and Creative Destruction: The Charles River Bridge Case* (1971).

For internal improvement, see John Lauritz Larson, *Internal Improvement: National Public Works and the Promise of Popular Government in the Early United States* (2001); Maurice Baxter, *Henry Clay and the American System* (1995); Ronald E. Shaw, *Canals for a Nation* (1990); Carter Goodrich, *Government Promotion of American Canals and Railroads, 1800–1890* (1960); and George Rogers Taylor, *The Transportation Revolution* (1951). Robert G. Albion's two classic studies, *Square-Riggers on Schedule* (1938) and *The Rise of New York Port* (1839), set the stage for understanding this commercial revolution. On the Erie Canal, see Ronald E. Shaw, *Erie Water West* (1966); and Nathan Miller, *The Enterprise of a Free People* (1962). For its social and cultural impact, see Carol Sheriff, *Artificial River* (1996); and Paul Johnson, *A Shopkeeper's Millennium* (1978). For steamboats, see Kirkpatrick Sale, *The Fire of His Genius: Robert Fulton and the American Dream* (2001); Harry P. Owens, *Steamboats and the Cotton Economy* (1990); and Louis C. Hunter, *Steamboats on the Western Rivers* (1949). The economic impact of river transportation is evaluated in Erik F. Haites, James Mak, and Gary M. Walton, *Western River Transportation: The Era of Early Internal Development, 1810–1860* (1975).

The communications revolution, in addition to supplying the central motif of Daniel Walker Howe's *What Hath God Wrought* (2007), is the subject of Richard R. John, *Spreading the News* (1995); Menahem Blondheim, *News over the Wires: The Telegraph and the Flow of Public Information in America* (1994); Gerald Baldasty, *The Commercialization of News in the Nineteenth Century* (1992); Richard Kielbowicz, *News in the Mail* (1989); and Alan R. Pred, *Urban Growth and the Circulation of Information* (1973). Two works by Richard D. Brown consider the cultural impact of information flow: *The Strength of a People: The Idea of an Informed Citizenry* (1996); and *Knowledge*

Is Power: The Diffusion of Information in Early America, 1700–1865 (1989). For the link between the communications revolution and abolition, see James Brewer Stewart, *Holy Warriors* (1976); and Leonard L. Richards, *Gentlemen of Property and Standing* (1970).

For early railroads, see the excellent overview essays in *The Encyclopedia of North American Railroads*, eds. William D. Middleton, George M. Smerk, and Roberta L. Diehl (2007); James D. Dilts, *The Great Road* (1993); and John F. Stover, *Iron Road to the West* (1978). Impact studies include John Lauritz Larson, *Bonds of Enterprise* (1984); Albert Fishlow, *American Railroads and the Transformation of the Antebellum Economy* (1966); and Lee Benson, *Merchants, Farmers, and Railroads* (1955). James A. Ward, *Railroads and the Character of America* (1986), explores the cultural impact of railroad transportation.

Economic development in antebellum America was driven in part by the spread of agriculture into the Midwest. For general explanations, see Wilma Dunaway, *The First Frontier* (1996); Malcolm J. Rohrbough, *The Transappalachian Frontier* (1978); and Robert D. Mitchell, *Commercialism and Frontier* (1977). Rohrbough's *Land Office Business* (1968) explains the antebellum land system. Michael Williams, *Americans and Their Forests* (1989), contains a wealth of detailed information about deforestation and land-use practices. The agriculture that dominated frontier economies can be explored in R. Douglas Hurt, *American Agriculture: A Brief History* (1994); Mart Stewart, *"What Nature Suffers to Groe,"* (1996); Joyce E. Chaplin, *Anxious Pursuit: Agricultural Innovation and Modernity in the Lower South* (1993); and Jeremy Atack and Fred Bateman, *To Their Own Soil: Agriculture in the Antebellum North* (1987). For technological innovations, see Peter D. McClelland, *Sewing Modernity: America's First Agricultural Revolution* (1997); and Charles Danhoff, *Change in Agriculture* (1969).

The process of creating communities and states in the new West can be studied in a number of local and regional studies. See, for Missouri, Stephen Aron, *American Confluence: The Missouri Frontier from Borderland to Border State* (2006); for Kentucky, see Aron, *How the West Was Lost* (1996); for New York State, see Charles Brooks, *Frontier Settlement and Market Revolution: The Holland Land Purchase* (1996); for Indiana, see Andrew R. L. Cayton, *Frontier Indiana*

(1996); for Ohio, see Cayton, *Frontier Republic* (1986); and R. Douglas Hurt, *Ohio Frontier* (1996); for Michigan, see Susan Gray, *The Yankee West* (1996); and for Illinois, see John Mack Faragher, *Sugar Creek: Life on the Illinois Prairie* (1986). Still useful is R. Carlyle Buley, *The Old Northwest*, 2 vols. (1950). Two good studies of butter and dairy production are Sally McMurry, *Transforming Rural Life* (1995); and Joan M. Jenson, *Loosening the Bonds: Mid-Atlantic Farm Women, 1750–1850* (1986). For the South, see Stephanie McCurry, *Masters of Small Worlds: Yeoman Households, Gender Relations, and the Political Culture of the Antebellum South Carolina Low Country* (1995); and Lacy K. Ford, *Origins of Southern Radicalism: The South Carolina Upcountry, 1800–1860* (1988).

Commercial networks were essential to moving all that agricultural produce to market. For the evolution of commercial practices and systems (in addition to Albion, *Rise of New York Port*), see Kim M. Gruenwald, *River of Enterprise* (2002); William Cronon, *The Great Metropolis: Chicago and the Great West* (1991); Conrad Edick Wright and Katheryn P. Viens, eds., *Entrepreneurs: The Boston Business Community, 1700–1850* (1997); Thomas Doerflinger, *A Vigorous Spirit of Enterprise* (1986); and the early chapters of Alfred D. Chandler, Jr., *The Visible Hand* (1977). The rise of credit reporting is addressed in Josh Lauer, "From Rumor to Written Record: Credit Reporting and the Invention of Financial Identity in Nineteenth-Century America," *Technology and Culture* 49 (2008): 301–25; and James D. Norris, *R. G. Dunn & Co., 1841–1900: The Development of Credit-Reporting in the Nineteenth Century* (1978).

A recent interest in lower-level commercial functionaries can be seen in Brian P. Luskey, "Jumping Counters in White Collars: Manliness, Respectability, and Work in the Antebellum City," *Journal of the Early Republic* 26 (2006): 173–219; Michael Zakim, "The Business Clerk as Social Revolutionary; or, a Labor History of the Nonproducing Classes," *Journal of the Early Republic* 26 (2006): 563–603; and Thomas Augst, *The Clerk's Tale: Young Men and Moral Life in Nineteenth-Century America* (2003). Failure too has received recent attention in Scott A. Sandage, *Born Losers* (2005); Bruce Mann, *Republic of Debtors* (2002); and Edward Balleisen, *Navigating Failure* (2001). On gentleman-crooks such as the "swindling Harry Lee," see

Charles Royster, *Light-Horse Harry Lee & the Legacy of the American Revolution* (1981).

The plight of artisans and other working people during the market revolution has engendered an enormous outpouring of scholarship. Start with Jacqueline Jones, *American Work: Four Centuries of Black and White Labor* (1998); David Montgomery, *Citizen Worker: The Experience of Workers in the United States with Democracy and the Free Market during the Nineteenth Century* (1993); Bruce Laurie, *Artisans into Workers* (1989); David Brody, "Time and Work during Early American Industrialization," *Labor History* 30 (1989): 5–46; and the classic article by Herbert Gutman, "Work, Culture, and Society in Industrializing America, 1815–1919," *American Historical Review* 78 (1973): 531–88. Paul A. Gilje, *Liberty on the Waterfront* (2004), details the working class of the coastal economy. The very poor and least skilled are examined in Seth Rockman, *Scraping By: Labor, Slavery, and Survival in Early Baltimore* (2008); Peter Way, *Common Labour* (1993); and Sharon V. Salinger, *"To Serve Well and Faithfully": Labor and Indentured Servants in Pennsylvania, 1682–1800* (1987). For the special concerns of the higher-skilled traditional artisans, see Paul Gilje and Howard B. Rock, eds., *Keepers of the Revolution* (1992); Rock, Gilje, and Robert Asher, eds., *American Artisans: Crafting Social Identity, 1750–1850* (1995); and William J. Rorabaugh, *The Craft Apprentice* (1986). See also Michelle Gillespie, *Free Labor in an Unfree World* (2000).

Because working-class history is best done close to the ground, much of the best work is organized by locale. For studies of labor in New York, see Joshua Greenberg, *Advocating the Man* (2006); Richard B. Stott, *Workers in the Metropolis* (1990); Sean Wilentz, *Chants Democratic* (1984); and Howard B. Rock, *Artisans of the New Republic* (1979). Other good local studies include Christopher Phillips, *Freedom's Port* (1997), covering Baltimore; Ronald Shultz, *Republic of Labor* (1993), covering Philadelphia; and Stephen J. Ross, *Workers on the Edge* (1985), covering Cincinnati. Studies organized by industry include Michael Zakim, *Ready-Made Democracy: A History of Men's Dress in the American Republic* (2003); Donna J. Rilling, *Making Houses, Crafting Capitalism* (2000); and Rosalind Remer, *Printers and Men of Capital* (1996). Three classic works examine the shoe industry: Mary H. Blewett, *Men, Women, and Work: A Study of Class, Gender, and*

Protest in the Nineteenth-Century New England Shoe Industry (1988); Paul G. Faler, *Mechanics and Manufacturers in the Early Industrial Revolution: Lynn, Massachusetts* (1981); and Alan Dawley, *Class and Community: The Industrial Revolution in Lynn* (1976).

The transformation of women's work is explored in Wendy Gamber, *The Boardinghouse in Nineteenth-Century America* (2007); Jeanne Boydston, *Home and Work: Housework, Wages, and the Ideology of Labor in the Early Republic* (1990); Jane H. Pease and William H. Pease, *Ladies, Women, and Wenches* (1990); Christine Stansell, *City of Women* (1986); and three by Thomas Dublin: *Transforming Women's Work* (1994); "Rural Putting-Out Work in Early Nineteenth-Century New England: Women and the Transition to Capitalism in the Countryside," *New England Quarterly* 64 (1991): 531–73; and *Women at Work* (1979). For primary source material, see Benita Eisler, ed., *The Lowell Offering: Writings by New England Mill Women, 1840–1845* (1998); and Dublin, ed., *Farm to Factory: Women's Letters, 1830–1860*, 2nd ed. (1993). For new work on the sex trade, see Helen L. Horowitz, *Rereading Sex* (2002); Patricia Cline Cohen, *The Murder of Helen Jewett* (1998); and Timothy Gilfoyle, *City of Eros* (1992).

Violence and misbehavior in one of New York's most notorious neighborhoods is chronicled in Tyler Anbinder, *Five Points* (2001). See also Paul A. Gilje, *The Road to Mobocracy* (1987). Another mob action is reported in Daniel Cohen, "Passing the Torch: Boston Firemen, 'Tea Party' Patriots, and the Burning of the Charlestown Convent," *Journal of the Early Republic* 24 (2004): 527–86. For a rowdy period autobiography, see William Otter, *History of My Own Times*, ed. Richard B. Stott (1835, 1995), which contrasts nicely with another self-conscious performance in *The Autobiography of Benjamin Franklin* (1850). For thoughts on Franklin, see David Waldstreicher, *Runaway America: Benjamin Franklin, Slavery, and the American Revolution* (2004), and compare with Gordon S. Wood, *The Americanization of Benjamin Franklin* (2004). Immigrants commonly participated in and often bore the brunt of urban violence. See Roger Daniels, *Coming to America: A History of Immigration and Ethnicity in American Life*, 2nd ed. (2002); and Ruth Wallis Herndon, *Unwelcome Americans: Living on the Margin in Early New England* (2001). Recent scholarship also focuses on "whiteness" as an ethnic characterization and a property. See Matthew Frye Josephson,

Whiteness of a Different Color: European Immigrants and the Alchemy of Race (1998); and David Roediger, *The Wages of Whiteness* (1991).

Whiteness conjures up race, which is naturally the focus of a rich literature on work and working people during the market revolution. For slavery in general, see Gavin Wright, *Slavery and American Economic Development* (2006); Adam Rothman, *Slave Country* (2005); Peter Kolchin, *American Slavery* (1993); James Oakes, *Slavery and Freedom* (1990); and Robert W. Fogel, *Without Consent or Contract* (1989). On race more generally, see the essays in Michael A. Morrison and James B. Stewart, eds., *Race and the Early Republic* (2002). For evidence of a surprisingly porous color line in private affairs, see Joshua D. Rothman, *Notorious in the Neighborhood: Sex and Families across the Color Line in Virginia, 1787–1861* (2003).

Oddly enough, the cotton culture (the centerpiece of antebellum slavery) has been somewhat neglected by historians. Recent localized studies include David J. Libby, *Slavery and Frontier Mississippi* (2004); Steven F. Miller, "Plantation Labor Organization and Slave Life on the Cotton Frontier: The Alabama-Mississippi Black Belt, 1815–1840," in *Cultivation and Culture*, eds. Ira Berlin and Philip Morgan (1993); and Daniel S. Dupre, *Transforming the Cotton Frontier: Madison County, Alabama, 1800–1840* (1997). Angela Lakwete unpacks the Eli Whitney myth in *Inventing the Cotton Gin* (2003). Mark A. Smith, *Mastered by the Clock* (1997), finds modernization at work on cotton plantations.

Variations on slavery can be seen in Thomas Buchanan, *Black Life on the Mississippi: Slaves, Free Blacks, and the Western Steamboat World,* (2004); David S. Cecelski, *The Waterman's Song: Slavery and Freedom in Maritime North Carolina* (2001); W. Jeffrey Bolster, *Black Jacks: African American Seamen in the Age of Sail* (1997); and Ann Patton Malone, *Sweet Chariot: Slave Family and Household Structure in Nineteenth-Century Louisiana* (1992). The racial borderland in Baltimore is covered in T. Stephen Whitman, *The Price of Freedom: Slavery and Manumission in Baltimore and Early National Maryland* (1997); and Barbara Jeanne Fields, *Slavery and Freedom on the Middle Ground* (1985).

Urban and industrial slavery can be seen in many of the urban labor studies already cited as well as Charles B. Dew, *Bond of Iron* (1994).

See also older studies such as the essays in James Newton and Ronald L. Lewis, eds., *The Other Slaves: Mechanics, Artisans, and Craftsmen* (1978); Claudia Golden, *Urban Slavery in the American South* (1976); and the pathbreaking work by Robert L. Starobin, *Industrial Slavery in the Old South* (1970).

Free black laborers filled out the workforce North and South. See Leslie M. Harris, *In the Shadow of Slavery: African Americans in New York City, 1626–1863* (2003); Graham R. Hodges, *Root and Branch: African Americans in New York and New Jersey, 1613–1863* (1999); James Oliver Horton and Lois E. Horton, *In Hope of Liberty: Culture, Community, and Protest among Northern Free Blacks, 1700–1860* (1997); Shane White, *Somewhat More Independent: The End of Slavery in New York, 1770–1810* (1991); and Suzanne Lebsock, *The Free Women of Petersburg* (1984).

Finally, slaves as property have received new attention from Robert H. Gudmestad, *A Troublesome Commerce; The Transformation of the Interstate Slave Trade* (2003); Walter Johnson, *Soul by Soul: Life Inside the Antebellum Slave Market* (1999); and Michael Tadman, *Speculators and Slaves* (1989). See also Sharon Ann Murphy, "Securing Human Property: Slavery, Life Insurance, and Industrialization in the Upper South," *Journal of the Early Republic* 25 (2005): 615–52; and Peter C. Mancall, Joshua L. Rosenbloom, and Thomas Weiss, "Slave Prices and the South Carolina Economy, 1722–1809," *Journal of Economic History* 61 (2001): 616–39.

Industrialization triggered many of the structural changes that gave the market revolution such force in people's lives. For a general introduction to the subject, see David R. Meyer, *Roots of American Industrialization* (2003); Walter Licht, *Industrializing America: The Nineteenth Century* (1995); and Thomas C. Cochran, *Frontiers of Change* (1981). For a recent study focusing on innovative entrepreneurs (including Samuel Colt), see Barbara M. Tucker and Kenneth H. Tucker, Jr., *Industrializing Antebellum America* (2008). Technological change can be followed in Ruth Schwartz Cowan, *A Social History of American Technology* (1997); Brooke Hindle and Stephen Lubar, *Engines of Change: The American Industrial Revolution* (1986); David R. Hounshell, *From the American System to Mass Production, 1800–1932* (1984); and Elting E. Morison, *From Know-How to Nowhere: The Development of American Technology* (1975). On power sources, see Louis C. Hunter, *History of Industrial Power in the United States,* 3 vols. (1979–85). For manufacturing on the fringes of development, see Margaret Walsh, *The Manufacturing Frontier* (1972). On the cultural significance of technological and industrial change, see David Nye, *America as Second Creation* (2003); and Laura Rigal, *The American Manufactory* (1998).

Specialized studies focus either on particular industries or places. On cotton textiles, in addition to the works of Thomas Dublin cited previously, see Barbara M. Tucker, *Samuel Slater and the Origins of the American Textile Industry* (1984); Jonathan Prude, *The Coming of Industrial Order* (1980); and Peter J. Coleman, *The Transformation of Rhode Island* (1963). Local studies dominated by textiles include Cynthia Shelton, *The Mills of Manyunk* (1986); and Philip Scranton, *Proprietary Capitalism* (1983). For iron and machinery, see John Bezis-Selfa, *Forging America: Ironworkers, Adventurers, and the Industrial Revolution* (2004); John K. Brown, *The Baldwin Locomotive Works* (1995); Maureen K. Phillips, "'Mechanic Geniuses and Duckies,' a Revision of New England's Cut Nail Chronology before 1820," *APT Bulletin* 25 (1993): 4–16; Amos Loveday, Jr., *Rise and Decline of the American Cut Nail Industry* (1983); and Merritt Roe Smith, *The Harpers Ferry Armory and the New Technology* (1977). For clocks, see Michael O'Malley, *Keeping Watch: A History of American Time* (1990); and John Joseph Murphy, "Entrepreneurship in the Establishment of the American Clock Industry," *Journal of Economic History* 26 (1966): 169–86. The definitive (and elegant) study of paper making is Judith McGaw, *Most Wonderful Machine* (1987).

The impact of the market revolution on Native Americans can be found in almost every account of interactions between European Americans and the indigenous peoples of America. For entree into that literature, see Theda Perdue and Michael D. Green, *Cherokee Nation and the Trail of Tears* (2007); Daniel K. Richter, *Facing East from Indian Country* (2001); Andrew C. Isenberg, *The Destruction of the Bison* (2000); Daniel H. Usner, Jr., *American Indians in the Lower Mississippi Valley* (1998); and Richard White, *The Roots of Dependency* (1983). For a detailed knowledge of Cherokee acculturation, I am indebted to William G. McLoughlin, *Cherokee Renascence in the New Republic* (1986). For an introduction to antebellum Indian removal, see Anthony F. C. Wallace, *Long Bitter Trail* (1993).

The phenomenon of the financial panic is analyzed technically and historically in Charles P. Kindleberger, *Manias, Panics, and Crashes,* 5th ed. (2005). For particular details, see Jane Knodell, "Rethinking the Jacksonian Economy: The Impact of the 1832 Bank Veto on Commercial Banking," *Journal of Economic History,* 66 (Sept. 2006): 541–74; Daniel S. Dupre, "The Panic of 1819 and the Political Economy of Sectionalism," in *The Economy of Early America,* ed. Cathy Matson, 263–93 (2006); Richard S. Chew, "Certain Victims of an International Contagion: The Panic of 1797 and the Hard Times of the Late 1790s in Baltimore," *Journal of the Early Republic* 25 (2005): 565–613; Peter L. Rousseau, "Jacksonian Monetary Policy, Specie Flows, and the Panic of 1837," *Journal of Economic History* 62 (2002): 457–88; Clyde Haulman, "Virginia Commodity Prices during the Panic of 1819," *Journal of the Early Republic* 22 (2002): 675–88; and Sandra F. Van Burkleo, "'The Paws of Banks': The Origins and Significance of Kentucky's Decision to Tax Federal Bankers, 1818–1820," *Journal of the Early Republic* 9 (1989): 457–87. Three classic studies continue to be useful: Peter Temin, *The Jacksonian Economy* (1969); Samuel Rezneck, *Business Depressions and Financial Panics* (1968); and Murray N. Rothbard, *The Panic of 1819* (1962). Jessica Lepler's recent Brandeis University dissertation, "1837: Anatomy of a Panic" (2008), promises to make an important addition to this literature.

The idea of free labor has been explored in a number of works, starting with François Furstenberg, *In the Name of the Father: Washington's Legacy, Slavery, and the Making of a Nation* (2006), and "Beyond Freedom and Slavery: Autonomy, Virtue, and Resistance in Early American Political Discourse," *Journal of American History* 89 (2003): 1295–1330; Robert J. Steinfeld, *Coercion, Contract, and Free Labor in the Nineteenth Century* (2001) and *The Invention of Free Labor* (1991); James L. Huston, *Securing the Fruits of Labor* (1998); Jonathan A. Glickstein, *Concepts of Free Labor in Antebellum America* (1991); and Eric Foner, *Free Soil, Free Labor, Free Men* (1970).

For the run-up to the Civil War, see two works by William Freehling: *The Road to Disunion: Secessionists at Bay, 1776–1854* (1990); and *The Road to Disunion: Secessionists Triumphant, 1854–1861* (2007). See also James L. Huston, *Calculating the Price of Union: Slavery, Property Rights, and the Economic Origins of the Civil War* (2003); Gary J. Kornblith, "Rethinking the Coming of the Civil War: A

Counterfactual Exercise," *Journal of American History* 90 (2003): 76–105; Michael A. Morrison, *Slavery and the American West* (1997); and Thomas R. Hietala, *Manifest Design: Anxious Aggrandizement in Late Jacksonian America* (1985). On Lincoln, I relied on Orville Vernon Burton, *The Age of Lincoln* (2007); and David Herbert Donald, *Lincoln* (1995). For the Compromise of 1850, see Peter B. Knupfer, *The Union as It Is* (1991). The narrow limits of the gift of emancipation are discussed in Amy Dru Stanley, *From Bondage to Contract* (1998); and Eric Foner, *Nothing But Freedom* (1983).

For the writings of Adam Smith, I relied on the Oxford World Classics edition of *The Wealth of Nations*, ed. Kathryn Sutherland (1993); and for the writings of Karl Marx, *The Portable Karl Marx*, ed. Eugene Kamenka (1983). One useful commentary on Smith is Jerry Z. Muller, *Adam Smith in His Time and Ours* (1993). On the misappropriation of Smith by neoclassical fundamentalists, see Warren J. Samuels and Steven G. Medema, "Freeing Smith from the 'Free Market': On the Misperception of Adam Smith on the Economic Role of Government," *History of Political Economy* 37 (2005): 219–26. On the historical process of development, I find much to recommend in Karl Polanyi, *The Great Transformation* (1944); as well as Walt W. Rostow, *The Stages of Economic Growth*, 2nd ed. (1971). Always provocative and stimulating is work on global capitalism by Immanuel Wallerstein, *The Modern World System*, 3 vols. (1974, 1980, 1989), and recently his reflections in *After Liberalism* (1995). Among the hundreds of titles touching present-day conditions, I have drawn on Joseph E. Stiglitz, *Globalization and Its Discontents* (2002); Kevin Philips, *Bad Money* (2008); and Thomas L. Friedman, *Hot, Flat, and Crowded* (2008).

Index